# THE PUBLIC SECTOR

# THE PUBLIC SECTOR

## Concepts, Models and Approaches

Jan-Erik Lane

SAGE Publications
London • Newbury Park • New Delhi

First published 1993    Reprinted in 1993

SAGE Publications Ltd
6 Bonhill Street
London EC2A 4PU

SAGE Publications Inc
2455 Teller Road
Newbury Park, California 91320

SAGE Publications India Pvt Ltd
32, M-Block Market
Greater Kailash – I
New Delhi 110 048

**British Library Cataloguing in Publication data**

Lane, Jan-Erik
  Public Sector: Concepts, Models and Approaches
  I. Title
  350

  ISBN 0–8039–8818–4
  ISBN 0–8039–8819–2 pbk

**Library of Congress catalog card number 92–50698**

Typeset by Mayhew Typesetting, Rhayader, Powys
Printed in Great Britain by The Cromwell Press Ltd,
Broughton Gifford, Melksham, Wiltshire

# CONTENTS

# PREFACE

Public administration as an academic discipline has more or less crumbled during the recent decades of research into the public sector. It has become outdated, losing its status as the main approach to the interpretation of the state or government. Christopher Hood (1990) describes the predicament of the science of public administration well in an article named 'Public Administration: Lost an Empire, Not Yet Found a Role?'

Replacing it there is now a proliferation of concepts, frameworks and theories. Public sector processes of decision-making and implementation in the modern state are approached through a variety of models from such different fields as public policy, policy implementation, management and evaluation as well as the public choice approach and neo-institutionalism. This overview of these multiple approaches aims to give students an introduction to the analysis of policy-making, to policy implementation as well as to public sector management and administration.

This volume presents the main theories of policy-making, implementation and management in the modern state, stating their pros and cons from a theoretical point of view. No attempt is made to propose any new solutions to the basic problems of modelling decision-making and implementation in state institutions. The purpose is to introduce students taking their first courses in public policy-making, policy analysis and public management or public administration to the state of the art, that is, to the basic conceptual paradigms and salient theories or sets of theoretical hypotheses.

For a political scientist, the concept of the public sector includes both what kind of activities public institutions carry out and how decisions are made and implemented by these institutions. Thus, on the one hand, we have the theory of the public sector as a branch of government involved in allocation, redistribution and regulation, with all kinds of concepts involved in the analysis of these three branches of government. On the other hand, we have the dynamic policy perspective of a public sector involved in the making and implementation of policies. The public sector requires both descriptive and normative concepts in order to understand not only what goes on in public institutions but also whether the outputs and outcomes are efficient or desirable. Fundamentally, the public sector is a set of institutions that coordinate the interests of different groups that ask in various ways for public activities of different kinds.

I have drawn somewhat upon a few articles that I published in edited volumes and international journals. In addition I have drawn upon an article written jointly with Torgeir Nyen, 'Neoinstitutionalism and the Public Sector', *Statsvetenskaplig Tidskrift*, 95 (4), 1992. However, besides much new material, all of the text has been thoroughly revised in order to be used as an undergraduate textbook. I should thank Andrew Dunsire (York), Ed Page (Hull) and Richard Rose (Strathclyde) for helpful comments on an earlier version of the manuscript. Some of the chapters in the book have arisen from papers presented at COCTA (Committee on Conceptual and Terminological Analysis) sponsored panels at IPSA and ISA conferences. They form part of a project sponsored by the International Social Science Council (ISSC) to focus on key social science concepts and develop awareness in the social science community of theoretical issues.

# INTRODUCTION

# PUBLIC INSTITUTIONS AND INTERESTS

The public sector (though variable) has an enormous impact on us all. How can we tell whether it is doing too much or too little, whether or not it is doing the job efficiently and effectively, whether or not it serves the public? According to a traditional model it served the public through a set of hierarchical structures responsive to politicians. Speaking generally, politicians were to take care of the normative side of things, pursuing public interests as it were, and effective bureaucracies were to ensure that goals were carried into effect. Many studies have questioned the responsiveness and efficiency of this model and its applicability to the real world.

In the liberal democracies or the so-called capitalist democratic societies there is an important divide between two sectors of the economy or society: the public and the private. This basic dichotomy refers to both institutional differences and interests or individual preferences.

The institutions of politics, government and bureaux populate the public sector whereas various market institutions inhabit the private sector. Persons, groups and élites often use the so-called public interest as a criterion for problem-solving in the public sector, whereas self-interests prevail in the private sector. Traditional public administration used to be the academic field of study of the making and execution of decisions in public institutions.

A system of public institutions is an asset to a nation. If properly used, public institutions for the making of policy, implementation and administration are as important to national development as economic resources. The problem, however, is that it is far from clear how systems of public institutions are to be built up so as to function 'properly' from administrative or management perspectives. In fact, if we look at the analysis of public institutions we find different theories advanced about what constitutes a set of 'good' or 'effective' public institutions.

The traditional conception of public administration used to supply a set of principles with which to understand the public sector and which could be employed to reform public institutions. However, several of the notions of public administration have been more or less abandoned during the post-Second World War period (see Shafritz and Hyde, 1978; Lynn and Wildavsky, 1990). Here, we will outline some of the objections raised in the critique of public administration as a scholarly discipline, although it probably never existed as a set of clear-cut principles or precise concepts.

## PRINCIPLES OF PUBLIC ADMINISTRATION

It is not easy to summarize the public administration approach to the public sector. There is no single source that provides us with a hard-core set of beliefs, although a few basic texts may be identified, including, for example, *Principles of Public Administration* (1927) by W.F. Willoughby, *Papers on the Science of Administration* (1937) by L. Gulick and L. Urwick, *The Administrative State* (1948) by Dwight Waldo and *Public Administration* (1950) by Herbert A. Simon, Donald W. Smithburg and Victor A. Thompson. Andrew Dunsire in his *Administration* (1973) offers a clear examination of the discipline of public administration.

Public administration was inspired by a set of theoretical or normative principles identified by scholars like John Stuart Mill (*Representative Government* in 1861, see Mill, 1964), Woodrow Wilson ('The Study of Administration' in 1887, see Shafritz and Hyde, 1978) and Max Weber (*Gesellschaft und Wirtschaft* from 1922, see Weber, 1978). Public administration as a discipline was also influenced by the emerging school of 'scientific management' in the early twentieth century (F.W. Taylor and H. Fayol) as well as by mainstream organization theory (Mintzberg, 1983; Morgan, 1986; Morgan, 1990).

A set of maxims may be used to construct a so-called ideal-type general public administration model, that is, with slight exaggerations and a few omissions in order to pin-point what is typical of the public administration approach. The following would be the basic public administration principles according to which the public sector is or should be structured, involving the institutional structure, the motivation of public employees and the status of the public interest:

1 The tasks of public institutions are to be decided by politicians but executed by administrators in order to satisfy the model of rational decision-making.
2 Administration is based on written documents and this tends to make the office (bureau) the heart of modern government.
3 Public tasks are organized on a continuous, rule-governed basis.
4 The rules according to which work is conducted may be either technical or legal. In both cases trained individuals are necessary.
5 The tasks or functions are divided into functionally distinct spheres, each furnished with the requisite authority and sanctions.
6 Officers as well as tasks are arranged hierarchically, the rights of control and complaint being specified. There is a preference for centralization, all other things being equal.
7 The resources of the organization are quite distinct from those of the members as private individuals.

8 The office holder cannot appropriate his or her office for private aims.

9 Public employees orientate towards the tasks within the public sector in terms of vocation or a sense of duty to fulfil the obligations of their roles.

10 In the public sector there is one dominating interest, the public interest, which sets limits to the influence of self-interests in politics and administration.

Basically, there have been three kinds of reactions to the public administration model. Some have seen it as primarily a normative model for the conduct of the operations of the modern state. Others have criticized the model for its lack of descriptive accuracy. Finally, there is the criticism that the public administration model fails to identify the mechanisms that are conducive to public sector effectiveness and efficiency, meaning that its capacity to explain how the public sector actually works is low. The new theories of the public sector have oriented towards a sort of post-Weber or post-Wilson conception of public administration in order to arrive at models that are radically different from the classical conception.

In the attempts to develop new approaches to public institutions – policy-making, implementation and management – features other than those included in the classical public administration model have been emphasized. In essence, the new principles of public policy-making and implementation constitute more than an attempt to model existing public institutions in liberal democracies more truthfully, because they also involve a different theory about human motivation and efficiency or effectiveness in the public sector. Thus, the new frameworks comprise, inter alia, principles such as the following:

1 The distinction between politics and administration is irrelevant and dubious (Appleby, 1949).

2 Rational decision-making is not feasible in public institutions, only bounded rationality (Simon, 1947; Lindblom, 1959; Wildavsky, 1984).

3 Top-down policy implementation does not work, therefore there cannot be automatic accomplishment of objectives in the public sector (Wildavsky, 1979; Pressman and Wildavsky, 1984).

4 Public administration is best handled by self-steering groups (Argyris, 1960).

5 Public administrators cannot be constrained by rules of procedure, as what matters is goal achievement and effectiveness (Novick, 1965).

6 Centralization in the public sector may be conducive to rigidity and hierarchy in public administration could result in an implementation deficit (Crozier, 1964; Hanf and Scharpf, 1978).

7  Systems of public institutions operate most efficiently when they are decentralized (Williams and Elmore, 1976).
8  In public administration there may exist tendencies towards irrationality or a substantial risk of so-called garbage can processes (March and Olsen, 1976).
9  Public employees do not have a special type of motivation, but act in order to maximize self-interests like income, prestige and power (Downs, 1967; Tullock, 1970).

Although we examine these ideas more closely in the chapters to follow, a brief discussion of some of these maxims will clarify the distance between the traditional public administration model and the post-public administration models.

Weber claimed for his interpretation of the public administration model that public administration or bureaucracy is capable of the 'highest extent of rationality' (Albrow, 1970). Anti-Weberian approaches argue that in reality rational behaviour is not a typical feature of modern organizational life, particularly not of public bureaux (March and Simon, 1958).

First, it was argued that only bounded (limited) rationality, not complete rationality, could be achieved by 'administrative man' (Simon, 1947). By eliminating certain alternatives and outcomes the choice of a course of action takes place within the context of a confined set of opportunities. Secondly, it has been argued that public institutions could only handle minor decisions on the margins of social impact (Braybrooke and Lindblom, 1963; Lindblom, 1965). Thirdly, new theories of public institutions state that the rational assumptions of the Weberian model are irrelevant to the operating modes of public organizations. Typically, there exist no consistent preference functions and there is no reliable knowledge about administrative technologies (Rose, 1984; March, 1988).

Public ends are ambiguous and shifting, the means are unreliable and controversial; decision rules may vary from one situation to another. Instead of rational processes for the making and implementation of public policies we may expect to find irrational events in the public sector: solutions looking for problems, participants searching for choice opportunities and outcomes which seek some relation to organizational goals (Hogwood and Peters, 1985).

Proponents of the public administration model have argued strongly in favour of the specialization of divisions and personnel in administrative systems. Functional specification of various departments in bureaux as well as role differentiation for various kinds of staff is a sine qua non for the efficient and safe operation of public administration. The counter-argument from modern organizational theory is that people matter more than formal structure (Argyris, 1960).

Organizational outputs are not a function of a grand overall organizational scheme defining the functions to be carried out and coordinating the contributions of each employee by extreme division of labour. The so-called classical principles of management result in the mechanization and routinization of administrative work which is counter-productive to the accomplishment of goals in the public sector. The human relations school argued that functional specialization and role differentiation are detrimental to bureau efficiency and effectiveness.

The structuring of public institutions must be based on factors that are conducive to job satisfaction. The alternative to the sharply delineated systems of division of labour in public administration is a complete restructuring that allows employees to work in multiple roles and make an individual contribution to the completion of end products, a holistic approach instead of a mechanistic one.

The standard public administration model favours hierarchy and centralization. The credo in implementation analysis implies a preference for the bottom-up alternative against top-down implementation, requiring extensive decentralization of the public sector (Williams, 1982). A decentralized strategy is superior to a centralized structure, because it makes adaptation easier, promotes the mobilization of local motivation and enhances flexibility.

Actually, the more centralized an administrative structure is, the more likely is the occurrence of policy failure due to inherent implementation difficulties. Successful implementation presupposes bottom-up implementation, trusting that basic operating units will reinterpret and innovate in relation to the ends and means of public policies (Elmore, 1982).

Moreover, public policy-making and implementation is not the efficient accomplishment of a clearly delineated goal function, because in reality there is no perfect administration (Hood, 1976; Dunsire, 1978). What we find is only a policy evolution, a kind of flux where ends and means replace each other in a consecutive fashion (Pressman and Wildavsky, 1984).

## MOTIVATION IN PUBLIC ADMINISTRATION

The public administration model approaches the public sector on the basis of a conception of public service as a *vocation*. The administrator is to be solely occupied with the carrying out of the tasks that are inherent in the administrative role. The purpose is to safeguard an important distinction between the private and public roles of a public sector employee. One criticism of the public administration model states that such a sharp distinction is neither feasible nor desirable. The behaviour of public administrators is not typically oriented in terms of a clear private–public dichotomy (Niskanen, 1971; Breton, 1974).

The public choice approach assumes that public administrators maximize a private utility function which depends on the size of their bureau as well as the power and prestige they may command in their public roles. Personnel in bureaux are in reality not the unselfish servants of their political masters, devoted to the neutral and objective fulfilment of a vocation. Quite the contrary, public administrators fulfil their duties out of selfishness, reducing the public goals of a bureau to the status of a means in relation to more basic personal objectives such as pecuniary reward, personal power and prestige as well as security of employment (Mueller, 1989).

Public administration approaches behaviour in the public sector in terms of a norm for administrative efficiency requiring that the role of the administrator takes precedence over the status as employee. The participation approach to the structuring of a system of public institutions amounts to a rebuttal of the public administration model for the role of the public office holder. Participation as employees in bureau decision-making could be both a goal in itself and a means to administrative efficiency.

Employee participation in governing boards or in structures for co-determination involving trade unions representing public employees would increase the involvement of the employees in the running of the public bureau, which may be conducive to job satisfaction and efficiency. The acceptance of private motivation aspects in public sector structures is anathema to the traditional model of public administration, as it challenges the relevance or predominance of the concept of the public interest. However, the well-known assumption that rational behaviour maximizes self-interests should be applied also to big government, as it throws new light on the public sector.

## THE PUBLIC INTEREST

Crucial to the discussion about the validity and applicability of the public administration model and its modern competitors is the concept of the public interest. It stands for both objectives and institutions by which to make and implement public decisions. Public sector spending, it is argued in the standard textbooks of political science and public administration, aims at the accomplishment of the public interest. Is this true, or perhaps we should first ask: what does it really mean?

'Public interest' has two elements: 'public' and 'interest'. Both these concepts are important, yet hard to pin down. If there are various interests, then how do we identify those that may be called 'public'? The concept of interest has an individualistic import as 'interest' denotes basically what various persons wish.

One may certainly speak of a variety of personal interests, selfish or altruistic ones. However, the concept of the public has a holistic import as 'the public' somehow refers to a collective entity. There is therefore constant tension between the individualistic connotation of 'interest' and the holistic connotation of 'public'.

Implicit in public policy-making is the making and implementation of public policy as a *principal–agent* problem. At the heart of the operation of public institutions is the notion that politicians, bureaucrats and professionals as agents are contracted to act in the interests of the citizens as principals. The attempt by the principal to monitor the agent is critical according to this framework. How can one design a compensating system (contracts) that makes the agent act for the principals' interests according to his/her self-interests? Typical principal-agent problems such as behaviour opportunism, moral hazard, small numbers problem and asymmetric information (Williamson, 1986), also plague the relationship between politicians on the one hand and public employees of various kinds on the other.

Among the new approaches to the modelling of the public sector, the public choice school questions the notion of the public interest as the foundation for principal–agent relationships in the public sector (Buchanan, 1986). New theories model the process of public sector expansion among rich countries as driven by fiscal illusions, egoistic behaviour by special interest groups and institutional failures in the public sector (Tarschys, 1975; Larkey et al., 1981; Wildavsky, 1985). What exists in the public sector are only mundane interests, self-interests and more or less narrow collective interests (Olson, 1965, 1982).

Proponents of the basic public administration model claim that the public interest notion is a valid one, either substantially or in a procedural sense. They argue that the public interest will be forthcoming if the procedures of public institutions are the correct ones, or it states that the public interest is some specific objective that ought to be pursued (Leys and Perry, 1959; Schubert, 1960; Downs, 1961).

The concept of the public interest in the public administration approach is both a descriptive and an evaluative notion – a highly value-loaded term. Public interests may be referred to as if they had a normative existence to be revealed by some method. Or public interests may be invoked as moral guidance in public activities. The descriptive and normative meanings of 'public interest' are so closely intertwined that they are very difficult to separate.

It is tempting to resolve the confusion surrounding the contested notion of public interest by simply stating that it is devoid of meaning or that it is only a word recommending some action, or by quoting from a dictionary: 'Public Interest. A term used in several Nationalization Acts. It was declared that an industry after nationalization was to be operated in "the public interest", a phrase to which no precise meaning can be attached' (Hanson, 1974: 394).

However, this is like cutting the Gordian knot by a sword without attempting any serious analysis of the basic problems involved in the labyrinthine mixture of the variety of different interests in relation to politics, administration and management in the modern tax state.

If people in the welfare state have conflicting interests or are in disagreement about what objectives government should pursue, then what about the public interest? The interpretation of the public interest as what people actually want has to be qualified, recognizing the fundamental fact of opposing interests or values in social life (Thompson et al., 1990). The public interest could be what a majority of society wants, or the majority will. However, this definition will take the public interest concept into all the difficulties of majority decision rule according to the social choice literature (Riker, 1982; Kelly, 1986).

The identification of public interests with some procedure for the aggregation of individual wants or preferences is often rejected by invoking the ideal or value component of the concept of the public interest. Interests are public, not simply because a majority share them, but because they are the interests that each and everyone would want the state to pursue were they rational or enlightened.

The requirement of rationality may be interpreted differently. Rational interests may be simply those interests that persons would pursue if they calculated carefully how to achieve their objectives. Or rational interests could be those wants that persons would pursue if they focused on essential matters from a universalistic or impartial point of view, such as, for example, from under a veil of ignorance (Rawls, 1971).

The public interest concept in the standard public administration model may be qualified by the requirement of a special type of rationality, namely impartiality. Only those interests could be public that would be pursued by persons who not only disregard their irrational or non-rational interests but also by-pass their selfish interests. The public interest concept would require a person to consider only those wants or needs that he/she would pursue if they acted without personal stakes involved. Walter Lippman states:

> Living adults share, we must believe, the same public interest. For them, however, the public interest is mixed with, and is often at odds with, their private and special interests. Put this way, we can say, I suggest, that the public interest may be presumed to be what men would choose if they saw clearly, thought rationally, acted disinterestedly and benevolently. (1955: 42)

The public interest could consist of some highly desirable things in the substantive interpretation which leads to well-known normative models of the state and policy-making. Or the public interest would emerge from the operation of some ethical acceptable decision process that would somehow aggregate the individual preferences of the social community in the procedural interpretation (Mueller, 1989).

The public interest is a labyrinthine notion with several difficulties. The focus of traditional public administration on public interests needs to be critically assessed and broadened to recognize that a variety of interests may occur in public institutions and take part in policy-making, policy implementation or just administration and management. The ambiguity of the concept of the public interest is augmented by its fuzzy boundaries in relation to other kinds of aggregated interests.

First, there is the notion of state interests, which may be interpreted as either descriptive or normative. State interests may be the interests that existing states pursue or they may be the interests that express the essence of the state. Secondly, there is a set of officially stated interests that may or may not agree with state interests. One should be aware of the possibility of non-official state interests which are exemplified in geopolitical notions. It is an entirely open question whether state interests or official interests could be called 'public interests'.

Thirdly, there is a variety of group interests. In a minimal sense the concept of a group interest only stands for a collective interest pursued by a small or a large set of people. Group interests may be egoistic or altruistic. And they may be state or bureau interests, official or non-official. Authorities or state agencies (bureaux) pursue both official and non-official interests whether these be state interests or merely self-interests.

The notion of private interests has many meanings. It may stand for egoistic interests or merely individual interests. The set of self-interests could include egoistic interests, whether they are personal or group interests. The concept of public interests has also been interpreted as the mere aggregation of private interests, meaning simply individual preferences.

The multifarious nature of the interest concept means that the concept of the public interest is not very helpful when one attempts to propose a conceptual framework with which to model policy-making and administration in the public sector. It seems that the theory of motivation that is at the heart of the public choice school is more plausible than the public interest conception. But we also have to take into account that the play of self-interests in the public sector is constrained by institutional factors, as the new institutionalism underlines (Bromley, 1989).

## CONCLUSION

The public sector comprises a number of institutions for the making and implementation of decisions with regard to interests of various kinds. How interests are handled depends on both the nature of the interests and the type of public institutions involved. Public sector institutions will not automatically locate or implement the public interest.

The state is a special set of *institutions* that take *interests* of various kinds into account in decision-making, administration and management. Its public institutions affect the way interests are decided upon as well as policy outcomes that are highly relevant for a variety of interests.

The state may be regarded as a set of institutional mechanisms for the aggregation or coordination of interests into collective decisions and outcomes. In a democracy it is required that there is 'government of the people by the people for the people' in the Abraham Lincoln interpretation. Since a rule of continuous referenda on every social choice would result in staggering transaction costs, if at all implementable, the modern democratic state is based on a set of principal–agent relationships in the public sector. These principal–agent relations involve both the relationship between the population and its elected leaders and the relationship between the government and its agencies or bureaux.

Whereas in the private sector market institutions offer mechanisms for coordinating interests, public institutions coordinate interests by the making and implementation of policy. This book is about some of the problems that the modelling of these institutions face.

Although the general public administration framework is outdated, it remains vital to discuss abstract concepts for the interpretation and evaluation of public institutions that handle policy outputs of the public sector resulting in social outcomes. In the chapters to follow we look at how policy-making, policy implementation and policy management may be approached by means of alternative conceptual schemes for the modelling of the public sector, with particular reference to problems in liberal democracies or societies with an advanced economy (Hill, 1992).

The structure of the book is as follows. First we examine the notion of the public sector to see if it is possible to unpack such a complex concept. Perhaps the familiar public finance models could tell us what to expect in the public sector? Then, we analyse the notions of bureaucracy to see how the modelling of public institutions may give rise to different images of the public sector. Thirdly, whatever the composition of the public sector may be, it will – at least partly – be the outcome of the dynamics of public institutions which stem from public policy-making. How is policy-making achieved? We survey a number of policy-making models, asking to what extent such alternative decision-making models really contradict each other. Fourthly, we take on the so-called missing link in the traditional public administration framework: implementation models.

Another neglected aspect of the public sector – the invisible state – is analysed by means of contrasting regulation models. Chapter 6 takes up management models concerning leadership in the public sector, which have relevance for the question of privatization. In Chapter 7 the basics of the public choice framework are discussed, even though a number of public choice models are dealt with occasionally in other parts of the volume. Then, the new institutionalism is inquired into in its sociological and economic versions. Finally, we move to normative concerns about public sector efficiency and equity models that attempt to identify what good or just policy-making amounts to.

# 1
# DEMARCATION OF THE PUBLIC SECTOR

Much of the literature on the welfare state has focused on the growth problem of identifying the factors – environmental, institutional and cultural – which are conducive to public expenditure expansion (Tarschys, 1975; Frey, 1978; Tufte, 1978; Whiteley, 1980; Larkey et al., 1981; Hibbs and Fassbender, 1981; Castles, 1982; Wildavsky, 1985; Lybeck, 1986). An increasing part of the literature is now orientated towards the outcome problem, or the study of the consequences of governmental expansion and big public budgets. It is argued that unrestrained public sector expansion results in public policy failure due to communication problems or the lack of coordination and of reliable means–end technologies, as well as lack of appropriate public revenues (Rose, 1980, 1984).

The same literature takes up the problem of shrinking the public sector in two ways. Either it outlines alternative ways of delivering services, emphasizing privatization and the feasibility of public–private partnerships mixing market allocation forms with bureaucracy (Bridge, 1977; Ostrom and Ostrom, 1977; Savas, 1982), or decision techniques are discussed that would contain governmental growth (Wildavsky, 1980). Statements to the effect that government or the public sector is too large in rich liberal democracies must be based on ideas about the proper size of government, which implies that there is choice, which is neglected in the literature on the structural forces conducive to growth in government (Borcherding, 1984; Wildavsky, 1985).

When Anthony Downs (1960) argued that the size of the government budget tends to be too small, or James M. Buchanan stated that the public sector is too large, the budgetary expansion of the government being beyond control (Buchanan and Wagner, 1977; Brennan and Buchanan, 1980), then it is pertinent to ask for the normative criteria upon which such statements are based. It has been suggested that the public sector should not be larger than some proposed magic figure, Colin Clark's 25 per cent in 1945 or Milton Friedman's 60 per cent in 1976 (Rose, 1981).

An urgent problem in much of the literature on the emerging new field of political economy, concerned with the identification of determinants of public expenditures in the short and long run, is the need for a clear conception of the public sector. Here, we search for the variety of meanings of 'public sector' by focusing on the rationale of criteria that are employed to make a distinction between the public and the private sectors. Thus, we look for the reasons why items of expenditure should appear on the political budget.

The basic problem here is what could be called the 'demarcation problem'; it involves deliberations about what the concepts 'public' and 'private' refer to. as well as about the criteria that may guide the choice of what is to be public, private or some public–private mixture, and how such decisions may be implemented. The demarcation between the public and the private involves semantic questions, issues involved in the derivation of an optimum or feasible solution to the problem of what is to be private or public and matters concerning the practicality of implementing any such solution (Margolis and Guitton, 1969).

It is not possible to justify a public sector of a specific size without commitment as to how various amounts of national, regional and local goods are to be combined to produce a government of a certain overall size and at a specified level (Tiebout, 1956; Buchanan, 1965; Oates, 1972). The solution to the size problem is a function of the solution to the problems of choosing the proper size for the national government budget, the regional government budget or the local government budget: the model of fiscal federalism. The focus in this chapter is on the so-called public finance models that attempt to identify the public sector mainly by economic criteria. Are there inherent properties of goods and services that make them 'naturally' public goods and services?

## PUBLIC SECTOR CONCEPTS

First, we consider what the expression 'public sector' stands for. It is often taken for granted that the public sector is the budget(s) enacted by political assemblies. The emphasis is on political budgeting, the resources mobilized and disposed of by political assemblies at various levels of government. Such a definition is only one among several possibilities.

It does not recognize another major source of governmental impact on society, namely legislation. However, the impact of legislation is difficult to trace. Is it always the case that governmental legislation results in a uniform reduction in the freedom of citizens or that the outcome of such legislation is always an increase in relative cost to the individual compared with free choice? It could be the case that sometimes government legislation merely recognizes a spontaneous order (Hayek, 1973), but this is difficult to establish.

A most general definition of 'public sector' may be rendered formally like this:

(DF1) 'Public sector' = def. 'Government activity and
   its consequences'

The concept of the public sector implied here involves the traditional
approach to the public sector as public administration or public
authority (Ostrom and Ostrom, 1971); DF1 may be replaced by:

(DF1') 'Public sector' = def. 'State general decision-making and
   its outcomes'

It must be emphasized that definition DF1' focuses on legislation and
authority more than budget and allocation; it is conceivable that the
public sector could be all-inclusive in the sense DF1, if the govern-
ment(s) would lay down comprehensive directives as to what citizens
should do, to be followed from a belief in the legitimacy of authority
or from fear of the cost of disobedience (Eckstein and Gurr, 1975). DF1
or DF1' could be called the authority interpretation of the concept of
the public sector. In Chapter 5 we will take a closer look at a few
concepts that may be used for modelling the end and means of public
legislation, particularly government regulation of the private sector.
   Focusing again on the budget, the public sector would consist of
government consumption, investment and transfers. Thus:

(DF2) 'Public sector' = def. 'Governmental consumption,
   investment and transfers'

Definition DF2 is reasonably adequate, as specifying a public sector for
every country would not present insurmountable difficulties. However, DF2 is amorphous, since its three elements may vary considerably in relation to each other. The distinction between public
consumption and investment on the one hand and public transfers on
the other hand is vital for the solution of the size problem; one may
wish to argue for some particular size of government consumption and
investment on the basis of deliberations about the principle of
consumer choice, while admitting another size for the transfer part
based on consideration about social justice in an equity argument. DF2
may thus be replaced by the more precise:

(DF3) 'Public sector' = def. 'Government consumption and
   investment'

DF3 would be the allocation interpretation of the concept of the public
sector, a core definition as it were. Arguments about the proper size
of the public sector would then have to be supplemented by a statement regarding the proper size of transfer payments. DF3 minus DF2
would constitute the distribution interpretation of the public sector. It
does not follow from the fact that a government allocates goods and
services that it also must produce them. A fourth definition of 'public
sector' could be as follows:

(DF4) 'Public sector' = def. 'Government production'

DF4 needs clarification as it could refer to two different states of affairs: government provision or public ownership of the means of production. One needs to make a distinction between the provision and the ownership interpretations, because the first may occur without the second. Moreover, there is the employment interpretation, as governments may provide many services without much government employment as well as employ many people without owning a substantial portion of the capital.

Thus, DF4 is ambiguous as it may refer to government provision (DF4'), ownership (DF5) or employment (DF6). Typical of the public sector expansion in the advanced capitalist democracies has been the emphasis on government provision and public employment (Rose, 1985). These distinctions reappear when the ambiguous concept of privatization is dealt with in Chapter 6.

The purpose of these distinctions is to emphasize that the public–private distinction is not one distinction but several. If the opposite to the public sector is sought, then we have to admit that there will be many different entities.

In relation to the first concept of the public sector – government authority – we have private freedom; in relation to the second concept of the public sector – public consumption and investment – the private would simply be private consumption and investment or net income after the government has taken its share in the form of taxes and reallocated part of these as transfers. That part of the total resources of society that governments offer as public consumption almost free and use for investments constitutes the sphere of governmental choice, the opposite being private choice. The third concept – public redistribution – affects private choice but does not replace it. The private counterpart to the fourth, fifth and sixth concepts of the public could be private provision of goods and services under, for example, contracting or franchising, private ownership of the means of production and employment in private organizations.

The size problem is in reality several different problems; asking about the proper size of the public sector may imply at least six questions:

1  What is the proper place of governmental authority in society? Or, how much private autonomy are we to recommend? (The problem of individual freedom.)
2  What proportion of the total resources of society should be left to government choice as public consumption and investment? And how much should be turned over to private choice? (The allocation problem.)
3  How large should the governmental budget be? Or, how much private income should be generated without governmental

influence in the form of transfers? (The distribution problem.)

4  How much of the goods and services provided by government should also be produced by government? (The production problem.)

5  How much of the means of the production should be owned by government? (The ownership problem.)

6  How much of the workforce should be employed in governmental organizations? (The problem of bureaucracy.)

Unpacking the concept of the public sector leaves us with a set of basic questions which have to be discussed one by one.

## MARKETS AND BUREAUX

It may be argued that what matters is not the manifestations of the public and the private in various spheres like allocation, income distribution, production and employment. The demarcation problem concerning the proper size of the public vis-à-vis the private is in essence a choice between two fundamentally different modes of social interaction. Let us quote a classical text, 'there are two methods for the conduct of affairs within the frame of human society, that is, peaceful cooperation among individuals. One is bureaucratic management, the other is profit management' (Mises, 1962).

To the so-called Austrian school, including, inter alia, Ludwig von Mises and Friedrich von Hayek, the demarcation problem concerns whether society should be organized on the basis of private ownership of the means of production (capitalism, the market system) or on the basis of public control of the means of production (socialism, communism, planned economy) (Schumpeter, 1965). Capitalism means free enterprise, sovereignty of consumers in economic matters. Socialism means government control of several spheres of the individual's life and the unrestricted supremacy of the government in its capacity as the central board of economic management. There is no compromise possible between these two systems (Mises, 1935).

Mises lumps the distinctions between private ownership and public ownership as well as the distinction between planned economy and consumer sovereignty into the market versus state demarcation. But it must be emphasized that the distinction between market and bureaucracy in no way coincides with the other equally important distinctions.

A step towards conceptual clarity about the fundamental concepts involved in the demarcation problem may be to identify the variety of interaction concepts employed to make the separation between the public and the private. The following concepts are related to the public–private demarcation problem: exchange and authority, competition and hierarchy, laissez-faire and planning, market economy and command economy, capitalism and socialism, and freedom versus authority.

Let us cross-tabulate these distinctions in order to see how they relate to each other analytically. It is conceivable that some of these concepts are logically related and that they draw on some of the aspects of the public–private distinction, but it is hardly likely that all these conceptual pairs are reducible to one major conceptual demarcation, such as, for example, market versus bureaucracy. It could be that Mises' market–bureaucracy demarcation needs clarification in terms of the interaction concepts listed above.

It is often stated that in principle there are only two mechanisms for the allocation of resources, the market and the public budget. How do we characterize the difference between the two? The ownership distinction – private versus public ownership of the means of production – is different from the separation between market and public budget. The relationship between these conceptual pairs may be represented in a 2×2 table (Table 1.1).

Table 1.1  *Ownership versus allocation mechanism*

|         | Market | Public budget |
|---------|--------|---------------|
| Private | I      | II            |
| Public  | III    | IV            |

Although the ideal-types of capitalism and of communism are oriented towards combinations I and IV respectively, combinations II and III are logically possible. Combination II is practical, but the status of III is a contested issue. Some socialist theoreticians argue that market allocation is feasible even if the means of production are no longer privately owned (Lange and Taylor, 1964; Le Grand and Estrin, 1989), whereas adherents of the market economy deny this (Hayek, 1944). Combination I may be described as decentralized capitalism, while combination IV would constitute hierarchical socialism.

However, the distinction between types of ownership does not coincide with the separation between competition and hierarchy (Demsetz, 1982). Private ownership of the means of production is not necessarily tied to a competitive pattern of interaction, although welfare economics states that such a competitive pattern of interaction leads to a social optimum (Rowley and Peacock, 1975). Table 1.2 shows the combination possibilities.

The occurrence of hierarchy in the private sector is manifested in trends towards monopoly or oligopoly, which have traditionally been

Table 1.2  *Ownership versus interaction pattern*

|          | Competition | Hierarchy |
|----------|:-----------:|:---------:|
| Private  | I           | II        |
| Public   | III         | IV        |

considered a target for public regulation by the state (II). However, the new institutionalist economics defence of hierarchy in the firms of the private sector states that hierarchy is often more rational than the market when transaction costs are taken into account (Williamson, 1975; Coase, 1988). Moreover, it has been stated that a kind of capitalism involving extensive hierarchy in the private sector is to be expected due to the development pattern of modern society (Schumpeter, 1965).

From a logical point of view, the occurrence of competition is also possible in a system of publicly owned means of production. It is open to debate whether combination III is likely to occur, but in any case the fact that the government owns the means of production does not imply that hierarchy must drive out competition (IV). Just as it is vital to separate the question of ownership of the means of production from the question of type of interaction pattern, it also seems important that the two basic mechanisms of allocation may be independently combined with the interaction types. Table 1.3 shows the possible combinations.

Table 1.3  *Allocation mechanism versus interaction pattern*

|             | Market | Public budget |
|-------------|:------:|:-------------:|
| Competition | I      | II            |
| Hierarchy   | III    | IV            |

The extent to which markets adhere to the model of perfect competition is not easily determined, and even more problematic is the hypothesis that markets on the whole tend to move away from the conditions of perfect competition. In any case, combinations I and III are not simply theoretically possible, they actually exist.

The hierarchical interaction pattern between those requesting and those appropriating money is typical of the public budget, but this

Table 1.4  *Forms of control and types of allocation mechanism*

|  | Market | Public budget |
|---|:---:|:---:|
| Laissez-faire | I | II |
| Planning | III | IV |

characteristic of the budgetary process does not exclude competitive elements. The provision of services may be contracted out to the highest bidder and competition between bureaux may be introduced by means of efficiency-promoting mechanisms that allow the ranking of the various bureaux in terms of output criteria (Mierlo, 1985; Jonsson, 1985).

If public budget-making is the same as planning, then perhaps market allocation is the opposite of planning – what may be called 'laissez-faire'. It is far from clear what is to be understood by the concept of planning (Wildavsky, 1973), but one may identify two polar forms of social control. Generally speaking, production and consumption may be either planned or left to the choice of the participants in production and consumption. How do these two types of social control, planning versus laissez-faire, compare with the allocation distinction (Table 1.4)?

Since market allocation exchange feeds on diffusion processes and public budget-making expresses the authority of political decision-makers, it may be assumed that the only possible combinations are I and IV. Rational budgeting, it is claimed, must be based on planning and planning is a substitute for the spontaneity and unpredictability of the laissez-faire of markets.

However, these formulas equating markets with laissez-faire and public budgeting with planning have been seriously challenged. On the one hand, the idea of a PPB-system has been criticized as not representative of the way public budget-making works (Wildavsky, 1986; Gunsteren, 1976). On the other hand, combination III could be relevant to an understanding of modern society. Charles Lindblom (1977, 1988) has argued in favour of the concept of planner sovereignty to denote a social state where planners make choices in a market environment (III). It seems that this Lindblom model differs from his version of the general competitive socialist model, where the public sector would own all capital but markets would allocate the resources.

To sum up, the distinction between the public and the private sector is not the same as the distinction between public and private ownership, nor the same as the separation between a planned economy and a laissez-faire system. The problem of drawing a demarcation line between the public and the private does not totally coincide with the problem of how to mix competition with hierarchy. A large public sector may operate with elements of choice and competition using charges on the demand side and bidding on the supply side of the public household. Moreover, a large private sector may include considerable hierarchy.

The size of the public sector in the budget interpretation is a function of how much government allocation or redistribution there is, neither of which implies a comprehensively planned economy, or public ownership of the means of production. Rather than being mutually exclusive, a public sector may interact with the market based on a system of predominantly privately owned means of production.

In the traditional caretaker model of the state a public sector of a certain size has been a necessary condition for the existence of a market mechanism. Government regulation may benefit rather than oppose the workings of the market mechanism. It is equally true that an expansion of the total resources mobilized by the budget does not necessarily imply a weakening of the market mechanism. If these resources are transferred back to private citizens, then the operation of the markets for goods or services may sustain no damage.

Government consumption and investment per se do not imply a command economy. First, an increase in public allocation would imply moving consumption and investment decisions from the private sector – citizens and organizations – to public authorities only if the goods so allocated could be allocated by the market mechanism. Secondly, even if public budget-making replaces the market in public consumption, it does not ipso facto replace market operations with regard to production. The distinction between consumption and production is vital (Table 1.5).

Table 1.5  *Production and consumption versus market and public budget-making*

|              | Production | Consumption |
|--------------|:----------:|:-----------:|
| Market       | I          | II          |
| Budget-making| III        | IV          |

Although the reliance on public budget-making in the production or consumption spheres may reduce the scope for the market, two points must be emphasized. When the planning procedure introduces hierarchy or command, it may not actually replace the operations of the market but may supersede hierarchy in the private sector or result in the provision of goods that the market could not have allocated anyway (Holler, 1984). Market and public budget-making may be combined in the same sphere of economic activity (Grant, 1985; Konukiewitz, 1985).

The two collective choice mechanisms – public budget-making and the market – have their own areas, which may be combined without conflict. The problem of choosing between a planned economy and a market economy does not exhaust the possibilities of mixing the public and private sectors. It is possible to argue for the existence of a large public sector without favouring comprehensive planning. Let us look at those criteria for determining the size of the public sector that do not imply that planning is to be preferred to the market. Thus, we will focus upon the justification for government allocation and redistribution, not on the use of the planning procedure or extensive government ownership instead of market, choice and competition.

## NATURE OF GOODS

A social choice mechanism may provide citizens with goods or services they believe they need; citizens may disagree about the quantity or quality to be provided, since the choice mechanism must provide for rules of arbitration between opposing interests. However, there seems to be a set of goods which few citizens would not consider necessary: protection of internal and external peace, equality before the law and due legal process, and the enforcement of contracts. These goods and services have to be provided by means of public policy, because they have properties that the market as an allocation mechanism fails to meet, since they are indivisible.

The market mechanism is constructed around voluntary exchange for the interaction between citizens, the applicability of which is constrained by the occurrence of the free-rider phenomenon (Buchanan, 1968). Consequently, there is a set of goods or services that has to be provided by means of authority, because a voluntary exchange approach results in a prisoners' dilemma situation as the size of the citizen group increases (Mueller, 1989). Thus, there must be public policy as a function of market failures of various kinds (Layard and Walters, 1978). A generalization of this argument in favour of policy as against market is the pure theory of public goods (Samuelson, 1954).

According to a basic and traditional theme in the public finance approach (Musgrave and Peacock, 1967), there is a set of goods characterized by non-excludability and jointness that the market mechanism cannot supply but that citizens want. The decision to use the collective choice mechanism would thus follow from a consideration of the technical and economic properties of goods (Ostrom and Ostrom, 1977) (Table 1.6).

Table 1.6 *Typology of goods*

|  | Jointness | Rivalry |
|---|---|---|
| Non-excludability | Public goods | Common pool goods |
| Excludability | Toll goods | Private goods |

On the one hand, non-excludability implies market failure because it is only one side of the more general concept of non-appropriability (Head, 1974) or externality (Pigou, 1962), which means that the price mechanism cannot be employed to appropriate the full social benefits or charge the full social costs. Jointness, on the other hand, implies market failure, because if everyone may consume a good or service, then why charge a price if the marginal cost is zero?

Public policy would accordingly be responsible for the allocation of a special set of goods, the public goods characterized by the combination of jointness and non-excludability, like defence and the legal order, whereas the market would take care of the other types of goods. The choice between institutions – voting and bureaucracy on the one hand and market mechanisms on the other – would be a strict consequence of citizens' preferences in relation to the possible mixes of public goods and other kinds of goods.

## The logic of collective action

The problem of allocating public goods is but one version of the general problem of collective action (Olson, 1965, 1982). There are two fundamental problems in collective action that provide public goods of some kind: for example collective wage bargaining or economic growth.

First, there is the free-rider problem that anyone, even a non-union member, can benefit from the good, although he/she does not contribute to paying the cost. This predicament may be called the $N-1$ problem: if a group of $N$ persons allocate a public good, then $N-1$ could free-ride as long as one person goes on providing the good. However, if everybody followed this logic, then no public good would be forthcoming.

Secondly, there is what may be termed the $1/n$-problem in the sense that if some people allocate a public good, then each person can only have a $1/n$ share of the good as $n$ or all other individuals in a society also may consume the good. Thus, if among ten equally large trade unions one union declines to demand any wage increase in order to hold inflation down or stimulate economic growth, it can only have a 1/10 share of these public goods. If the trade union is small, then its ambition to decline a wage increase in order to enhance low inflation or high economic growth for a society will be of no significance as the quota 1/n becomes infinitesimally small.

## The caretaker or guardian state

It has been maintained that this approach to determining the scope of institutions by means of the nature of the goods is the same as the classical minimal theory of the state – the guardian state of Manchester laissez-faire liberalism. However, there is nothing to prevent the allocation of most of the resources of society to the provision of public goods – a maximum theory of the state such as at times of full-scale war, for example.

The difficulty about the theory of public goods is that its basic concept – non-appropriability – is not a very precise one. Positive or negative externalities in production and consumption may be identified for almost all goods; there is no such thing as a neatly identifiable set of goods to be described as non-excludable, whereas all other types of goods would be characterized by excludability. If externality is a property that occurs to a greater or lesser extent among all types of goods, then there would hardly be any limit to the size of public policy in relation to the market. We need an independent criterion that will inform us which externality is to be the target of public policy.

Such a criterion would include considerations not only concerning bad or good externalities but also concerning the capacity of government to take action (Coase, 1960; Buchanan and Stubblebine, 1969). Thus, the existence of non-appropriability in itself can never be a sufficient condition for public policy; not only do we have to know the preferences of citizens in relation to non-excludable goods or social wants, but we must also recognize the cost of implementing public policy in some institutional set-up. Consequently, it is difficult to maintain a sharp distinction between the nature of the goods and the allocation mechanism. If the combination of non-excludability and jointness is an argument for public policy, then how about the combination of non-excludability and rivalry?

## The tragedy of the commons

If the nature of goods is to govern the selection of the collective choice mechanism, then institutional considerations should not enter into the description of the salient properties of goods. However, the notion of common pool goods shows how tenuous the distinction is between technical characteristics and properties that derive from the institutional set-up. It has been argued that public policy should be resorted to when exclusion is impossible, but what does 'impossible' mean? Not possible given the present state of technology, or not economically feasible given the present state of economic institutions?

Once it is realized that the description of goods in terms of the fundamental 2×2 figure is not fixed for all time but is dependent on the evolution of technology and institutions, then the idea of a close relationship between goods and allocation mechanisms must be modified. Non-excludability may be a reason for public policy, but it may equally well enter an argument for an improvement in technologies and institutions so that a good or service become the subject of exclusion.

A large number of resources in society are held in common, as exclusion is ruled out, but they are not characterized by jointness in the Samuelson (1954) sense: 'each individual's consumption of such a good leads to no subtraction from any other individual's consumption of that good' (1954: 387). The problem here is not the provision of goods but the protection of goods. How is such protection to be provided? If protection, that is exclusion, does not work, then the market mechanism cannot work either. Taking an exchange approach the prisoners' dilemma problem is even more acute in relation to common pool goods than with regard to public goods, since consumption by one individual leads to a subtraction from any other individual's consumption.

Thus, individual rationality would result in a rapid depletion of the common pool since the free-rider would not only get something for nothing but also reduce the benefits of the others. Whereas some citizens may accept the free-rider phenomenon in relation to pure public goods because they themselves value the good so highly – the exploitation by the poor of the rich (Olson, 1965) – this cannot be expected in relation to common pool goods. Every person will have a strong incentive to use up the pool but not to make any agreement about providing the protection.

Are common pool goods, then, reason for public policy? Where exchange may fail authority could work, or maybe the solution lies in the transformation of the nature of the goods involved (Hardin and Baden, 1977)? Instead of resorting to public policy the common pool goods problem may be solved by changing the technology and institutions surrounding these resources with the result that exclusion is no longer impossible and market allocation is possible. If such goods are definable in terms of private property institutions, then exclusion becomes possible and the prisoners' dilemma situation is removed.

Transforming the common pool good into private property may involve other kinds of costs, but it demonstrates clearly that non-excludability is not a sufficient condition for public policy. What matters is not that public policy should do what markets cannot do at all, but the relative balance of the two sets of institutions in terms of both pros and cons. Instead of possibility we must look at efficiency.

## Non-subtractability

The fact that citizens may be excluded from consuming a good does not imply that market provision is not problematic. There is a set of goods that is characterized by jointness while simultaneously full exclusion is feasible, so-called toll goods. The collective choice problem vis-à-vis toll goods is to find a choice mechanism that recognizes the public nature of these goods when the principle of exclusion is applied: what is the advantage in excluding citizens from consuming the good if their consumption of the good does not reduce its value with respect to others?

Consequently, the provision of toll goods like roads, parks and some types of communication systems involves a paradox: in contrast to purely public goods excludability is not technically or economically impossible, that is, the costs of providing these goods may be covered and there will be no prisoners' dilemma; but on the other hand it is not socially advantageous to exclude citizens since the marginal cost of consuming the goods is very little. To employ the exclusion principle in relation to toll goods would mean that there could be an under-supply of them. There would be the risk that the full benefits arising from economies of scale would not be taken advantage of; actually jointness is an extreme version of non-subtractability which may be modelled as an economy-of-scale phenomenon.

What allocation mechanism is appropriate in relation to non-subtractability when combined with excludability? A distinction between two different types of non-subtractability may be introduced in order to facilitate the discussion of the pros and cons of the two basic allocation mechanisms, that is, public policy or the market.

*1. Economies of scale in consumption* Jointness implies that each citizen consumes the same good and that the variety of citizen preferences regarding the good is expressed in terms of differences in the marginal willingness to pay (Lindahl mechanism). Thus, the social demand curve will be the outcome of a vertical summation of the individual demand curves and the quantity provided will be determined where the supply curve intersects with the vertically derived demand curve (Figure 1.1).

When there is rivalry, then the demand curve will be the outcome of horizontal summation of the individual demand curves; the price will be the same for all individuals but the quantity consumed will vary (Figure 1.1a). This is quite the opposite to jointness where the Lindahl prices will differ but the same quantity is consumed by all (Figure 1.1b).

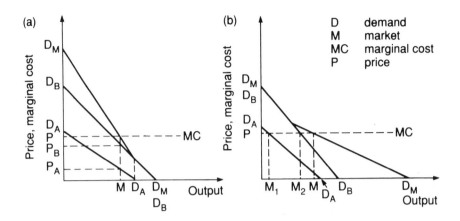

Figure 1.1  *Public goods, private goods and optimality*

An efficient market allocation of the toll good will require a system of differential prices in order to match the variety of individual demand curves. Is such a system of price discrimination possible? It has been argued that one type of market allocation mechanism – perfect competition – cannot handle this problem, because in a perfect competition the price is outside the control of producers and consumers (Head, 1974: 79). However, Harold Demsetz suggests:

> Price differences for the same good in the world of private goods are inconsistent with perfect competition. But price differences can be consistent with competition because a firm that sells a unit for $R_2$ or $R_1$ in markets $D_2$ and $D_1$ does not forgo the sale of the same unit to market $D_3$ at a price $R_3$. (1970: 302)

The difficulty with a market allocation of toll goods lies perhaps not so much in what type of market is the proper one – perfect competition or monopolistic competition. Both would face the same problem which becomes increasingly difficult as the size of the citizen group demanding the good becomes larger: how is knowledge about the variety of citizen preferences for the jointly supplied goods to be secured so that a system of differential prices may be employed which reflects these different preferences? Could such an information base ever be devised to make so-called Lindahl prices feasible as charges or taxes?

Beyond a certain limit for a group of citizens there would no doubt be a strong case for public policy or the public provision of toll goods, as the market allocation of these goods by means of price discrimination may result in considerable social costs. If the price is varied over groups of citizens in a manner that does not correspond to the differences in citizens' preferences, then private cost may be larger or smaller than social cost. In addition, if the price varies between groups of citizens reflecting their different demand schedules, then each citizen would have an incentive to distort his/her preferences. Whilst the free-rider problem creates fundamental problems for the market allocation of public goods and common pool goods, the preference distortion problem lies at the core of a market provision of toll goods.

Actually, the whole idea of a system of differential prices for jointly consumed goods appears to be unrealistic. When toll goods such as theatres, cable TV or telephone services are provided by markets, then either a homogeneous price is employed or the good is transformed into a variety of more or less similar goods to be sold in various markets.

*2. Economies of scale in production* The provision of toll goods may create another kind of difficulty in relation to market allocation as certain types of toll goods display the phenomenon of decreasing marginal cost (Musgrave, 1959: 137). Even if excludability is in principle possible, perfect competition may be impracticable due to the production conditions involved in, for instance, the provision of electricity. The standard analysis of the case for monopoly applies (Bilas, 1971). If there are increasing returns to scale, then the long-term marginal cost could be less than the long-term average cost, meaning that perfect competition cannot be employed (Layard and Walters, 1978).

The monopoly mechanism allows for the provision of these toll goods as the price may be made equal to the long-term average cost, thus avoiding losses to the producer (Ramsey optimum price). However, this is not an efficient solution from the point of view of society. Since the price does not equal the marginal cost there would still be a case for public policy intervention in the market. The government may initiate regulations paying the monopoly to expand output until price equals marginal cost or establish some kind of public utility controlling price and quantity.

Thus, decreasing cost phenomena may be one reason for public policy because the market – either as perfect competition or as monopoly – may not meet the standard efficiency condition; however, it must be strongly emphasized that public policy in relation to non-subtractability is not a sufficient condition for social efficiency. Of course, it does not follow from the fact that there is market failure that there will be policy success. Public intervention, in one form or the other, with regard to the provision of toll goods will only be an improvement in comparison to market provision if the defects inherent in the public production of these goods are fewer than the standard market failures (too little output at too high a price). What are the difficulties involved in the public allocation of goods? Let us look at

the arguments in favour of government allocation of private goods –
the great debate between socialism and capitalism (Bergson, 1982).

## The Barone theorem

Private goods are the opposite of public goods, that is they satisfy the
principle of excludability and the utility derived from their consumption is internalized by the citizens consuming the good. Presumably,
these are the types of goods that are suited for the operations of the
market as an allocation mechanism: there are no externalities and there
is full subtractability, that is, each citizen may act independently of
others. What are the conditions for an efficient allocation of this type
of good? Does (or do) public policy and/or the market satisfy these
conditions? Allocative efficiency has two components following the
basic approach in welfare economics: exchange efficiency and production efficiency (Bergson, 1969; Lange, 1969).

Exchange efficiency refers to a state where further trade cannot
advance the utility of any one citizen without lowering that of another,
that is, the marginal rates of substitution between any pair of goods
are the same for all the individuals who consume the goods. And efficiency in production means that no change in factor inputs will bring
about a larger output of any one good without reducing the output of
another good, that is, the marginal rates of transformation between
any pair of goods is the same for all producers of these goods. An
optimum optimorum is reached when the marginal rate of substitution
equals the marginal rate of transformation for all pairs of goods in
society.

It may be shown that if there is perfect competition, then the price
system reaches such a maximum if the production possibility set is
correct. May we then conclude that the provision of private goods
should be left to the market as the appropriate allocation mechanism
and that public policy could not satisfy individual wants for private
goods? Perfect competition in market institutions is a sufficient condition for social efficiency with regard to allocation of private goods.

It follows from the Barone theorem that public policy may also
satisfy the efficiency conditions (Barone, 1935). The ministry of
production in the socialist state may achieve exchange efficiency,
production efficiency and maximum overall efficiency to the same
extent as the market, if government has the same information as that
utilized by the market. And this is one crux of the matter: is the
acquisition of such a vast knowledge of citizen preferences and
production possibilities practically feasible (Hayek, 1935)?

The controversy between a planned economy and a market economy
boils down to the information and incentive problems. Could public
policy assemble and process the same amount of information that is
contained in a decentralized market system? Could public institutions

motivate choice participants to find socially rational solutions? According to socialist economists this is indeed possible, not only theoretically, but also from a practical point of view (Lange and Taylor, 1964). However, this view has been sharply challenged by those who argue that planning is not conducive to efficiency with regard to the allocation of private goods (Caiden and Wildavsky, 1974).

The welfare economics theorem about the necessary conditions for efficiency in allocation has been turned against the market and its institutions to be used in favour of public policy, government planning or ownership of the means of production (Lerner, 1944; Radomysler, 1969; Little, 1973). It is argued that the market as it actually operates in real life falls far short of the perfect competition model with its monopolies, oligopolies and the phenomenon of monopolistic competition (Schumpeter, 1965). This means that the market allocation of private goods fails to fulfil the efficiency conditions, which could be attained by means of public policy and planning (Bohm, 1976). Thus, in terms of socialist economics the Barone ministry of production should replace the market, even for divisible goods.

Again, we must remind ourselves of the fact that the occurrence of market failure is only a sufficient condition for public policy if it can be shown that public policy entails policy failure less often than existing markets entail market failure. Nobody has ever been able to prove this, nor does the available empirical evidence concerning the amount of efficiency in planned economies indicate that this is the case.

Efficiency considerations as a foundation for the choice between public policy and the market imply that the principle of citizen sovereignty should be upheld. The fundamental question is which mechanism of allocation is the most suitable one, given the preferences of citizens in a democracy. But it is now time to look at an approach that states a case for public policy by-passing the principle of citizen sovereignty.

## Merit goods

To what extent should the outcomes of a collective choice mechanism reflect the preferences of citizens? Some would argue that the principle of citizen sovereignty is inviolable and that social choice is a procedure for the summation or aggregation of individual preferences. Following this approach, it becomes vital to ascertain the extent to which market choice or public policy is in agreement with the preferences of a majority of citizens, or socially consistent.

A quite different approach is to demand that social choice be normative, that is, that it satisfies ethical requirements whatever the preferences of the citizens may be. According to one version of this doctrine, public policy must be employed to assure the allocation of merit goods, that is, goods that are meritorious according to some standard set by public policy (Musgrave, 1959). The identification of merit wants opens up the possibility of extensive public policy-making to replace market behaviour and market outcomes.

There is no limit to how many merit goods there should be apart from those that the normative standard implies. On the other hand the concept of merit goods identifies a crucial dimension in the concept of a social state or a collective outcome, namely the fact that as citizens we may wish to·consider individual rationality as being different from collective rationality (Hardin, 1982). Even if not all individual citizens value education, culture and art, a bare majority may agree that these goods are in the interest of the entire collectivity and thus should be provided for by means of public policy.

The problem is the definition of the concept of individual wants or preferences; is collective choice to be based upon the actual or ideal preferences of the citizens for both private and public wants? Once normative considerations come into the picture alongside the positive deliberations, the problem of demarcation between market and public policy moves into the area of ethics or social justice. Typically these normative considerations arise in the demarcation problem as redistribution criteria or principles of equity.

## JUSTIFICATION OF PUBLIC RESOURCE ALLOCATION

According to the public finance tradition the public sector has a proper place in society – a place that may be determined unambiguously through an investigation of the combined technical and economical properties of goods. If these entities are known for a society, then we know the size of the public budget. It is a sort of 'theory of the state' by which we attempt to determine in which circumstances people in an economy find that an extension of the authority of their government is requisite for the most efficient pursuit of their own economic interests (Baumol, 1965: 51).

Thus, we must see if there is a set of properties that may be employed as decision criteria to derive a set of goods which government is to allocate in accordance with consumer preferences. The preceding examination suggests that the following decision criteria are relevant: non-appropriability and non-subtractability.

In principle, a good is non-excludable when potential consumers cannot be excluded from consuming the good. However, with a slight change, the criterion may be economic in nature: it is not economically feasible to exclude potential consumers once the good is supplied to one consumer. However, it matters whether exclusion is to be technically or economically feasible. Whereas the technical criterion indeed delimits a set of goods so that they may properly be designated non-excludable, the economic criterion on the other hand is much less sharply applicable: when is it economically unfeasible to exclude people from consuming a good?

The application of the economic criterion appears to require a supplementary criterion that reveals what exclusion is to be allowed to cost. What goods are strictly non-excludable following a definition of the exclusion principle as 'enjoyment of a commodity after paying the price set by its owner' (Musgrave, 1959: 9)? Ostrom and Ostrom mention the following goods: peace and security of a community, national defence, mosquito abatement, air pollution control, fire protection, streets, weather forecasts, public TV (1977: 12).

One could argue that it is not quite clear in relation to some of the items mentioned – streets, public TV and weather forecasts – whether they are non-excludable on the grounds of a technical or economic interpretation of the principle of exclusion. But – and this is the crux of the matter – is non-excludability a necessary and/or sufficient criterion for public resource allocation?

Most of the items now included in public budgets hardly satisfy a technical criterion of non-excludability, from which follows that it is in fact not a necessary criterion for public resource allocation. It could not possibly be a sufficient criterion, because there are many goods that are non-excludable by means of the market mechanism and we need a criterion that tells us which of these goods the government should allocate and in what amounts.

It appears that non-exclusion is simply the pure type of the concept of externality (Head, 1974: 51). Thus, if we want to use the criterion of non-excludability as an argument for government resource allocation we must have a new criterion that tells us in addition which externality will be the basis for how much of government action. Of course, the non-excludability criterion cannot help us here as it needs for its application the very same criterion that we are looking for.

Jointness in supply or demand seems to imply market failure, because jointness implies a system of differential prices for one and the same good, whereas perfect competition implies uniform prices for different amounts of the good supplied by competing producers. Jointness would thus constitute the second type of market failure. But is jointness a necessary or sufficient condition for public resource allocation?

Very few goods are truly non-subtractable or carry zero marginal cost. In fact, there is a large set of goods often allocated by government that is characterized by limited subtractability or decreasing marginal cost: health care, electricity and gas services, water and sewage systems, education, and so on. Owing to overcrowding, all such goods display non-subtractability up to a certain limit only. We thus need a new criterion which will indicate when the extent of non-subtractability is such as to necessitate public resource allocation.

Pure non-subtractability could hardly in itself constitute a necessary condition for public resource allocation, because there are hardly any such goods. Even for such typical Samuelsonian goods as national defence or clean air, there are trade-offs: one part of the country may be supplied with the good so that the availability of the good in other parts of the country decreases or increases. The fact that one subset of citizens consumes a certain amount of such a good may certainly have clear implications for the consumption of the good by other citizens.

It seems difficult, not to say impossible, to argue that jointness is a sufficient condition for public resource allocation, because there may be many goods characterized by some non-subtractability or decreasing cost that may conveniently be allocated by the market mechanism: swimming-pools or various kinds of sports facilities, higher education, health care, and so on. Obviously, we need a new criterion that will tell us when the amount of jointness reaches a level that necessitates public resource allocation.

Even if it followed from the occurrence of market failure in the face of non-subtractability or decreasing cost that a good should be allocated by means of public resource allocation, we still need to know how much of the good is to be provided by government action. The criterion of jointness is a type criterion, not an amount criterion. It could help us understand what kinds of goods are suitable for government provision, but it does not carry any implication whatsoever as to the size of good to be provided. The missing link is, of course, preferences.

In fact, the properties of non-excludability and non-appropriability hardly suffice to delimit a discrete set of goods or services that may be designated the proper sphere of public budget-making, because these properties are better conceived of as ordinal variables. This means that we may order goods and services on the basis of extent of externality and extent of jointness. What are the public policy implications of various degrees of externality and various degrees of jointness?

The public finance literature states that government should counteract negative externalities and realize increasing returns to scale. By talking about degrees of non-excludability and degrees of jointness we may move away from the simplistic notion of a neat set of goods which the government should allocate.

The occurrence of externalities as the basis for government action is a typical argument in the welfare economics tradition. Baumol only considers externality as the criterion for public resource allocation (1965: 52). What is an externality? The phenomenon of externality is usually approached as a divergence between private marginal utility (cost) and social marginal utility (cost) in production or consumption. Externality may be (1) positive, when private marginal utility is less than social marginal utility, or (2) negative, when private marginal cost is less than social marginal cost (non-rejectability).

The government employs a number of measures to create equality between private utility and social utility as well as between private cost and social cost (Johansen, 1978a: 178–84). Are we to conclude that externality is a sufficient condition for public resource allocation? Most fundamental is the objection that government must resort to other criteria in order to arrive at a conclusion as to how to handle the variety of externalities. How is government to know the level of social utility or social costs associated with a good if the market mechanism is not to be trusted?

The crux of the matter is that whereas the operation of market mechanisms allows for the aggregation of individual decisions into social outcomes, no corresponding institutional mechanism lies in the hands of government or bureaucracy. In order to arrive at conclusions about the level of marginal social utility, government must know not only how each single individual values the goods in question but also how to aggregate these various individual values. Only if government knows the preferences of citizens in relation to various externalities as well as how to add them together is it possible to arrive at definitive conclusions about how much to allocate.

Thus, we end up again with the need for a new criterion – preferences that will help us sort out the implications of externalities for public policy. If consumer preferences govern the market, then citizens' preferences may govern the size of the public sector only if there are institutions that reveal and aggregate these: 'the decision to satisfy one or another social want must be derived, somehow, from the effective preferences of the individual member of the group as determined by his tastes and his "proper" share in full-employment income. A political process must be substituted for the market mechanism' (Musgrave, 1959: 10–11).

In order to determine the size of the public sector we need, in addition to the economic and technical criteria, political criteria that state how the preferences of the citizens with regard to those goods which satisfy the criteria of externality and jointness are to be aggregated into a collective decision – what economists call a *social welfare function* (Mishan, 1981).

Market failure occurs in relation to the allocation of goods that display two different types of reciprocities or interdependence between human beings: in the case of externality, reciprocity implies that the actions of one person affect the actions of another person; in the case of jointness, the utilities of each person depend upon the consumption of the very same good by several individuals.

Any society faces a choice with regard to these two types of reciprocities: how much of them do we want? If a society wishes to favour interaction based on jointness, then the public sector will no doubt be large. Similarly, if a society cares about externalities, there will be a great deal of public resource allocation. However, if the actions of independent utility maximizers are considered more important than reciprocities, then the public sector will be small.

The size of the public sector is a function not simply of properties of goods, nor only of the preferences of citizens, but of the prevailing values or culture in a society identifying what is an externality and a jointness. How to handle the problem of reciprocities versus independence or autonomy is a task for ideologies, and the solution to the problem cannot be derived by investigating 'economic' matters only.

## FISCAL FEDERALISM

The classical public finance model restricted the allocation branch of government to goods and services that were clearly public, like external and internal defence (Musgrave, 1959; Buchanan, 1968; Tullock, 1970). Recent public finance models have enlarged the scope of the theory by pointing out that the public goods properties may be transformed into criteria for public policy actions as various goods and services may be characterized by more or less excludability and more or less jointness (Baumol, 1965; Prest and Barr, 1979). The basic criterion would then be whether externalities and scale economies are more efficiently handled by government or by market institutions (Bohm, 1976).

In addition the public finance approach contains some simple economic principles for the structuring of the entire state, that is, the fiscal federalism theory (Oates, 1972). In order to achieve an optimal institutional set-up involving national government and regional and local governments, tasks and functions should be allocated in a determinate way between the various levels of government. These principles apply not only to federalist states but also to the mix of centralization and decentralization in unified states. Yet it must be

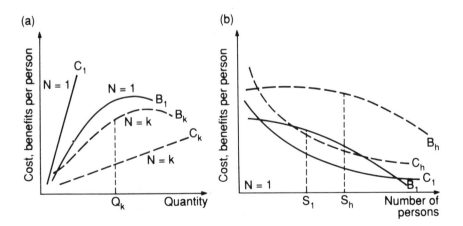

Figure 1.2  *Local goods and optimality*

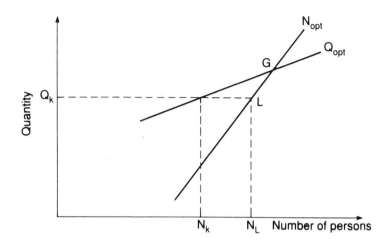

Figure 1.3  *Optimal local clubs*

emphasized that these economic rules of thumb may come into conflict with power interests that also govern the structuring of the public sector.

The idea of fiscal federalism is closely connected with the concept of club goods (Buchanan, 1965). Local government should concentrate on the allocation of goods and services that display jointness or economies of scale but that are not pure public goods. Consider some indivisible good that several people in a neighbourhood of a certain size could use. Then they could create a club for this facility, deciding its optimal size as a function of how many pay and how many use the facility (Figure 1.2a). It would also be possible to derive the proper size of the club given that it operates infrastructure of a certain size, or to derive the proper size of the local community given the existence of infrastructure, as shown in Figure 1.2b.

Combining the two graphs into Figure 1.3 we arrive at the optimal allocation of so-called local public goods, or goods that are indivisible but whose utility tapers off and that may experience congestion. An economic theory of local government would state that local governments should be formed in response to the need for such local public goods.

First, the principle of fiscal equivalence implies that benefits and costs should be tied together as closely as possible, meaning that charges should be used to pay for the consumption of local public goods (Cornes and Sandler, 1986). Secondly, equity considerations are the concern of the central or national government to be handled by means of general redistribution programmes. Finally, the inefficiencies created by local government taxation should be corrected by means of national government grants.

However, these principles concerning a suitable combination of economic efficiency and social justice are not implemented in actually existing institutions. The relationships between central and local government are to a considerable degree based on practical circumstances involving trade-offs between political power and economic efficiency that do not follow the fiscal federalism model.

## MARKET FAILURE OR POLICY FAILURE?

To public finance scholars the market fails because of the nature of goods – non-appropriability as well as non-subtractability – whereas believers in a planned economy observe market malfunctioning in terms of institutional deviants, monopoly, oligopoly and monopolistic competition. The weakness inherent in both positions is that there is no estimation of the likelihood of public policy failure.

Theoretically, we cannot compare the probability of market failure with an ideal model of public policy-making and implementation. Instead, we must move to a relative comparison of the pros and cons of each allocation mechanism; thus we must base the choice between market and state on some theory about the probability of policy failure.

Given the objective of collective choice, be it efficiency in production or consumption or equity in the distribution of resources, the probability of market failure must be balanced against the likelihood of policy failure as the basis for evaluation of the choice mechanism to be employed. The mere existence of market failure is not a sufficient condition for public sector programmes, because there may also be policy failure.

The argument in favour of the public sector is often based on the assumption of an ideally perfect fiscal system, the expenditures of which achieve what the market cannot accomplish where the financing of these items is neutral with respect to market operations (Buchanan, 1967). Recent literature has gone a long way towards shattering such simplistic notions. These *institutional problems* will be discussed at length in the chapters below on models of policy-making (Chapter 3) and implementation (Chapter 4).

The advantages of the market exceed those of public budget-making if its probable benefits minus its costs exceed the expected value of the latter. It may well be the case that government can deliver where markets fail; market failure may be extensive in relation to goods and services which are very much in demand by citizens, meaning that there is a real necessity for public policy. The public household has a rationale no doubt; and many would argue the redistribution case of equity for public policy.

## TAXATION POLICY DILEMMAS

Public households carry costs. How do we pay for the public household? Markets have their revenue logic, which implies the identification of a budget constraint for the provision of goods as well as a natural way of eliminating whatever does not meet the criterion of fiscal solvency. Whilst there may be a case for public expenditure because of market failure, the revenue aspect of the public household is much less impressive. Basically, government may be paid for by means of benefit taxation, the ability to pay taxation or deficit spending besides lump-sum taxes (Musgrave and Musgrave, 1980; Buchanan, 1967; Brennan and Buchanan, 1980).

Benefit taxation is only possible to a limited extent, because total application of the principle of benefit taxation to pay for public policy would require an elaborate information system that would indicate each citizen's willingness to pay in relation to each good. This is not feasible due to the preference revelation problem, nor are redistribution policies possible under benefit taxation. Resorting to the principle of ability to pay implies that the relationship between sacrifice and benefit becomes obscure in public policy. And large-scale deficit spending opens up the possibilities for big government expanding beyond the size where marginal cost would equal marginal value in its programmes. Actually, existing taxation systems tend to follow the politics of taxation (Peters, 1991) more than public finance recommendations about efficient tax structures (Atkinson and Stiglitz, 1980).

What emerges for political strategies in policy-making about taxation at various levels of government is the fact that taxation decisions involve deliberations about both efficiency and equity, goals which often contradict each other. The logic of taxation institutions invites opportunistic behaviour among several groups in order to maximize their gains. Since there is no natural connection between those who benefit from and those who pay for the public household, the politics of taxation has its own basic problems divorced from the politics of public policy-making and implementation (Fenno, 1966).

The criterion of efficiency implies that dead-weight losses and static and dynamic efficiency costs are to be minimized, in so far as this is possible given all the uncertainties of tax incidence and behaviour reactions to various kinds of taxation, such as taxes on income, on wealth, on corporate profits, on property and indirect taxes of various kinds. The criterion of justice may be interpreted in different ways, depending on the position taken with regard to the troublesome concept of social justice.

Whereas there used to be a strong utilitarian argument for progressive taxes (see Chapter 10), it is now emphasized that the efficiency losses of such a taxation scheme could be substantial to society. Actually, only a special kind of tax – so-called lump-sum taxation –

satisfies the efficiency criterion, but lump-sum taxes cannot be employed for redistribution purposes. A lump-sum tax is fixed in amount and of such a nature that the taxpayer cannot in practice have an impact on the liability to pay.

The inherent conflicts between various goals that a taxation system may be evaluated against make the construction and implementation of taxation systems difficult, judged by the standard neo-classical model of such a system (Musgrave, 1959). However, the very same discrepancy between tax realities and ideal taxes opens up a broad scope for political strategies in the making of public policy with regard to the many instruments of taxation.

There are several goals that are relevant in the normative theory about taxation. First, the tax system on the input side of the public household must raise enough revenue to pay for the programmes on the output side of this household. Secondly, it should be economical in the sense that it involves minimal waste in terms of excess burden and dead-weight losses. Thirdly, it should be usable in stabilization policies, contributing to economic growth and external balance. Fourthly, it must be equitable in some sense.

Employing many different forms of taxation where several allow for tax avoidance, there is bound to be opportunistic behaviour in the making and implementation of tax policies. Special interest groups may be very effective in lobbying for tax loopholes when Parliament is to decide on changes in one or another tax.

## JUSTIFICATION OF REDISTRIBUTION

The public finance model may be interpreted in terms of Knut Wicksell's (1967) approach equating (Pareto-)efficiency in budget-making with the unanimity decision rule. It would need to be supplemented by a theory about the distribution branch of government. Efficiency considerations have to be supplemented by deliberations about justice, both ex ante and ex post the calculation of the efficiency implications of public policy. However, the public finance model, recognizing the necessity of distributional criteria, has little to say about the criterion of social justice to be employed in public policy.

The attempt to derive implications about public resource allocation from an argument about the properties of public goods is based on the idea of aggregating individual preferences. Any optimum allocation of resources will result in a distribution of income. But the resulting distribution of income may not be just, because the initial income distribution was not equitable. Though the workings of the efficiency criteria are neutral, the outcome may still be socially unacceptable. The application of the allocative principles requires that matters of equity be relegated to the distribution branch, which may secure a just, initial distribution of income before the beginnings of exchange and public goods provision (Musgrave and Peacock, 1967).

The idea of an ex ante welfare distribution criterion has the same function as the general idea of a social welfare function that is a necessary complement to the efficiency framework (Bergson, 1954, 1969; Bator, 1957a,b). What economists refer to as a social welfare function is a perspective that contains a set of normative principles or an equity criterion, which may be employed for redistributive choices, either ex ante or ex post. It will be discussed at length in the chapter on normative models. In the words of Head:

> In welfare maximization analysis for both a private goods world and a world with a public good, we obtain a utility possibility locus or infinite set of Pareto-optimal points corresponding to different distributions of welfare. In both cases the choice of unique optimorum or optimum optimorum requires the strong value judgements of a social welfare function. (1974: 94)

Whether the social welfare function is to be employed ex ante or ex post the operation of the allocative principles is a contested issue; here, the important point is that the efficiency argument is supposed to govern the size of the public sector in the allocation interpretation, whereas the equity argument expressed in a social welfare function is assumed to solve the problem of arriving at a size for the public transfer. Technically speaking, the problem of deciding how equity is to be combined with efficiency is usually approached in terms of a utility possibility curve (U) and a social welfare function (W) applied to that curve (Figure 1.4).

This means employing an ex post procedure to solve the problem, the equity consideration being applied after the resources have been

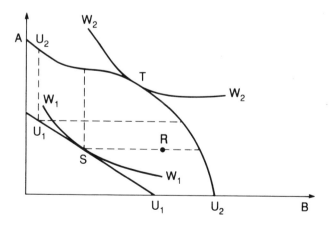

Figure 1.4 *Ex ante and ex post equity*

allocated and the incomes distributed by whatever decision mechanism is considered efficient (T). All discussions about the equity–efficiency combination proceed on the basis of the assumption that the private goods world is to be regulated by the market with the government supplying the public goods. Obviously, if we know the welfare function we could apply it ex ante making sure that the working of the efficiency principle does not exacerbate the original inequities (S).

Using the social welfare function construction as a tool to bridge the gap between the allocation branch (efficiency) and the distribution branch (equity) of the public budget raises important theoretical issues concerning the relationship between the principle of social justice (equity) and the nature of collective choice.

First, the working out of the efficiency principle following, basically, consumer preferences for public goods and private goods would depend for its final outcome on the initial distribution of incomes. If the initial distribution of income is not in accordance with the equity principle, how can we apply a social welfare function ex post? If the initial distribution of income is equitable, then we do not need a social welfare function ex post. If the resulting distribution of income is not in accordance with the principles of equity, then of what use would the ex ante criterion be?

The problem is that in determining how much income redistribution there should be, no distinction can be made between the ex ante and ex post application of a social welfare function. When a government decides how much equity it wants in terms of income distribution it has to face the fact that the prevailing outcomes are efficient only in a conditional sense, given the initial distribution of income; moreover, it necessarily changes the efficiency operations when it redistributes income. In a dynamic perspective, including both ex ante and ex post situations, efficiency and equity cannot be separated.

Suppose we have a society of two individuals A and B, whose utility situations ex ante and ex post are depicted in Figure 1.4. If A and B are at S and the ex ante equity criterion is considered satisfied, then we do not need to make a new equity decision ex post (T). If A and B are not at S at some non-equitable point – a false start – the outcome of the efficiency principle may constrain the ex post choices in such a way as to make an optimum ex post situation impossible. But how is government to know what would have followed had we started from S or outside S? Could it choose the trade-off at R?

Moreover, the ex ante and ex post criteria do not have to be the same as we may wish to apply a Rawlsian maximin rule to the outcomes of a primary state of equity. But if we want to employ two equity criteria why bother about ex ante equity? Secondly, there is the even more fundamental problem of specifying a principle of equity in the first place. What is social justice?

## EQUITY

The standard approach to equity is to argue that efficiency considerations are necessary but not sufficient for the derivation of a social state. Allocative efficiency offers a number of efficiency loci, the choice amongst which has to be made on the basis of redistributive criteria or social justice (Graaff, 1957; Samuelson, 1965; Mishan, 1981). How are principles of social justice to be identified in a social welfare function?

If equity is interpreted as equality we get the famous distinction between equality ex ante and equality ex post (Thurow, 1980). Of course, the market cannot afford these equity principles, since they are supposed to be relevant to collective choice before or after (or both) the operations of the market. The choice between market and government with regard to social justice is related to the valuation of merit versus equality of result. The equity–efficiency trade-off models how much redistribution of income and wealth society government may be prepared to pay for in terms of economic output forsaken (Okun, 1975).

However, this does not imply that equity must be at odds with market principles. It is possible to conceive of principles of equity which legitimate the market. If the established order of rights and duties is accepted as the starting point for the derivation of an efficiency locus, then public policy may be dispensed with. It can be shown that perfect competition tends to distribute income in accordance with the marginal product value of the factors of production (Varian, 1987). And it could be argued that the profits derived in market situations might be regarded as justified, because they may be used for risk-prone activities (Schumpeter, 1989).

Any social welfare function (SWF) implies principles of equity which reflect the moral principles one adheres to. Such principles may offer a straightforward defence of the market, the 'contractarian man' of Buchanan (1977) or the minimal state of Nozick (1974), or they may suggest far-reaching intervention in either the presuppositions of the market or the outcomes of the market, as in the Rawlsian maximin and difference principles (Rawls, 1971).

The social welfare function introduces a political maxim into the attempt to derive a government size from the preferences of consumers/citizens. It may be challenged by various ideological principles. Only if the social welfare function is derived by means of some aggregation rule from individual welfare functions is the public finance requirement of consumers' sovereignty satisfied (Musgrave, 1959: 13).

Even if it were possible to allocate public goods in strict accordance with the diversity of individual preferences by means of an intricate system of differential prices (Lindahl prices), the applications of the distribution principle changing the outcome of the allocation by means of transfer payments must be zero-sum. The social welfare function must contain criteria for how conflicting interests are to be accommodated.

We need political criteria that will inform us as to when it is proper for a majority of citizens to implement a social welfare function against the will of the minority. Such criteria for the aggregation of citizens' preferences cannot be justified merely by referring to the principle of consumer sovereignty. Actually, the idea of a functional correspondence between private goods and public goods – supply follows demand – has already been abandoned by the acceptance of a third category – merit goods. According to Musgrave: 'They [social wants] become public wants if considered so meritorious that their satisfaction is provided for through the public budget, over and above what is provided for through the market and paid for by private buyers' (1959: 13).

Merit goods may be interpreted as redistribution. Redistribution may be in cash or in kind. Various kinds of redistribution may be identified: broad horizontal, life cycle and insurance type, vertical as well as fragmented horizontal redistribution among minority groups, besides redistribution to organized interests (Lindbeck, 1984: 1). The existence of categorical equity has implications for the distinction between the public and the private.

The public finance school makes a distinction between the allocative and redistributive branches of government, the former providing goods and services in accordance with the criteria of externality and jointness whereas the latter would concentrate on ex ante or ex post transfer payments. Redistribution in kind means that we cannot make a simple distinction between efficiency and equity, between public resource allocation and public resource distribution. The public provision of goods and services has clear distributive implications whatever the nature of the goods involved.

It is not only the case that the public allocation of private and semi-public goods carries redistributive consequences, but also the provision of pure public goods may be employed for redistribution (Tullock, 1959). Under majority rule there is no guarantee that the groups that benefit from the composition of the budget are the same groups that pay the costs or that benefit equals sacrifice. The simple framework of efficiency and equity in determining the proper size of the state is muddled by the recognition that public resource allocation is not neutral in relation to considerations of social justice.

It is not easy to derive a social welfare function from individual preferences; as a matter of fact it may contain more than individual values and some aggregation rule, that is, an equity maxim. If a cardinal utility aggregation is impossible because the utility ranking of individuals is not strictly interpersonally comparable (Samuelson, 1965) and if the political decision process cannot generally devise an aggregation rule that satisfies a few elementary choice criteria, then how do we arrive at the necessary criterion?

Will the actual workings of the political process suffice? No, social outcomes may fail to satisfy ethical criteria that make collective choice a function of individual values. Eugene Mishan is explicit on this point:

> a SWF for society giving expression to a distributional ordering is not to be regarded as a sort of synthesis of the individual SWFs of a society of economic men or political men; . . . society's SWF ought to be regarded as a synthesis of the individual SWFs of men in their capacity as ethical beings, in which capacity their deliberations are guided solely by considerations of what is right and just. (1981: 130)

Thus, we are back to the ideal interpretation, but a solution to the size problem concerning the public sector cannot await the arrival of ethical reasoning at a principle of equity that meets with acceptance – among reasonable people, contractarians or those in the state of veiled ignorance.

An ad hoc solution is used in the public finance model. Assume that there is a social welfare function that is ethical and satisfies the Pareto principle for being a function of individual preferences. What is the best or ideal state of the world for such a simple system? Samuelson answers: 'To answer this ethical, normative question we must be given a set of norms in the form of a social welfare function that renders interpersonal judgements. For expository convenience, let us suppose that will be supplied later' (1955: 351–2).

We may wish to know who is to give us the social welfare function and how it is going to handle zero-sum changes. This is a problem for normative policy models, examined in Chapter 10.

## MACRO- OR MICRO-DEMARCATION

By failing to use the properties of goods as a starting point, and bearing in mind that the possibility of exclusion and the existence of jointness are decisive for the use of allocation mechanisms, the solution to the demarcation problem will be determined by the properties of the allocation mechanisms themselves. If public policy has the properties ascribed to it by Tullock (1965) – bureaucratic waste – and by Buchanan – revenue-maximizing Leviathan – then why not devise a solution to the demarcation problem by restricting the scope of public policy as much as possible (Tullock, 1965; Brennan and Buchanan, 1980)?

The traditional approaches to the demarcation problem proceed along a micro-perspective, taking each type of good and service by itself and discussing the relative merits of the two allocation mechanisms, seeking a solution that is adequate in terms of efficiency and equity. The weakness of the micro-solution is that it implies a public policy preference; if public policy is prima facie to do what markets cannot do, then there is hardly any limit to what public policy may be trusted to do. The outcome is that public policy will drive out markets if there is no awareness of the danger of policy failure or the weak financial restrictions on policy-making.

One macro-solution could be to tie public sector growth to economic growth so that the public–private balance will not be upset. If the number of resources in society grows then public policy may expand, but not otherwise, except in national emergencies (Wildavsky, 1980). The strength of the macro-solution to the demarcation problem is that it identifies another dimension in the problem, the system level.

The use of allocation mechanisms has, from the point of view of a systems level, profound implications for basic values in society, including the confrontation between individualism and collectivism. Those who adhere to a macro-solution, by fixing the public policy sector once and for all, argue that markets are an essential ingredient in a free society as they are based on the exit option.

Fundamentally, public policy rests upon authority not exchange, and authority may be backed by power and coercion, however large the voice option may be. Moreover, collective allocation mechanisms like public policy feed on fiscal illusions that make citizens blind to bureaucratic strategies and to overspending by politicians (Buchanan and Wagner, 1977). A constitutional spending limitation decision would curb those forces conducive to over-expansion in the public sector.

The disadvantage of the macro-solution is that there is no way of knowing if the fixation of the size of public policy is a desirable decision in terms of efficiency. Maybe the actual preferences of consumers in combination with some criterion of efficiency in allocation imply that markets ought to be expanded and public policy reduced, or that public policy should be used even more.

Will policy failure diminish if the rate of expansion of public policy is limited? It seems important not simply to identify some overall desirable size for public policy but to identify the causes of policy failure in each circumstance in order to discover whether the market could have performed better. If taxation or inefficiency is the major problem in public policy then it is not absolutely certain that a spending limitation decision will be the answer.

Even after a constitutional amendment, which would limit the decision-making capacity of parliaments in a way that might be difficult to accept, we would still be looking for ways of solving the demarcation problem in order to put the allocation mechanism to its most efficient use in providing goods and services for the citizens.

The macro-solution may be an important step towards such objectives as saving markets, but it does not solve the demarcation problem. Besides, such a demarcation solution does not solve the problem of the proper size of the domestic economy and the unofficial economy which may substitute for the official economy at times (Rose, 1989).

## CONCLUSION

It is often argued that the distinction between the public and the private sectors has become more diffuse in the mixed economies of the rich countries with representative governments. Government is about to drive out the market, intervening in several different ways with the operations and outcomes of market allocation mechanisms.

There is no single way to make the private–public distinction. Several interpretations of the public sector should be borne in mind: (a) bureaucracy, (b) planned economy, (c) authority, (d) public resource allocation, (e) public distribution of income, (f) public ownership, (g) public employment.

One cannot simply state a case for government over and above market failure; the probability of policy failure has to be taken into account, but is it feasible to calculate the expected value of the market and of public policy in order to arrive at an acceptable system solution? Perhaps we ought to try a constitutional solution to the demarcation problem, fixing in some way the relative sizes of public policy and market once and for all.

The prevailing public finance approach states that the size of the allocation branch follows from the technical and economic properties of goods and the preferences of citizens. Similarly, the size of the distribution branch would complement, not replace, the market operations on the basis of a social welfare function expressing the preferences of citizens in relation to equity.

The public finance framework is both simple and packed with interesting concepts. However, as there seems to be much more to public policy than non-excludability and jointness, its applicability is rather narrow. Is ongoing policy-making really an attempt to find an efficient solution to the problem of satisfying social wants? Do we understand a public programme structure or a public budget when we call attention to the free-rider problem or the rational ambition to take advantage of scale economies? What about human motivation in public policy?

It seems that a crucial element has been left out when the public finance model tries to derive a size for the public sector: political criteria. The implications of technical or economic properties of goods and services for public resource allocation are indeterminate without criteria that state how government is to handle various degrees of externality and jointness. To derive these decision criteria on the basis of some aggregation rule from the preferences of citizens begs the fundamental institutional question: how are collective decisions made in the public sector? We must begin to look at institutional models. Moreover, the necessary justice principles require the use of ethical criteria which fall outside the public finance framework.

We have examined the public finance models that state guide-lines as to how to make the demarcation line between the public and the private sectors. We established a rationale for some kind of a public sector: public goods allocation. However, how large the public sector is in a country depends upon factors that have an impact on broad public resource allocation, public redistribution and public regulation. Before we turn to the policy models we will survey the bureaucracy models in order to arrive at a perspective on one very important kind of public institution, the bureau.

Looking at the demarcation is not enough if we wish to understand the distinction between the public and private sectors. What is missing is the logic of interests that cluster around the public sector. Anthony Downs argued in a well-known article (1960) that the government budget in a democracy tends to be too small because of the staggering costs of information about the potential benefits for rational citizens. As we embark upon the analysis of the role of public institutions in relation to various group interests we will see that the exactly opposite argument is sometimes used in the research on bureaux and public policy-making.

# 2

# CONCEPTS OF BUREAUCRACY

A public household in general and public resource allocation in particular would be impossible without the existence of a structure of bureaux at various levels of government making and implementing decisions as to which goods and services are to be supplied in what amounts to various groups of citizens/consumers. Public resource redistribution depends on the existence of administrative personnel who handle transfer payment tasks in accordance with a publicly enacted system of rules. In the welfare states the role of bureaux is extensive as a considerable part of the total resources is allocated over the budget (Dunleavy, 1985, 1991).

Public regulation is conducted by means of bureaux monitoring those whose behaviour the state wishes to control or govern. The concept of the bureau seems to be at the very heart of the public sector as James Wilson argues in *Bureaucracy: What Government Agencies Do and Why They Do It* (1987), but the basic problem is to come up with a plausible theory about the logic of bureau operations that has empirical support (Aberbach et al., 1981).

Although there is unanimous agreement about the necessity of bureaux in the welfare state, there is wide disagreement about the basic characteristics of bureau behaviour or bureaucracy. It is readily recognized that 'bureau' and 'bureaucracy' are not synonymous; whereas the meaning of the word 'bureau' tends to be rather un-ambiguous, 'bureaucracy' presents quite a semantic predicament.

The *Oxford English Dictionary* states as one of the meanings of 'bureau': 'an office for the transaction of public business; a department of public administration'. Sometimes 'bureaucracy' has the same denotation. However, often 'bureaucracy' does not stand for some object or entity like a set of people, but refers to some institution or a set of properties of organization.

In the extensive literature on public authorities or agencies one may discern mutually inconsistent propositions about bureau operations such as:

1  Bureaucracies are capable of the highest level of rationality or efficiency (Weber, 1978).
2  Bureau behaviour is characterized by economic inefficiency as well as administrative waste (Tullock, 1965; Niskanen, 1971).

3  The logic of bureau operations is irrationality (March and Olsen, 1976; Hogwood and Peters, 1985).

The basic issue of contention concerns how efficient bureaux tend to be or could be. How do we test these propositions in order to find out which one has greatest empirical support (Goodsell, 1983)? It seems important to insist upon an empirical procedure to find out how bureaux operate, but it is impossible to by-pass theoretical problems as to how bureaucracies are conceptualized in opposing theories. What is the meaning of the key terms 'bureau', 'bureaucracy behaviour' and 'efficiency'?

By looking at the concept of bureaucracy implied in general statements about bureau characteristics, not only may we find out how the key terms are defined, but also such an examination will give us clues to the kind of test that is appropriate to such statements. It cannot be taken for granted that these terms are employed in similar senses.

There are two main types of distinct approaches to bureaucracy: the organizational framework and the public choice approach. Theories of bureaux and bureaucracy behaviour derived from mainstream public choice theory tend to be individualist, atomistic and economic in their assumptions (McLean, 1987); the organizational approach displays an emphasis on structure, wholes and power (Benson, 1982). How to integrate these two research traditions is a major task facing the study of bureaux, as the one proceeds from the assumption of individual utility maximization, whereas the other emphasizes complexity and unintended functions (Chisholm, 1987).

## THE SEMANTIC APPROACH TO BUREAUCRACY

A look at usage or definitions reveals ambiguity as well as confusion between the descriptive and normative employment of 'bureaucracy' which is shown in Martin Albrow's *Bureaucracy* (1970). Fred W. Riggs (1979) examines the variety of meanings of 'bureaucracy', concluding that the concept may denote aggregates or systems, wholes or parts as well as a variety of properties having various emotive connotations. It is unlikely that such a set of different meanings may be reduced to a common conceptual core.

It appears that 'bureaucracy' is what is referred to as a 'theoretical term', that is, it derives its meaning from the theoretical context in which it operates and as an abstract concept it needs the elaboration of indicators to be applied to observable phenomena (Kaplan, 1964). The theoretical nature of the concept of bureaucracy means that it is necessary to look at the specific context in which propositions concerning bureaucracy behaviour are stated. Let us begin with the classical bureaucracy analysis: the Weberian 'idealtypus'.

## BUREAUCRACY AS RATIONALITY

Max Weber is considered to be the chief spokesman of the theory of bureaucracy as efficiency. He makes a number of claims in *Economy and Society* that point towards a theory about bureau rationality or efficiency, for example:

> Experience tends universally to show that the purely bureaucratic type of administrative organization – that is, the monocratic variety of bureaucracy – is, from a purely technical point of view, capable of attaining the highest degree of efficiency and is in this sense formally the most rational known means of exercising authority over human beings. (Weber, 1978: 223)

The association of bureaucracy with efficiency is clear in Weberian administrative theory; yet, there are some key problems of interpretation in relation to the quotation that must be resolved (Rudolph and Rudolph, 1979). What is meant by 'bureaucracy', 'experience' and 'capable of'? Note that Weber did not state that bureaucracy is efficiency, but that bureaucracy is capable of efficiency; the use of the phrase 'experience tends universally to show' indicates that the theory is intended as an empirical generalization about the contribution of various administrative forms to efficiency.

Weber's is not an absolute concept of efficiency, but a relative one, comparing the historical evidence about various types of authority structures (*Herrschaft*) in order to rank three types in terms of their relative efficiency (traditional, charismatic and legal authority).

The Weberian claim about bureau efficiency rests on his famous model of bureaucracy – an ideal-type comprising the following properties (Weber, 1978: 220–1): impersonal authority structure, hierarchy of offices in a career system of specified spheres of competence, free selection based on achievements in accordance with specified rules, remuneration in terms of money based on clear contracts, discipline and control in the conduct of office. The formal model of bureaucracy contains nothing about bureaucratic motivation, but Weber's notion of *Beruf* or vocation is assumed.

Of course, bureaucratic efficiency cannot simply be a function of the formal structure of the bureau, but depends crucially on what goals are expressed in the behaviour of bureaucrats as well as what means are considered. Maybe the lack of any requirements concerning the motivation of bureaucrats in the model explains the phrase 'capable of', since it opens up the possibility that bureaucracies that are close to the Weberian ideal-type characteristics nevertheless perform poorly simply because the bureau officers do not care too much about efficiency or productivity.

How bureaux operate will depend on more factors than those specified in the model, though we are not told what these other factors are. Formal bureaucratic organization in accordance with the model makes bureaux only 'capable of . . . the highest degree of efficiency'.

The missing link is supplied in the Weberian theory of bureaucratic behaviour as a vocation:

> Rather, entrance into an office, including one in the private economy, is considered an acceptance of a specific duty of fealty to the purpose of the office (*Amtstreue*) in return for the grant of a secure existence. It is decisive for the modern loyalty to an office that, in the pure type it does not establish a relationship to a person, like the vassal's or discipline's faith under feudal or patrimonial authority, but rather is devoted to impersonal and functional purposes. (Weber, 1978: 959)

Weber argued from a historical perspective comparing modern bureaucracy with other types of government or authority; judged in relation to other types of authority and government modern bureaucracy is more efficient, but it does not follow that modern bureaucracy is efficient according to other criteria. Thus, Weber may be both right and wrong: the relative efficiency judgement may be correct depending on experience, but the strong efficiency judgement that modern bureaucracy is capable of 'the highest degree of efficiency' – an absolute comparison as it were – does not follow from experience.

The basic Weberian idea is that the transition from a personal relation to a impersonal one establishes the concept of an office to which the office holder is more devoted than to any person (the ethics of *Beruf*). This may be a step towards more efficiency, but it does not make modern bureaucracy efficient in an absolute sense. We have here a sort of fallacy: the fact that a bureaucrat is devoted to his/her office does not entail that the motivation problem is solved; it is still possible that the office holder is thus devoted because it maximizes his/her own personal utility or because he/she wishes to maximize the utility of the bureau. Both these objectives may not be conducive to efficiency.

The emphasis in the Weberian analysis is too much focused on formal institutional structure emerging from a historical perspective; what is crucial to efficiency in bureaucracy behaviour is the ends and means of bureau behaviour. And it does not follow that bureaucrats pursue ends and means that are in the public interest simply because they are oriented more towards their office than towards personal loyalty to someone else.

The Weberian ideal-type of bureaucracy makes no claim with respect to descriptive realism. It is an open question how it relates to reality. The model may be employed for the purpose of evaluating actual practices in two distinct senses: it may identify deviants from the rationality or efficiency requirement or it may hold up an ethical challenge that may be conducive to changes in existing practices. The model is in no way a realistic one claiming that public administrative bodies typically or on average have the properties specified.

Weber's model may also be employed for comparative purposes in order to pin-point the range of variation in the bureaucratic phenomenon by looking at how the basic properties in the model vary from one country to another (Page, 1985). Even if it is true that public agencies are not bureaucracies in the Weberian model sense, the relevance of the model may in no way be affected by the lack of correspondence between model and reality. As an ideal-type it could direct the reform zeal in the public sector, if indeed it rightly identifies the efficiency mechanism in public authorities.

## DYSFUNCTIONS IN BUREAUX

Much of the research about bureaux and bureaucracy behaviour has been conducted within the framework of the Weberian model. It has been the starting point for numerous investigations within public administration and organizational sociology. Although the Weberian model was used as a framework for analysis, it did not meet with unanimous agreement, because several findings indicated that there was a gap between theory and reality. Not questioning the basic mechanism of the Weberian model – bureaucracy as a neutral and rational machinery – several scholars revealed that bureaucracies could display other traits than rationality and efficiency. There was a risk of so-called dysfunctions in bureau operations.

Robert K. Merton argued that the sharp distinction between means and ends typical of the Weberian model tends to be blurred in bureau operations. The older a bureaucracy is the stronger the tendency to a displacement of means and ends. From the beginning the bureau was a means to promote external social ends, but as a result of organizational inertia the interests of the bureau itself tend to replace the promotion of external goals. The bureau itself becomes the end of its operations. Merton stated in *Social Theory and Social Structure* (1957) that bureaux cannot be understood if one does not pay attention to unintended consequences of bureaucracy behaviour: dysfunctions.

Philip Selznick in *TVA and the Grass Roots* (1949) came to a similar conclusion. Selznick showed that a bureaucratic apparatus tends to develop in a democratic organization. The drive towards autonomy of the bureaucracy derives, according to Selznick, from its possession of specialized knowledge about the operations of the organization. Technical expertise and the specialization of the knowledge base of the organization is typical of bureaux, which can be conducive to a vicious circle where the bureaucracy within the organization tends to over-emphasize the need for expertise. In due time the experts will take over the organization – one of the dysfunctions of bureaucracy. Selznick suggested a number of methods to counteract this, including a broad composition of the board of the organization and an explicit emphasis on the democratic ideology of the organization.

It may be generally argued that the Weberian model did not fully realize the implications of expertise for the structuring of bureaucracies. It is necessary to introduce another distinction between two kinds of personnel within bureaux: administrative personnel and professionals (Parsons, 1947).

Harold Wilensky showed in *Organizational Intelligence* (1967) that bureaux cannot operate without strong elements of specialists and expertise knowledge, which counteract the tendencies of bureaucracies towards centralization and homogeneity. There is an inherent conflict between the professionals in a bureau, on the one hand, who base their position on the possession of a monopoly of expertise knowledge, and the administrative staff, on the other, who conduct the bureau on the basis of their authority. Since the employment of knowledge has become increasingly important for bureaux, the tension between administrative power and expert knowledge within bureaucracies may lead to dysfunctions.

In *Patterns of Industrial Bureaucracy* (1954) Alvin Gouldner critiqued the emphasis on subordination in the Weberian model. According to Gouldner this element in the model by-passes the negative consequences of control of the behaviour of the subordinates. A strong surveillance of people within a bureaucratic organization may lead to a severe dysfunction: control strengthens the tensions already in existence in the organization which surveillance should counteract. Gouldner argued that it is not possible to direct the organization towards goals upon which all would agree. Organizations consist of different groups of individuals with varying interests and goals that only partly complement each other.

The theme of dysfunctions was developed into a general reaction against the Weberian administrative theory in the human relations school. Criticizing various organizational theories – scientific management, theories of division of labour and the Weberian administrative perspective – various authors developed a number of hypotheses about the individual in the organization which broke off from the prevailing notions about rationality and mechanization.

Instead of hierarchy they emphasized the informal structure of the organization and the need of the individual for integration into the organization. 'Bureaucracy' denoted the inhuman, the formal external framework of the organization, whereas what really happened in an organization was what Weber had not noticed: implicit norms, personal individual motivation and satisfaction, group integration and identification (Likert, 1961; Pfeffer, 1982; Morgan, 1986).

The idea that bureaucracies may be plagued by dysfunctions amounts to a minor criticism of the Weberian perspective. The idea that bureaucracy is a predictable machine that operates in a rational mode under normal circumstances had to be revised. Bureaux display inherent tendencies to operate suboptimally due to unintended and unrecognized consequences of behaviour in a complex structure. However, the theme of the human relations school implies a more serious criticism of the Weberian model, because it denies the basic mechanism implicit. Crucial for the capacity of the organization to accomplish its goals is the informal structure, according to Chris Argyris in *Understanding Organizational Behavior* (1960).

There exists according to Argyris an undeniable conflict and tension between the demands of the formal organization and the legitimate needs of the individual. What characterizes bureaucracies – division of labour, subordination, hierarchical structure and control – is not in agreement with the needs of the individual in his/her mode of functioning in an organization. Informal behaviour systems compensate for the inhuman and mechanistic nature of organizations. These informal behaviour patterns are more crucial for the capacity of the organization to operate successfully than the formal characteristics of the Weberian model (Argyris, 1964).

## BUREAUCRACY AS RIGIDITY

Contrary to Weber's position, bureaucracy is often equated with rigidity. To some scholars, who interpret 'bureaucracy' pejoratively, the distinguishing feature of bureaucracy and of bureau behaviour is rigidity. The following few quotations claim that bureaucracy behaviour is characterized by inflexibility, whether this may be true of the concept of bureaucracy as a definition of the term or as a general matter of fact concerning how bureaux function:

> Bureaucracies tend to reduce administration to the application of a set of rigid rules and formulas and to insist on a slavish devotion to routine, with the effect of exasperating the people and delaying public business. (Smith and Zurcher, 1944)

> Bureaucratism is usually characterized by adherence to routine, more or less inflexible rules, red tape, procrastination, unwillingness to assume responsibility and refusal to experiment. (Fairchild, 1955)

> The third usage corresponds to the vulgar and frequent sense of the word 'bureaucracy'. It evokes the slowness, the ponderousness, the routine, the complication of procedures, and the maladapted responses of 'bureaucratic' organizations to the needs which they should satisfy. (Crozier, 1964: 3)

In *Inside Bureaucracy* (1967) Anthony Downs developed a public choice theory of bureaucracy behaviour in which rigidity looms large. Downs identifies two sources of rigidity in bureaux, one is called 'normal', the other 'abnormal'. There will be a normal increase in rigidity as bureaux grow older and augment their size; however, there may also be a rapid abnormal outgrowth of rigidity when bureaux enter a rigidity cycle exemplifying the ossification syndrome.

The inherent tendency of bureaux to expand is, according to Downs, counteracted by an opposite force – the decelerating effect. As new bureaux reach their mature age further expansion becomes increasingly difficult due to a loss of their original function, to growing hostility from other bureaux, to difficulties in maintaining efficient output, to internal problems of recruiting talented people and of handling conflict.

The reaction on the part of the bureau to the 'inevitable' stagnation of the growth period is to resort to various expressions of rigidity in order to maintain the status quo and protect the organization against the threat of bureau death. The move towards rigidity measures takes different forms: for example, development of more formalized rule systems; shifting the emphasis from carrying out the goals of the bureau to protecting its size and autonomy; less capacity for innovation and more emphasis on routines and administration.

The combined effect of these rigidity trends is to make bureaux 'conservative' (Downs, 1967: 5–23), which means that large bureaux are seldom abolished and that the older the bureau the less likely is it that it will die. This theory about the normal development of rigidity in bureaucracy behaviour is certainly open to empirical test.

We may take a longitudinal perspective on the development of a bureau in order to investigate the extent to which there is a goal displacement from external objectives towards internal goals as well as to look at the relationship between innovation and administration in the bureau. This requires the construction of empirical indicators, but the test should be possible to carry out. The literature on administration includes empirical studies of innovation, formalization and administrative routines (Blau, 1955; Blau and Scott, 1963; Kaufman, 1976; Hogwood and Peters, 1983; Kaufman, 1985; Merritt and Merritt, 1985; Hill, 1992).

It is not clear if such a test of the rigidity hypothesis also covers the hypothesis about abnormal rigidity. Some bureaux tend to run into the so-called rigidity cycle. The hypothesis about the rigidity cycle implies that the rigidification of bureaucracy behaviour may be so severe that the bureau no longer produces any output and that it will face strong demand for reorganization or even that it be abolished. The answer to the rigidity cycle is the reorganization cycle, according to Downs. As there may be reasons for bureau reorganization other than ossification, it is hard to tell when there is a normal process of rigidification and an abnormal one.

Case studies in bureau development may be employed to find out what is going on in bureau growth: mere size expansion, rigidification or ossification. The basic problem is to separate the amount of formalization or rigidity that is neutral in relation to bureau operations, or that may even be eufunctional in relation to some bureau tasks, from the type of routinization that is dysfunctional for bureau operations (Ståhlberg, 1987).

# BUREAUCRACY AS 'BEAMTENHERRSCHAFT'

At this point one should bear in mind what Weber regarded as the inherent danger in bureaucracies – the drive of bureaucrats to become their own masters. The conflict between politicians and bureaucrats is endemic to the administration of modern society (Peters, 1987). According to the orthodox theory of bureaucracy it is a tool for efficient administration, but its goals are to be determined outside of bureaucracy. But how are bureaucrats to be confined to decision-making concerning the means of public policy and not its ends? Since there is really no neat and clear distinction between ends and means in public policy-making, how is a separation between politics and administration possible?

The growing complexity of modern society as well as the strong expansion of bureaux at all levels of government seems to have strengthened bureaucratic power. The literature on government overload (Rose, 1980), organized democracy (Olsen, 1983) as well as on intergovernmental dependency (Hanf and Scharpf, 1978) and on the relation between democracy and bureaucracy (Etzioni-Halevy, 1983; Saltzstein, 1985) suggests that typical of modern bureaucracy is its penetration into the spheres of political power. According to one conception of bureaucracy this is not just an accidental development typical of some historical period, but derives from the essence of bureaucracy behaviour.

New theories about the policy process model it as a network of organizations, both private and public, in which bureaux play an important role (Jordan, 1981, 1990; Rhodes, 1981, 1990). Policy-making within the structure of big government proceeds by means of inter-action between bureaux and private organizations in relation to both the making of public policy and the implementation of policy. Thus, bureaux tend to be dependent upon and interact with other organizations in society at the same time as this pattern of interaction enforces the independence of the bureaux in relation to government.

In the so-called mixed economy public programmes are initiated through interaction between bureaux and interest organizations and these programmes are often implemented in the form of collaboration between the public and the private (Hernes, 1978). The increasing complexity of society is conducive to the interdependence and inter-action between public authorities and private organizations in order to have well-functioning public programmes (Richardson and Jordan, 1979). Strong bureaux enter so-called policy networks that are responsible for various public programmes.

The interpenetration of the public and the private may strengthen *Beamtenherrschaft* in relation to government, but there is also a clear risk of what Weber called *Satrapenherrschaft* and what we may refer to as lobbying or interest group politics (Hogwood and Peters, 1985;

Page, 1985). Yet, Jim Sharpe (1985) emphasizes that bureaux as parts of a network of organizations may have a positive effect on the functioning of public programmes.

The literature on neo-corporatism argues along similar lines (Schmitter and Lehmbruch, 1978; Lehmbruch and Schmitter, 1982). Varying forms of corporatism at various levels of government feed on the interdependencies between public and private organizations within a policy area (Cawson, 1985; Streeck and Schmitter, 1985). The development of a so-called third sector between the public and the private or 'private interest government' (PIG) is another indication of the fact that bureau independence may be a necessary condition for a fruitful cooperation between the public and the private (Hood and Schuppert, 1987). But one must remain alert to the danger of the power of distributional coalitions (Olson, 1982), which may operate unrestrained under the auspices of either *Beamtenherrschaft* or *Satrapenherrschaft*.

## BUREAUCRACY AS CHAOS

A new set of principles modelling organizational choice has been suggested by critiques of rational choice models (March and Olsen, 1976, 1989). Organizational decision-making is to be understood in a way very different from that implied by a rational model:

> Suppose we view a choice opportunity as a garbage can into which various problems and solutions are dumped by participants. The mix of garbage in a single can depends partly on the labels attached to the alternative cans; but it also depends on what garbage is being produced at the moment, on the mix of cans available, and on the speed with which garbage is collected and removed from the scene. (Cohen et al., 1976: 26)

The model has been applied to general public policy-making, to be discussed in Chapter 3, and in particular to public sector organizations or bureaux, which we look at here. The garbage can model identifies four parts or 'streams' of decision-making: (a) problems, (b) solutions, (c) participants and (d) choice opportunities. And the model assumes that decision outcomes are a function of (a)–(d): 'Although we have treated the four streams as exogenous for most of our discussion, it should be clear that we view the understanding of the lawful processes determining the flows of those streams as fundamental to understanding what is happening in organizational choice situations' (Cohen et al., 1976: 36).

We argue that the garbage can model hardly amounts to a general theory of bureaucratic systems. However, it identifies certain tendencies in bureau operations towards inefficiency and even irrationality which may blossom at times. The relevance of this model to processes of bureau behaviour concerns whether its chaos hypothesis identifies something typical of the mechanisms of bureau behaviour – that is, some forces which belong to the essence of bureaux, yet which bring about disaster.

The garbage can model may be derived from a more general model of organizational choice building on Thompson's (1967) categories of preferences and technology. Bureaucracy behaviour, as with any organizational choice, is a function of the preferences involved and the technology to be employed. Collective preferences may be more or less ambiguous and technologies may be more or less certain. This can be illustrated by a 2×2 table (Table 2.1).

Table 2.1  *Organizational ends and means*

**Goal function**

|              |          | Unambiguous | Ambiguous |
|--------------|----------|-------------|-----------|
|              | Certain  | I           | II        |
| **Technology** | Uncertain | III       | IV        |

Whereas rational decision models would be applicable to decision situations I and III, they would obviously fail in situations II and IV. If bureaux always faced decision predicaments II and IV, then they would perform badly on any efficiency criterion. If the goals are not clear and if the technology is uncertain, then how could there be bureau efficiency? It seems somewhat exaggerated, however, to claim that all types of bureaucracy behaviour are to be found in the decision predicament most typical of the garbage can model, that is, situation IV. In short, the garbage can identifies how bureaux fail when they do not know what they want or how to go about doing things.

The Weberian model of bureaucracy has met with various kinds of response. One criticism was that it had neglected so-called dysfunctions stemming from an idealized model of abstract properties and their interaction. In reality unintended consequences and unrecognized functions were bound to occur. A more severe kind of criticism was launched within the human relations school which questioned the basic mechanism in the Weberian model. Organizational efficiency or productivity is not a function of the abstract model properties of the Weberian framework.

Finally, the introduction of the garbage can model in the study of bureaucracy means a radical rejection of the Weberian administrative approach. Bureaux, like all organizations, cannot in principle attain rationality in collective choice, as the likelihood of the occurrence of garbage can processes is not marginal.

There has been a trend towards a post-Weberian administrative theory that rejects more and more of the original Weberian model. Turning to the public choice approach to bureaucracy we find even more criticism of the classical model of bureaucracy. As a matter of fact, there are several models of bureaucracy anchored in the public choice approach. Before we turn to these we shall discuss why the public sector organizes a large number of transactions in a hierarchy like the bureau rather than in alternative forms: for example, in some contractual fashion in exchange institutions.

## BUREAUX IN ECONOMIC ORGANIZATION THEORY

Why do public bureaux exist? How does a bureau reduce transaction costs more than would alternative arrangements such as contracts between the government and private actors concerning the provision of public services (Moe, 1984: 759–62)? An application of the new economic organization theory (Williamson, 1985, 1986) would suggest that a public bureau is a superior solution to the problems of exchange between government and those who provide public services when the cost of measuring service output is high, when investments in asset-specific skills and capital will make one private contractor an indispensable monopolist and when uncertainty makes it impossible to write long-term contingent contracts.

Public bureaux are supposed to implement policies in accordance with the intentions of elected policy-makers. From the politicians' point of view the task is to design a structure of incentives which bring about bureau behaviour that is consistent with their intentions. The core of the problem of hierarchical control may be analysed by means of a principal–agent model. Information asymmetry is present when the political agent has relevant information which is inaccessible to the principal, or prohibitively expensive to acquire.

In any organization information asymmetry is inevitable. Consider the analysis of simple team production (Alchian, 1950; Demsetz, 1967). Individual input owners know what their contribution to the total product is, and each has no incentive to reveal that information to the other members of the team. In fact, knowing that his or her marginal productivity is unmeasurable, the input owner has the incentive to shirk. But since that is true for all input owners, the outcome is inferior to the outcome where no one shirks. In this prisoners' dilemma situation, the solution is to create an institutional constraint, that is, to hire a monitor.

Monitoring in organization cannot be perfect when monitoring each input's marginal productivity is costly. In an organization with a minimum of decentralization and division of labour, information asymmetry develops when specialized knowledge and skills are gained by subunits in the organization. The asymmetry can be used by these units to their own advantage but it often involves a cost when the effectiveness of the organization as a whole is considered.

The principals in the public sector suffer from the same asymmetry as their counterparts in the private sector because the same core problem exists in both sectors (Moe, 1984: 757). A few special problems arise in the theory of hierarchies in the public sector (Moe, 1984: 761–9). First, a concern for efficiency cannot be the principals' primary motivation. In the firm, after all payments have been made, the receiver of the residual reward (the owner) seeks to enhance efficiency because this will increase his or her reward. Clearly, efficiency in the supply of government services is not directly related to the return to the principal, the politicians. Lack of efficiency may in the long run contribute to electoral defeat, but a concern for interest groups and the symbolic side of politics will probably increase the possibility of being reelected more than will harsh efficiency measures.

In contrast to the owner of a firm in the private sector, the politicians in the public sector do not have strong incentives for promoting efficiency as their interests are not tied up with bureau efficiency. As there is no hidden hand of competition to weed out inefficient bureaux, public hierarchies cannot be seen as the most efficient way of handling the transactional problems involved in supplying public services or as developing towards increased efficiency.

Secondly, the principal's ability to design incentive structures is limited in the public sector. The manager of a firm may retain some of the residual normally accruing to the owner as one mechanism that induces the manager to act in the interests of the owner. As public bureaux do not run profits in the same sense that private firms do, this option is not open to the same degree for public principals. The principal pays the agent to produce, and the only profit the bureau may obtain is the difference between the budget and the costs of delivering the public service. If the principal let the bureau retain the difference between budget and costs if the same level of service were produced at a lower cost, measurement problems aside, then it would be in the interest of the bureau to cut costs but only in order to enjoy the benefits of a budgetary slack, an outcome which from the principal's point of view is no more efficient than the original outcome.

In the public sector, there are also other constraining factors such as a number of laws concerning public employees, administrative procedure and bureaucratic openness which put limits on the design of incentive structures. The constraints on principals are vital factors which must be considered when modelling bureau behaviour. Public choice models tend to emphasize the strategic advantages of the bureau, which may be employed for the purposes of opportunistic behaviour.

## BUREAUCRACY AS OVERSUPPLY

Even if it were true that in bureaux the bureaucrats are devoted to their offices and the functional purposes inherent in these, it may be the case that modern bureaucrats are so devoted to their functions that they care for them at the expense of other considerations. And the devotion to the office may be so pervasive that the enlargement of the bureau becomes the sole preoccupation of the office holder. Such a vocation may certainly not be conducive to efficiency; on the contrary, such a motivation could result in bureaucracy in the pejorative meaning of the word listed among other definitions in standard dictionaries: 'Bureaucracy: 1. government by bureaus. 2. the body of officials administering bureaus. 3. excessive multiplication of and concentration of power in administrative bureaus. 4. excessive governmental red tape and routine' (*American College Dictionary*).

A coherent theory derived from the public choice approach to bureaucracy behaviour that implies that the maximization of the bureau itself is a typical feature of bureaucrats has been put forward by William Niskanen in *Bureaucracy and Representative Government* (1971). Obviously, the hypothesis that bureaucrats maximize their budgets is intended as a fundamental characterization of bureaucratic behaviour. Niskanen pays little attention to the concept of bureaucracy employing it in the first two meanings listed in the quotation above. And an organization is a bureau only if it has two public features: 'Bureaus specialize in the supply of those services that some collective organization wishes to augment beyond that supplied by the market and for which it is not prepared to contract with a profit-seeking organization' (Niskanen, 1971: 20).

Thus, typical of a bureau is its public character, receiving a grant or appropriation from a government budget as the essential source of its revenues. The Niskanen bureaucracy model consists of a few equations modelling the interaction between the bureau and its government (sponsor) which allow some painstaking conclusions about the nature of bureaucratic outputs and inefficiency. The model is presented in Figure 2.1.

The basic derivation from the model concerns the nature of the equilibrium outcome of the interaction between the sponsor (demand) and the bureau (supply) in the budgetary process, characterized by the strategic advantage on the part of the bureau due to information asymmetry. How large will the bureau budget be? Given the peculiar economics of bureaux – there is a budget constraint that the total costs of the output of the bureau will be covered by the appropriation of the sponsor (Figure 2.1a) – Niskanen derives the implication that the output of this bureau is always larger than the optimal level. This is evident since output is fixed in a region where the minimum achievable marginal costs are substantially higher than the marginal value to

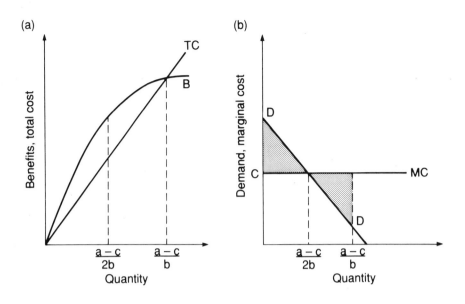

Figure 2.1 *Niskanen's budget-maximizing model*

the sponsor (Niskanen, 1971: 47–8). Thus, the size of the output of the bureau is always larger than the socially efficient level of output, where equilibrium is decided by equating marginal cost with marginal value (Figure 2.1b).

The conclusion must be that bureaucratic behaviour is fundamentally inefficient, as the size of bureau operations is not determined where marginal benefits equal marginal costs, namely the size that maximizes the net value to the sponsor (Niskanen, 1971: 50). Since the sponsor may be equated with government and, in a representative system, with the electorate, bureaucratic behaviour results in social waste, that is, an inefficient allocation of the resources of society given the preferences of its citizens.

Social inefficiency does not necessarily imply bureau inefficiency, however. Niskanen is careful to point out that his model of bureaucracy behaviour does not imply that bureaux operate with internal waste, that is, by means of production functions where a lower cost could be attained for the same level of output. Whether there will also be bureau inefficiency besides social inefficiency depends on other things, and one cannot rule out the combination of social inefficiency and bureau efficiency. If bureaucracy behaviour implies social waste, then what are the remedies?

Niskanen suggests a number of reforms in the structure of bureaux, which are all directed towards abolishing the information advantage of the bureaux. Thus, we have bureau competition for the supply of similar services, the recognition of private incentive mechanisms for efficiency-promoting behaviour, more use of private firms for public provision, as well as a strengthening of the control and review process.

These reforms would improve the social efficiency of bureaucracy behaviour but they would strip the bureau of the Weberian model's properties. The basic question is whether such drastic changes of bureaucracy would bring about an allocation where marginal benefit would equal marginal cost for the provision of the goods or services handled by bureaux. The validity of the Niskanen model may be tested from two angles.

Theoretically, it may be contested that the model is correctly specified given the present knowledge of budget behaviour in the public sector (Eavery, 1984; Bender and Moe, 1985; Moene, 1986; Sörensen, 1987), because there may exist system constraints on bureaucracy behaviour not recognized by Niskanen. Perhaps the relationship between politicians and bureaucrats is more symmetrical than assumed in the Niskanen model? It has been argued against Niskanen that the theory of the budget-maximizing bureau is inherently difficult to test. What could be the empirical consequences?

The Niskanen bureaucracy model does not simply state that the bureau budget will be a large one – whatever that could mean; nor is the model a longitudinal one predicting that bureau budgets will grow at a certain rate. The Niskanen analysis implies that bureaux are socially inefficient, meaning that their budgets are too large in relation to effective demand; thus, it is a cross-sectional hypothesis about the relation between demand and supply of the services and goods that bureaux provide. The criterion of size is the standard efficiency condition in micro-economic theory that is, that marginal value equal marginal costs.

The only way to find out whether a bureau is too large or too small or about the right size is to measure and compare demand and supply, but how can we do this for these kinds of goods? As a matter of fact, the difficulties of testing the Niskanen bureaucracy model are profound. What the marginal evaluation of an extra unit of bureau supply may be is often far from clear (Miller and Moe, 1983).

The Niskanen model does not predict that bureau inefficiency will be done away with if the control and review process is strengthened because it is a theory not about bureau waste but about the occurrence of bureau oversupply. Thus, the model implies that if the sponsor gets hold of enough accurate information, then the sponsor will cut back the size of the bureau operations until social efficiency is reached. However, the only way to test the implication is to conduct real life experiments changing the political system in rather drastic ways. In addition to bureau oversupply there could also be X-inefficiency in the Leibenstein (1966) sense that costs are not minimized.

The Niskanen model predicts that a shift to less bureaucracy and more market operations will be conducive to social efficiency. As it is hardly likely that the Niskanen reform proposals will be implemented – competition among bureaux without predetermined functions, private incentives of various kinds to bureaucrats who reduce bureau fat, privatization of bureau functions including even some types of military service – we have difficulty finding data that will corroborate or falsify the theory.

There is a limited amount of evidence concerning how bureaucracy compares with the market in relation to some services and goods (Borcherding, 1977; Borcherding et al., 1982; Mueller, 1989), but the conclusion is not straightforward; in any case, such comparisons are only possible outside the range of public goods which bureaux provide. A warning may be raised against an unreserved market preference implicit in the work of Niskanen. What matters beside efficiency is accountability and markets do not always perform better than bureaucracies in this respect (Rose, 1987).

## BUREAUCRACY AS SIZE MAXIMIZATION

Growth and size are often associated with bureaucracy. It is no accident that the list of defining properties in *Webster's Dictionary* contains amongst other characteristics the following:

> Bureaucracy: (1a) the whole body of nonelective government officials. (b) the administrative policy-making group in any large organization. (2) systematic administration characterized by specialization of functions, objective qualification for office, action according to fixed rules, and a hierarchy of authority. (3) a system of administration marked by constant striving for functions and power, by lack of initiative and flexibility, by indifference to human needs or public opinion, and by tendency to defer decisions to superiors or to impede action with red tape.

The 'constant striving for function and power' as the typical feature of bureaucracy behaviour has been seized upon by several scholars (Parkinson, 1957; Starbuck, 1965; Downs, 1967). The hypothesis that bureaucrats maximize their own utility and that their personal utility is a strict function of bureau size is a simple one. As simple is another version that argues that growth is the essence of organizations, including one species, namely bureaux: 'In fact, all organizations have inherent tendencies to expand. What sets bureaus apart is that they do not have as many restraints upon expansion, nor do their restraints function as automatically' (Downs, 1967: 16–17).

Not all versions of the size maximization argument argue that size is an uncomplicated property of bureaux. William Starbuck (1965) argues that growth is typical of organizations, because size has a number of separate effects: economies of scale, better chances of survival, more resistance to external pressures, more stability and less uncertainty.

If it were true that bureaux have one dominating goal – organizational growth – then we would expect the following to be true: new bureaux would grow rapidly; old bureaux would maintain themselves if not grow still more; the older the bureau the larger would be the bureau; new bureaux would grow either by internal diversification or by means of external merger; and bureaux would tend to grow steadily except when amalgamations take place.

These hypotheses may be subjected to empirical analysis (Meyer, 1985). Studies of the long-term development of bureaux do not corroborate the size-maximization argument (Kaufman, 1985; Mueller, 1989). The coming of bureaumetrics is a step towards an empirical evaluation of theories of bureaucracies. It has been argued that bureaux may have to face considerable cut-backs in periods of retrenchment (Hood and Dunsire, 1981; Dunsire and Hood, 1989).

It may be argued that bureau expansion is not to be taken for granted. When officials make priorities among their private goals, then security may loom large, as Herbert Kaufman has argued in *Are Government Organizations Immortal?* (1976). Growth is risky, it may bring bureau disaster.

## BUREAUCRACY AS UNCONTROL

The concept of bureaucracy often involves the notion of a quest for the concentration or power. The *Dictionary of the Social Sciences* contains the following definition:

> Bureaucracy, conceived as an ideal type, refers to principles of organization that find varying degrees of expression in a wide variety of organizations. The characteristics of the ideal type are rationality in decision making, impersonality in social relations, routinization of tasks, and centralization of authority. (Stone, 1969)

This typical feature of bureaux – to centralize power – may be interpreted in two ways: either the centralization tendency may inhere in the entire hierarchy in which the bureau is placed – system centralization; or the centralization drive may refer to the internal division of authority within the bureau.

According to the *Oxford English Dictionary* a 'bureaucrat' is an 'official who endeavours to concentrate administrative power in his bureau'. Yet, the outcome of such internal bureau processes may be the opposite of system centralization – bureau autonomy, and bureau irresponsibility. Gordon Tullock in *The Politics of Bureaucracy* (1965) considers bureau autonomy to be the typical characteristic of modern bureaucracy behaviour, and the outcomes of such 'bureaucratic free enterprise' are inefficiency, irresponsibility and waste. First:

> It can only be concluded that, in a very large organization of this type, for the greater part of its specific activities, the bureaucracy will be 'free' from

whatever authority it is allegedly subordinate to. 'It', the bureaucracy, will do things, will take actions, not because such actions are desired by the ultimate authority, the center of power, in the organization, but because such things, such actions, develop as an outgrowth of the bureaucracy's own processes. (Tullock, 1965: 168)

The phenomenon of bureaucratic free enterprise has its source in the hierarchical structure of bureaux with its implications for loss of communication reliability and preciseness as well as impossibility of control of the superordinate of the subordinate. Secondly:

We are saddled with a large and basically inefficient bureaucracy. Improved efficiency in this sector could, looking at the matter economically, raise our national income and improve our rate of growth. Politically, it could both increase the degree of control the citizen, qua voter, has over many fields of our national life and enlarge his personal freedom. This apparent paradox is the result of the peculiar form taken by the inefficiency of bureaucratic free enterprise. (Tullock, 1965: 221)

There is a growing literature about the tendency of bureaucracy to find its own goals and enlarge its discretion at the expense of its sovereign, the body politic. The traditional simple model of public administration with its distinction between politics or values and administration or facts as well as its naive conception of public administration as mechanical and impersonal execution has little relevance for the realities of politics and bureaucracy (Dunsire, 1973, 1978; Hood, 1976).

The uncontrollability hypothesis may be subjected to an empirical test by the derivation of some propositions. We wish to separate two ideas in the uncontrollability hypothesis: the notion that bureaux tend to become autonomous or that bureaucracy processes tend towards garbage can processes on the one hand, and the idea that these bureau trends result in inefficiency on the other. Bureaucracy as free enterprise is one state of affairs and inefficiency is another, as there may be causes of inefficiency other than bureau autonomy.

The analysis of productivity in the public sector requires the solution of a number of difficult theoretical and empirical problems (Murray, 1987). First, we have to find out whether bureau officials really tend to have a large or increasing amount of discretion; then, should this happen to be the case, we must inquire into the consequences of this. It does not follow that because there is a control problem leaving each bureau with more discretion than intended this autonomy will be employed for other purposes than carrying out the official tasks of the bureau. Actually, one implementation theory argues that autonomy is a precondition for successful implementation (see Chapter 4). Thus, it is an open question what the implications of far-reaching discretion will be for bureau operations.

Secondly, in order to arrive at the conclusion of Tullock that bureaucracy behaviour is inefficient because bureaucrats cannot be controlled,

ιe assumption is implicitly made about bureaucrats not caring about
..ieir public goals. This is a separate assumption that should be identified for special scrutiny.

## BUREAUCRACY AS PRIVATE CHOICE

Whereas it used to be claimed that there existed a special type of
behaviour or motivation – the bureaucratic vocation – it is often stated
in modern administrative theory and decision-making approaches that
the distinction between public and private choice is an invalid one. As
André Breton states in *The Economic Theory of Representative Government*:

> The hypothesis implies, even when stated in its simplified form
> (bureaucrats seek to maximize the relative size of their bureaus), that it is
> through the maximization of this objective that bureaucrats are able to
> achieve the highest possible income and prestige consistent with the
> constraints to which they are subjected. (1974: 162)

Such an objective function would perhaps not be conducive to the
propagation of the public interest or even more mundane public goals
of the bureau. However, such a bureaucratic mentality, or lack of one,
does not necessarily imply inefficiency. If the successful operation of
the bureau was made a function of the private incentives of bureaucrats, then the maximization of a private objective function in a
bureaucratic setting does not have to result in waste or bureaucratic
free enterprise. Efficiency-promoting mechanisms of a kind that tie
output to the private incentives of the officials may be introduced into
bureaux (Jonsson, 1985).

Two versions of the private objective function hypothesis may be
identified. According to a weaker version bureaucracy behaviour is
affected not only by the public interest but also by private motives,
whereas in the stronger version there is no such thing as the public
interest. In his cautious argument Downs follows the weaker version:

> Bureaucratic officials in general (all social agents) have a complex set of
> goals including power, income, prestige, security, convenience, loyalty (to
> an idea, an institution, or the nation), pride in excellent work, and desire
> to serve the public interest . . . But regardless of the particular goals
> involved, . . . every official is significantly motivated by his . . . own self-
> interest even when acting in a purely official capacity. (1967: 2)

Although the number of basic assumptions in Downs' theory is not
large they have so little content that almost anything is deducible. If
we happen to find bureau inefficiency, then this may be due to the
private motives of officials, but if we happen to find efficiency then
maybe another motive is at work – the public interest? Downs'
assumption about bureaucracy motivation is so general that hardly
anything specific can be deduced about bureaucracy behaviour.

The stronger version of the private choice argument in a bureaucracy setting is more specific; it states that public officials maximize their own interests whatever they may be and that bureau size is conducive to this maximization. How can we test the hypothesis that bureaucracy behaviour is the maximization of private gain? What would be the behaviour implications?

One set of test predictions would simply be the occurrence of a confusion of public and private roles in the traditional understanding of what is public. It is hardly likely that we will find massive private action in bureaucracy behaviour, like the use of the resources of the office for private ends or the manipulation of bureau resources for purposes quite different from those intended. A more sophisticated set of test implications would imply that private goals are enhanced at the same time as public targets are achieved, in particular bureau expansion.

It may not be entirely easy to separate the public interest hypothesis and the self-interest hypothesis concerning the fundamentals of motivation in bureaux. If the successful implementation of the official goals of the bureau also provides the office holders with their maximum pay-off, then there would be no incompatibility. The self-evident aura surrounding the private choice hypothesis should be replaced by empirical inquiries into the nature of bureaucratic motivation, which in fact tend to reveal a complexity of motives (Dunsire, 1987; Peters, 1987).

## CONCLUSION

There is peculiar tension between the reference and the meaning of the concept of bureaucracy. On the one hand, if it is taken for granted that 'bureau' refers to existing organizational entities within the public sector, then there hardly exists any single theory that adequately portrays the distinguishing characteristics of such entities. On the other hand, if we start from a specified concept of bureaucracy, then we must try to specify what its range of application is. It could be the case that the various properties discussed above are not generally true of existing bureaux.

Indeed, it seems difficult if not impossible to come up with some valid generalizations about what distinguishes bureaux or bureaucracies. We wish to emphasize the multidimensional nature of the phenomena of bureau operations within the public sector (Warwick, 1975; Jenkins and Gray, 1983). At the same time it is worth underlining that all models other than the Weberian rationality model refute the existence of the basic property of bureau efficiency.

One must recognize that alternative conceptions or theories of bureaucracy have validity in the sense of applicability in different fields of action. It is certainly the case that no single model of the theories surveyed here can do justice to all kinds of bureau behaviour in the huge public sector systems typical of advanced capitalist democracies. Bureaux are heavily involved in the making and implementation of public policy. How is this fact revealed in models of policy-making and of policy implementation?

# 3

# PUBLIC POLICY MODELS

Why are there several competing models of public policy-making? What are the characteristic features of the arrival at a collective choice and the implementation of the policy chosen within the public sector? In raising the question about the logic of an entity the focus is upon the basic elements as well as the theoretical principles that guide the composition of the elements. What are the fundamentals of public policy-making and which principles structure policy choice? Here we analyse public policy-making models, whereas Chapter 4 examines the modelling of public implementation or what takes place in the policy cycle after the enactment of collective choice (Ashford, 1978; May and Wildavsky, 1978; Hogwood and Peters, 1983).

The basic problem here is to compare alternative models of public policy-making. How are we to evaluate contrasting policy models? Models concerning public sector decision-making may be evaluated on their own terms or by comparing them to private sector choice models. It is not always clear whether a decision framework is supposed to model all kinds of choice situations or if the field of application is restricted to the public sector. To what extent are various models mutually exclusive? This is a problem of choosing between different theoretical languages.

## MODEL CHOICE AND MODEL EVALUATION

Confronted with a bewildering array of policy models we search for criteria for the arrival at a proper model choice on the basis of model evaluation in terms of explicitly stated methodological criteria. Which count?

An empirical model test is not enough; besides the requirement of corroboration or verification, as it were, models fulfil the function of integrating knowledge. Models systematize knowledge by creating a network between propositions. The implications of models are as important as their explicit content. Models of public decision-making which have a large set of implications are to be preferred to models that fail to integrate separate pieces of knowledge, all other things being equal (Popper, 1972).

What about truth or the extent of empirical confirmation (Scheffler, 1967a; Glymour, 1980)? Are we to make model choices on the basis of criteria like simplicity (Quine, 1960; Goodman, 1965; Quine and

Ullian, 1970) or aesthetics (Kuhn, 1962; Feyerabend, 1975)? Maybe we should use criteria like deductive power or theoretical coherence (Nagel, 1961; Hempel, 1965) or maybe understanding in terms of social science models is achieved by means of a pattern type interpretation (Kaplan, 1964).

Some argue that the test of a model is falsification, the confrontation with facts (Popper, 1959, 1963) though it remains doubtful how a theory could simultaneously satisfy the criteria of abstract generality and descriptive realism (Krupp, 1966). Maybe we are to evaluate public decision theories in terms of the realism of their assumptions (Simon, 1957); perhaps we would do better to follow those who advocate the potential fruitfulness of working with model assumptions that are abstract distortions of the observational world in order to derive powerful predictions (Friedman, 1953; Blaug, 1980; Caldwell, 1984).

Various models of the policy cycle may perform differently according to the evaluation criteria employed. Model evaluation then becomes the task of listing the pros and cons of different approaches. Equally true yet different models may perform differently in relation to various types of situations. Some models satisfy certain types of situations whereas other models perform in other types of situations. Instead of rejecting or accepting one public policy model we may point out the type of situations where a model performs well and the situations where it is inadequate.

Model evaluation is a complex judgement of how models score on criteria such as deductive power, falsifiability, degree of confirmation, coherence, simplicity and practical usefulness. Selecting the evaluation criteria is by no means simple. Are moral considerations not relevant to the evaluation of models of public decision-making and implementation such as social justice or overall utility?

The functions of public policy models are to explain, understand, interpret and organize data concerning the making of decisions by public bodies – government. Just as data without models are *blind*, so models without data are *empty*. Thus, model evaluation has to pay attention to how the models satisfy data – correspondence with fact – as well as to how the data are organized by the model assumptions or the internal consistency, deductive power and simplicity of the model. Policy models are perhaps much too oriented towards the output side of the state and tend to neglect the input side. Thus, we need to know more about the politics of revenue decisions (Manley, 1975; Peters, 1991).

The set of models may be divided into those that approach decision-making and implementation as a function of the environment or external factors and theories that model the policy-making as a result of internal processes.

## THE DEMOGRAPHIC APPROACH

The idea that policy-making is a reflection of the environment has a long standing in policy analysis. Actually, the demographic approach had many supporters up until the mid-1970s, because the early environmental studies scored high on one of the model evaluation criteria – the degree of empirical confirmation (Dye, 1966; Sharkansky, 1969; Hofferbert, 1974; Wilensky, 1975).

However, it has lately met with more and more criticism. Renewed analyses of the impact of environmental variables on policy indicators have not been able to come up with an acceptable degree of fit (Danziger, 1978; Sharpe and Newton, 1984). Whereas the demographic model used to be considered valid in local and regional government research, its status in national government policy research has been far more contested. The degree to which national policy-making is a function of environmental variables like affluence, social structure and the position of the trade unions and political parties is still undecided (Castles, 1982; Alt and Chrystal, 1983; Schmidt, 1982).

Although the demographic model approach may not be without relevance as far as one of the evaluation criteria is concerned – correspondence with facts – it seems as if it is far more problematic in relation to the other criteria. The attempt to find determinants of a policy variation in space variables describing the environment of policy-making suffers from all the weaknesses of crude empiricism: little deductive power, weak coherence between propositions and naive model specification. The research strategy is based on the atheoretical idea of maximizing the number of independent and dependent variables and resorting to the mechanical calculation of simple correlations as a tool for the specification of regression models.

A number of theoretical problems have been left undecided in this approach with regard to the interpretation of both the dependent and independent variables. Little effort has been devoted to the understanding of the findings as little has been done to integrate the estimation of a large number of demographic models. There is not much coherence in the interpretation of various relationships between variables, with the result that we cannot expect much in the way of deductive power. Since the whole procedure is based on an empirical strategy to maximize the variation in variables, the theoretical structure is barren.

However, it cannot be denied that, while acknowledging its weakness from a theoretical point of view, the demographic approach located an aspect of some types of policy-making. The demographic model appears to satisfy data on cross-sectional or longitudinal variation in policy-making concerning divisible goods and services. Its explanatory relevance is minimal in relation to classical public goods, that is, indivisible entities. It would no doubt be astonishing if public policy-making was not related to its environment, but the basic problem is the *nature* and *strength* of the links between environmental factors and decision-making in collective choice.

It would be just as unlikely that public policy would have no relationship whatsoever to its environment as that policy-making could be conceived as fully determined by the environment. Maybe what matters is how decision-makers take environmental factors into account and how they wish to give differential recognition to various factors in their preferences. Tore Hansen, Jim Sharpe and Ken Newton have done work in this direction reinterpreting the demographic approach more in terms of an internal perspective on policy-making (Hansen, 1981; Newton, 1981; Sharpe and Newton, 1984).

## INCREMENTALISM

The incrementalist approach to public decision-making is a combination of external and internal variables; incremental models concerning the policy process approach the relation between environment and decision-making in a more complex way than the demographic model approach. Incrementalism is thus more satisfactory from a theoretical point of view as it scores high on criteria like coherence and simplicity. In terms of the external perspective incrementalism claims that decision-making in general and in the public sector in particular is determined by time. Previously made decisions are crucial determinants of present policies.

This simple idea that policy is a function of itself in a time perspective is integrated as the conclusion of an elaborate decision theory consisting of a number of coherent propositions of values, cognitions and coordination (Lindblom, 1959, 1965; Braybrooke and Lindblom, 1963; Wildavsky, 1984). The theory has been tested in terms of budgetary models (Wildavsky, 1972, 1986).

Incrementalism appears to possess both theoretical content and empirical confirmation, a combination which may explain its attractiveness in policy analysis. However, the incrementalist approach does not score high on all evaluation criteria. The basic problem is the interpretation of the concept of the increment – a difficulty which has far-reaching implications for the deductive power of the incremental model as well as for its degree of confirmation.

The predictive power of incremental models would be impressive if the model could specify how large a programme change is allowed to be if it is to be designated as an 'increment'. Similarly, the theory would be formally adequate if it could specify the significance of a stable relationship between this year's policy and last year's policy. However, it appears to be theoretically very difficult to specify how large the addition positively or negatively is allowed to be (Dempster and Wildavsky, 1979).

It seems as if the specification of the permissible size of the increment depends upon the level of decision-making studied, as if the incremental model could safely predict future policies simply because the aggregation effects cancel out large positive and negative effects at higher levels of decision-making. Non-incremental changes would thus tend to be concealed by the natural process of summing expansion and cut-backs (Wanat, 1974).

What matters is the pattern of decision-making, whatever the size of changes. Incremental models satisfy decision processes which are stable over time, meaning that the future is a linear function of the past. At first it seems as if the incremental models adapted for the budgetary process received considerable support when estimated empirically. Then it was realized that there were considerable econometric problems involved in estimating the simple incremental equations. The resort to more complex incremental models has not been as successful as the early attempts at incremental modelling. Recent literature talks about shift-points in relation to policy, which defy incremental modelling and reduce the degree of confirmation of incrementalist models.

Thus, the incrementalist approach to policy-making is in a dilemma: its deductive power is constrained by the difficulty in specifying what an increment is whilst its degree of confirmation is reduced by the typical occurrence of shift-points in policy-making which defy the interpretation of the incrementalist equations as stable linear growth models. If the policy process is modelled as structurally unstable (Westlund and Lane, 1983), allowing for the occurrence of shift-points, then the deductive power of incrementalism is drastically reduced as there is as yet little knowledge of when and how shift-points take place.

For all its simplicity maybe incrementalism is too crude in relation to the complexity of the policy process. The idea that policies are heavily constrained by past commitments, that policy-making is the application of mechanical rules – standard operating procedures – that reduce complexity, calculation and uncertainty, and that policy-making never touches the base of its programmes may satisfy data for certain periods of decision-making in some countries. However, its general validity is doubtful and its theoretical appeal is decreased by the obvious voluntaristic aspect of action, including collective action. It may be the case that public policy-making could not consider all the alternatives and rank all the outcomes as incrementalism predicts, but it does not follow that decision-making is bound to be of limited scope at the margin.

Decision-making in the face of uncertainty, focusing only upon a few alternatives and values, does not ipso facto have to be marginal. Decision-making may be comprehensive in terms of the changes aimed at. If structural shift-points are at odds with incremental modelling, how do we explain the occurrence of these types of policy changes?

If the environment and its space and time dimensions do not suffice to account for policies, then we should turn to approaches that employ only internal variables – the internal perspective. There are a number of models of the decision-making process that emphasize the relevance of internal factors of various types. Let us begin with the classical rational choice model.

## RATIONAL DECISION-MAKING

The strength of the rational decision model derives from its attractive theoretical properties. The set of assumptions is characterized by coherence and simplicity: (1) the value function is consistent and integrated; (2) the model assumes complete knowledge about the alternatives and the environment; (3) it uses simple decision rules like the maximization of expected value or the mini-max or mini-regret rules (Simon, 1957: 244–5).

The weakness of the rational decision model stems from its lack of behavioural realism. Since its assumptions are seldom satisfied the model has a low degree of confirmation. This is true not only of individual choice behaviour but applies equally to collective choice in a political setting. Government, like any organization, acts under the rationality assumption as spelled out in *Organizations in Action* (Thompson, 1967), but it is an empirical question how closely actual behaviour meets with the expectations of the rational decision model.

Choice in an organizational setting is a function of the goals set up and the technology that is available. By making very special assumptions about the goal function and the level of knowledge about behaviour technologies the rational decision model maximizes deductive power, predicting unique solutions up to a certain limit where action reciprocities as displayed in two-person and N-person game theory make unique solutions impossible. At the same time the realism of the model is minimized as organizations seldom have connected and transitive goal functions covering every possible outcome and as organizations typically face uncertainty concerning the alternatives of action as well as the environment of behaviour.

Thus goals may be neither precise nor clear and the technology employed may be imperfect or unreliable. If this is the state of the goal and the technology functions, then it is far from evident that the behaviour rules devised by the rational decision model are the most appropriate. Such decision situations would call for decision rules like marginalism (Lindblom, 1965) or satisficing criteria (Simon, 1947; March and Simon, 1958).

Public policy may be modelled in terms of a means–end framework. Government typically defines a number of goals or targets for its programmes, some of which are to be achieved independently and simultaneously whilst others are to be accomplished reciprocally or sequentially. When various goals are interrelated so that the accomplishment of one goal has implications for the achievement of another we have a means–end chain or a means–end hierarchy.

The rational decision model requires that the acting organization is able to assign values to these various ends and means so that the organization can tell which ends and means are preferred when faced with goal conflicts. By-passing the methodological strife between cardinalists and ordinalists it is still the case that the rational decision model is unrealistic when it demands that the organizations be able to specify a connected and transitive value function for all conceivable means and ends, let alone assign these values on a ratio or interval scale.

Values are a necessary but not a sufficient condition for public decision-making. Besides means–end hierarchies public policy may comprise means–end technologies, based on knowledge about the causal relationship between action and outcomes.

Although organizations typically act on the assumption that their means are conducive to the achievement of their ends, it must be emphasized that such beliefs may be all but characterized by the knowledge requirements of the rational decision model. If public policy possessed knowledge about perfect and reliable programmes that result in the desired outcomes, then the technology problem would be solved. With a clear and precise goal function certain technologies would make the calculation of both technical and economic rationality possible.

However, there are several sources of uncertainty in public technologies. Knowledge at the present stage may be inadequate for various reasons, meaning that causal relationships may not be known or reality may be such that randomness implies that programmes cannot be trusted with a high degree of probability.

The difficulty is not whether uncertainty is to be placed with the decision-maker as a result of deficient knowledge or is typical of the actual situation of decision-making; the problem in public policy-making is that it may be very difficult to handle uncertainty, whatever its source, by means of a uniform assignment of probabilities. Often technologies fail to recognize all the interdependencies between ends and means, or the beliefs in causal relationships between the means and the ends may be unrealistic.

Although governments may have clear intentions, knowing what they wish to accomplish with recognized means, it is often the case that the relationship between programme and outcome is problematic. If the idea of a rational means–end hierarchy is unrealistic in relation to organizational action in a governmental setting, then the same judgement must be made with regard to the notion of rational technologies. Ambiguity in the goal function and uncertainties in the technology function severely limit the applicability of the rational decision model as its relevance is confined to choice situations with unambiguous goals and probable technologies (see Chapter 2, Table 2.1).

Consequently, by making strong theoretical assumptions the rational decision model limits its applicability. There is a striking contrast between the simplicity of the model and its rejectability. Its falsifiability in the Popperian sense is too limited, as it actually prohibits very little. Confronted with some falsified prediction it is always possible, it seems, to maintain an ad hoc hypothesis that one or two of the assumptions were not fulfilled (the ceteris paribus clause).

The rational decision model may be more attractive as a regulative notion than as a tool for the understanding of how policy-making actually takes place. In certain choice situations it may be normatively relevant to policy-makers; however, it fails to offer guidance to the understanding of policy-making characterized by choice situations involving multiple imprecise goals and extensive uncertainty.

Moreover, the assumptions of the rational decision model are not unproblematic when applied to collective choice. Actually, the application of a rational decision model to organizational behaviour raises a number of new problems about the value function and the technologies in policy-making. If the concept of rationality is troublesome in individual choice, then it is equally true that collective rationality has problems of its own (Riker, 1982).

We may wish to know not simply whether the assumptions apply or not, but how they come to apply. If organizations act under a rationality assumption, then how do organizations establish means–end hierarchies? And how is information about technologies collected and used? Organizations may take action to improve upon their technologies, but the rational decision model says little about how this is done.

Even if the rational decision model had performed differently in terms of empirical applicability and degree of confirmation, there would still be a need for models that account for how the value function in collective choice is established. Before we proceed to models of group choice that complement the rational decision model, whatever its validity may be, it should be contrasted with the garbage can model, applied here to policy decision-making and not to bureau behaviour as in Chapter 2.

## THE GARBAGE CAN MODEL

Evidently, the so-called garbage can model was intended as a way to represent organizational choice more realistically than the rational decision model, which was originally developed for individual choice behaviour. Like the rational decision model its theoretical simplicity is attractive: (1) the value function is ambiguous; (2) knowledge about the choice situation is uncertain; (3) decision rules are complex and symbolic (Cohen et al., 1972).

The garbage can model has been applied to decision-making in various types of organizations, and it is no exaggeration to suggest that its appeal has been most obvious in governmental-type organization (March and Olsen, 1976; Cohen and March, 1974; Clark, 1983; Olsen, 1983). The literature on so-called policy styles could be seen as an extension of the garbage can model (Richardson, 1982).

In relation to the evaluation criteria its degree of empirical confirmation is not the major problem. Undoubtedly there are sets of data about policy-making that satisfy the garbage can model as public decision-making often appears characterized by ambiguity, uncertainty and political symbolism.

The degree of empirical support is an issue of contention as the garbage can model over-emphasizes the irrational components of organizational behaviour, even in relation to its most typical empirical case – university decision-making (Trow, 1984). Its most serious weakness, however, is its lack of deductive power.

The rational decision model is undoubtedly very strong if judged by the criterion of deductive power. The problem with its suggested replacement – the garbage can model – is that it is far from obvious what its implications are. What can we deduce about organizational behaviour from these assumptions about value ambiguity, technology uncertainty and political ritualism?

If the rational decision model suffers from too much theoretical content, then certainly the garbage can model places too high a value upon descriptive realism. To state that organizational choice is irrational, that solutions look for problems instead of the other way around, that budget-making is ritualism and that technology is foolishness operates effectively as a critique of the rational choice model but it also demonstrates its strictly limited applicability.

However, as a behaviour theory on its own terms the garbage can model appears to raise as many questions as it answers. We may wish to know if rational organizational behaviour is ever feasible or even desirable, if it is impossible as the garbage can model seems to imply. Moreover, it is far from obvious that reality only contains two alternatives: rational behaviour or irrational behaviour. It may well be the case that organizations acting under the rationality assumption satisfy some other decision model which does not contain such strong assumptions as the rational decision model whilst also by-passing the amorphous nature of policy-making implied by the garbage can model.

Public policy-making bodies do have goals tied to their programmes and the emphasis on evaluation and implementation implies that programmes may find their outcomes, though the decision-making may fall far short of the requirements of the rational decision model. It is easy to point out the imprecise and vague nature of many goals in public policy-making – attention has often been called to the lack of technologies in the public sector (Rose, 1981) – and it is not difficult to find processes of policy-making that are oriented more towards the avoidance of a decision than the making of one, or that simply confirm by ritual action what has been decided elsewhere or not decided at all.

However, how do we identify when the goal function is more or less vague and imprecise, when the technology is more or less uncertain, and when political symbolism occurs together with real decision-making? Again, if systematic criteria are devised that allow us to classify choice situations as more or less rational then it turns out that the garbage can model covers an extreme case of decision-making as the polar opposite of rational decision-making.

If any deviation from the stringent requirement of the rational decision model means that the data satisfy the garbage can model, then it would indeed have a large coverage. If, on the other, its field of application is much more limited, then we will certainly be interested in knowing more about the many choice situations between rationality and irrationality.

The garbage can model raises some puzzling problems about the practical usefulness of theories modelling public sector decision-making. The rational decision model has a long standing as a useful tool for solving problems in the public sector. Actually, the adherents of planning, programming and budgeting (PPB) modelled public sector funding on the image of a comprehensive rational decision model (Novick, 1965, 1973), thus seriously overstating the case for rationality in organizations (Wildavsky, 1986).

Yet, it seems as if the practical conclusions of the garbage can model are none at best and useless at worst. If organizational choice is ambiguity and foolishness, then how do we change decision-making in the public sector? Is the garbage can model true of segments of the public sector at different time slices? If so, then we need additional criteria that will allow us to understand when and why some organizations or organizational behaviour is pathological (Hogwood and Peters, 1985).

To sum up: the garbage can model scores high on model simplicity but is weak in terms of deductive power and falsifiability. Its degree of empirical confirmation is contested whereas its practical usefulness is not obvious.

## COLLECTIVE CHOICE THEORY

The central place of goals in public policy can hardly be denied. At stake in public decision-making is the choice of values that are to govern the programme structure. Objectives or the objective function is basic in the collective choice processes that are the essence of public policy-making. None of the models thus far considered have explained how the collective values or the social objectives are established.

The incremental approach states that the objectives function will change only marginally, the demographic model implies that objectives will vary as a function of variations in the environment, and the rational model simply assumes the existence of an objective function. Of particular interest is the approach that models the derivation of the objectives of public policy – the so-called social welfare functions, in the economists' language.

It could be argued that the social welfare function models are a mathematical branch of decision-making theory with a mainly normative focus that is irrelevant to the understanding of ongoing policy-making. These models would constitute abstract collective choice theory as an elaboration of welfare economics without relevance for empirical research on public decision-making.

Actually, it has been argued that the famous Arrow impossibility theorem is irrelevant (Tullock, 1988) and that the whole idea of rational collective decisions contributes nothing to the understanding of policies (Buchanan, 1960). However, it is not difficult to point to the potential of the social welfare function approach to the understanding of policy-making (Sen, 1970).

Since in the social welfare functions (or SWFs) the object of choice is social states (Arrow, 1963: 17) and the problem is to define some acceptable ordering of the possible social states, the SWF is at the heart of public policy. To quote Ezra Mishan: 'The SWF . . . [is] any kind of criterion that might be used to rank alternative situations open to society subject to given economic constraints' (1981: 114).

The theory of the SWF concerns various mechanisms for the specification of the objective function in policy-making – something left unexplained in the rational choice model. Basically, two interpretations of the SWF are relevant here: the derived and the normative interpretations.

In a welfare state public policy cannot be dictatorial in the sense that it must somehow be a function of the way in which the various participating individuals order the relevant social states. Collective choice mechanisms enter at various levels in the public sector decision-making system and the participating individuals may vary from one choice situation to another; whether it is a matter of referendum or committee decision, local government or Parliament, public policy-making in democratic nations proceeds from some type of mechanisms for the aggregation of individual orderings of social states into a social decision.

Such choice mechanisms may have different properties besides the condition of non-dictatorship – properties that may help us understand public policy-making, its processes as well as its outcomes. The individualistic approach to the SWF is to display theoretically how various properties of social mechanisms may be combined; there is no reason why the analysis of the possible or impossible combinations of decision-making properties could not be employed in empirical policy analysis. Actually, the collective choice properties that are relevant in the SWF models are interesting in a practical policy perspective: rationality, Pareto-optimality, unrestricted domain, independence of irrelevant alternatives, non-dictatorship, acyclicity, anonymity, neutrality and positive responsiveness (Riker, 1982; Kelly, 1986; Nurmi, 1987).

It would be most interesting to investigate empirically the extent to which policy-making in various fields fails to satisfy each of these separate criteria on the social choice mechanism employed. That any social mechanism must fail to satisfy all these criteria we know from the Arrow findings, but the question of which criteria apply and which criteria must be dispensed with is still unresolved (Arrow, 1963; Kelly, 1986).

In the normative approach to the specification of the SWF the focus is not upon the derivation of the goal function of policy-making from the preferences of the participating individuals, but upon the identification of criteria that allow society to make the correct normative judgements about the possible social states. In effect, these models of policy-making state what goals of public decision-making are truly proper goals. Such models include the Rawlsian maximin model (Rawls, 1971) and the Buchanan (1977) contractarian model as well as the Harsanyi (1977) impersonality model.

Again, though these models presumably offer guidance more than understanding of policy-making, thus satisfying the evaluation criterion of practical usefulness, they are not without relevance for the analysis of ongoing public decision-making. The normative approach will be discussed in Chapter 10, but the decision focus should include considerations about how policy-makers enter judgements about justice and fairness into the making of decisions.

Public policies benefit various citizens differently and it is vital to unravel how the provision of goods and services affects the utility of various citizens and whether it is possible to improve the utility of some citizens while holding the utility of others constant. Maybe too much interest has focused upon external determinants of policy variations at various levels of government to the neglect of efficiency considerations. It would no doubt increase our understanding of policy-making if we knew how policy-makers compare alternative distributions on the basis of principles of effectiveness and justice.

We know little of the falsifiability and degree of empirical confirmation of the social welfare function approach. Yet, its simplicity and deductive power is such that it should be employed in empirical policy research to a much larger extent. Since we know fairly well how decision mechanism properties may or may not be combined it is an interesting and challenging task to study how existing institutions for policy-making compare judged by the collective choice properties.

Typical of the social welfare function models is that they cover all kinds of social choice mechanisms. In an empirical application these models would have to be pinned down to the special institutions that dominate ongoing social decision-making. Crucial distinctions between various types of collective choice mechanisms would have to be introduced, such as the distinctions discussed in Chapter 1: voting versus market, authority versus exchange, bureaucracy versus competition, planning versus laissez-faire.

According to one approach to the modelling of public policy-making there are natural limits to the specification of the objective function for public decision-making that derive from the distinction between politics and markets.

## PUBLIC CHOICE MODELS

The increasing popularity of the public choice approach to politics reflects its theoretical structure derived from rational choice theory. There is a set of theories that exemplify the public choice method – 'the economic study of nonmarket decision-making' according to Mueller (1979: 1). They refer to different aspects of politics – in a positive and normative perspective analysed with the basic economic-being assumption of self-interest maximization. Looking at the policy cycle two public choice models are clearly relevant for the analysis of ongoing policy-making and implementation: namely the model of the politician's motivation and of his/her strategic opportunism.

Why are there public policies in the amount and with the form and content that ongoing policy programmes display? Perhaps these policies reflect the public interest calculated by politicians in accordance with some technique related to altruism? The intent of the public choice theory of policy determination is to reject any such traditional notion of policy as the search for the public interest. Politicians are no different from private entrepreneurs and their supply of public policy is motivated by private concerns to the same extent as the private profit maximizer (Frohlich et al., 1971, 1978; Breton, 1974).

Public choice models score high on simplicity and deductive power as well as sometimes leading to surprising consequences; yet the basic assumptions are somewhat different from those of the public finance tradition and welfare economics. Typical is the self-interest axiom about the motives of public actors.

What is the objective function that a politician maximizes, and what are the implications for the understanding of policy-making? According to the well-known Hotelling–Downs model of the politician, a function consisting of the probability of reelection and private variables such as power, income, prestige and political ideals is maximized (Hotelling, 1931; Downs, 1957).

In *An Economic Theory of Democracy* (1957) Anthony Downs applied this hypothesis to the politician as individual actor as well as to an organized group – a political party. To move from one politician to a group of politicians one assumes that the group has found some mechanism for motivating the individual actors. A maximization of politicians' objectives results in the effort on the part of politicians to choose those policies during the election period that minimize the policy distance between the expectations of the citizens or voters and those supplied by government, given a memory function on the part of the citizens.

Downs' model predicts that each politician or political party chooses a bundle of policies such that the policy distance is minimized. This model can be accommodated to recognize competition between government and opposition by assuming that the opposition reminds the electorate about the size of the policy distance.

The variation in the efforts of the opposition will affect the government and its choice of public policies. The basic Hotelling–Downs model could be developed by relating the supply of policies by political parties to the demand for policies by the electorate ascending to spatial modelling (Mueller, 1979, 1989). Another line of model development relates to the political business cycle theme.

If politicians maximize the likelihood of winning elections, then perhaps manipulating the economy could be a crucial means to electoral victory. The famous political business cycle model predicts that the incumbent government will stimulate the economy before an election and deflate the economy after the election. In particular, the government will increase spending on programmes that are highly visible to the citizens ahead of an election only to raise taxes or reduce deficits after the election. Such opportunistic behaviour if effective is conducive to a cycle in the economy running over elections instead of over true depressions. The political business cycle predicts that left-wing governments will especially try to reduce unemployment whereas right-wing governments will focus on reducing inflation. In the large literature testing the political business cycle model there is hardly any clear conclusion as to its empirical import (Whiteley, 1986; Mueller, 1989).

Brennan and Buchanan (1980) model natural government as a revenue-maximizing Leviathan. Of all government revenues a portion is spent on public goods, leaving a surplus for government. Governments will try to choose a tax rate, and a tax base, such that revenues are maximized simply in order to maximize government surplus. A citizen will try to choose a public goods provision that minimizes government surplus. Thus, taxation is a struggle between Leviathan and the citizen over the parameters in the Leviathan model: the overall level of taxation, the share that funds public goods and government surplus.

The rather brutal nature of the basic assumptions has led to the criticism that public choice models score low on moral attractiveness as public policy is modelled as only rent-seeking behaviour from special interest groups (Buchanan et al., 1980). The counter-argument from some public choice scholars is the claim that the need for a constitutional reform of public policy principles is imminent in order to promote general interests (Brennan and Buchanan, 1985).

Public choice models of policy-making tend to have attractive model properties. Their chief weakness lies in the empirical base of the model, as the evidence is mixed and thus it is difficult to derive proper tests (Dunsire, 1987; Hood, 1987). When the public choice approach moves into spatial modelling or the political business cycle model, then the complexity of model building increases sharply. The well-known principle of Occam's razor, not to make things more complicated than they already are, comes readily to one's mind when one tries to arrive at an overview of the state of the art within these two fields of research. Moreover, the public choice models tend to over-emphasize the supply side in public policy-making.

Public policy-making often involves budgeting in the public sector, mobilizing resources and transforming these into an output of goods, services and money. One basic mechanism for operating the public sector is the budget, a national one supplemented by regional or local government budgets. These public budgets are collective for a group of people living within a geographical area.

The distinctive properties of the budget mechanism for allocating resources and redistributing money marks the public sector off from market allocation. Public budgets have a supply side as well as a demand side. According to the public choice approach, the interaction between supply and demand in public budget-making is basically asymmetric in favour of the supply side. The budget is too large in the sense of quantity supplied, but it is also too expensive in the sense of quality.

When making decisions about budget allocation and budget redistribution narrow interests in the supply of various budgetary programmes that benefit some at the expense of others have an edge over the interests of broad citizens' groups in the supply of goods and services that benefit all. The dividends from several budget items are vital to special interest groups whereas general interests tend to be diffuse and hard to motivate people to promote as they will not benefit differentially.

When producing goods and services in the public sector the budget only recognizes the costs as there exists no procedure by which demand could be effectively identified. Who could tell where the marginal value of a quantity or quality of a budgetary item equals its marginal cost? This means that producers may always claim that enough is not enough and that more resources will have a great impact in terms of effectiveness, with the result that requests will always chase appropriations whatever the level of budgetary expenditures. Since the goods and services produced in the public sector are often imponderables there is no natural way to evaluate whether the costs in the public sector are worth paying for.

Paying for the consumption of budgetary programmes is based on the formula that the total budget must somehow cover its costs whatever financial instrument is used. Since every programme costs very little in terms of its percentage of the total there will be an excess demand for each budgetary item. However, as the overall cost for the total budget is shared by so many, there is little incentive for everyone to combat general increases in overall finances. The incentive to look for the supply of special goods, services and money is stronger than the general interest in holding down the overall budget, the reason being the strong position of producer groups at the expense of broad consumer interests.

However, public choice theory tends to be too supply side oriented. There is a case for arguing in favour of demand side hypotheses when explaining policy-making, stating a variety of needs for comprehensive public resource allocation as well as redistribution in terms of transfer payments. It should be pointed out that there is one well-known public choice model that underlines the preferences or interests of citizens: the vote popularity model. It predicts that the popularity of a government depends on how the voters perceive the economy, in particular their reaction to the rate of inflation and the level of unemployment. Left-wing governments would be vulnerable if unemployment were high or rising whereas the Achilles' heel of right-wing governments is the level of inflation. As is the case with regard to the political business cycle there is disagreement about the strength of the empirical evidence for the vote popularity model (Hibbs, 1987).

To the public choice school the modern state rests upon a fundamental confusion of the two basic functions of budgeting: resource allocation and redistribution. The welfare state and its programmes have no basis whatsoever in the rationales for the use of the budget instrument, that is, provision of public goods proper and the shaping up of market failures. The welfare state is big government because it attempts redistribution in kind, not in terms of money. Choice is to be government choice so that everyone gets the same service for the same price – categorical equality.

This tension between demand side and supply side oriented public policy models recurs in the huge debate about the profound process of public expenditure growth in the twentieth century in advanced societies. Let us take a short look at some well-known models of the logic of public sector growth.

# MODELLING PUBLIC SECTOR GROWTH

The first attempts to account for the exceptional public sector growth in rich countries were demand side hypotheses. Demand theories suggested among other things that socio-economic development implies public resource allocation (Wagner's law), that increasing affluence implies larger budgets (Wilensky's law), that the dominance of the left in society or government would mean budget expansion replacing market mechanisms (Castles' law), that collective ideologies would promote public sector expansion (Wilensky's law), that sudden social shocks necessitated budgetary shift-points towards much higher levels of public funding (Peacock and Wiseman's law), that welfare spending by the neighbourhood state implied a demand for welfare programmes at home (Pryor's law), and that the increasing openness of the rich economies of the world created a demand for budgetary stabilizing of the erratic fluctuations of markets (Cameron's law).

These demand hypotheses may be classified as either economic or political. They are supported by no generally empirical evidence from policy-making in various rich countries. Either they lack outright substantial empirical confirmation or they model the relationship between determinants and budgetary decision-making inadequately, as demand models tend to lack one crucial variable: the institutional context for policy-making.

The second stage in the debate about public sector growth was supply oriented. Here we find the hypothesis that public spending involves bureaucratic waste (Tullock's law), that public sector growth is a function of bureau size maximization (Downs' law), that public sector productivity is negative, claiming more resources every year for the output (Baumol's law), that budget-making rests upon fiscal illusions about the relation between cost and benefit (Buchanan's law), that an invisible tax structure and high tax elasticities promote big spending (Oates' law); to these hypotheses we add the law that the basic structure of the public sector implies budget-making which favours the supply of goods, services and money at the expense of genuine demand for these entities (Niskanen's law and Kristensen's law).

The supply side approach basically concerns the logic of the interests that are to be found on the demand and supply side of the public household. It shares with Mancur Olson's law about distributional coalitions a distrust of the role of interest organizations in budgetary contexts; it agrees with Breton's law that public officials, whether bureaucrats or professionals, are motivated by a private interest function related to budget size, and it shares with Wicksell's law the idea that efficiency in budget-making presupposes that cost and benefit are closely interrelated somehow.

If either demand hypotheses or supply side models were generally true, then why has public sector growth now been halted? How, moreover, do we account for the differential growth rates in countries such as the USA and Switzerland on the one hand and the Netherlands and Sweden on the other? The third stage of public sector growth theory has seen the reemergence of more complicated models introducing the cultural context of policy-making such as value and belief systems (Wildavsky, 1985, 1987).

A most difficult problem in modern political economy is the explanation of public sector expansion in the advanced economies. The literature on determinants of government growth is now quite substantial. Theoretical ingenuity has not been lacking since a large number of different hypotheses have been suggested including some very bold conjectures. Nor has there been a scarcity of empirical labour because vast amounts of data have been examined in detail for most of the OECD countries, aggregating and disaggregating public finance information in a variety of ways. Why, then, are the results so meagre?

Maybe the gulf between scientific endeavour and findings is so striking that it is time to look more closely at the methodological assumptions underlying the public policy, public finance and public choice approaches to the interpretation of government growth. If a problem is intractable, then perhaps it should be framed differently. The explanatory approaches to the problem of public sector expansion may be cross-sectional or longitudinal, institutional or non-institutional, demand or supply oriented, and equilibrium or disequilibrium based.

Public sector expansion is a complex phenomenon which may be tapped by a variety of different indicators. As Bruno Frey (1988) has pointed out, the public policy literature has focused too much on the resource allocation and income redistribution data, simply because they were accessible to quantitative manipulation. If government regulation is added, then modelling public sector growth becomes even more difficult.

Looking at the public finance data, the variation to be explained by theories of public sector growth is substantial cross-sectionally and longitudinally in the set of rich countries after the Second World War. In 1960 the average share of government outlays among twenty OECD countries was 27 per cent of GDP which by 1985 had risen to an astonishingly high 47 per cent. The difference between the minimum in 1960 – Switzerland with 17 per cent as against 31 per cent in 1985 – and the maximum in 1985 – Sweden with a high of 64.5 per cent as against 31 per cent in 1960 – indicates a profound variation over time and between countries.

However, the typical models of public sector variation are either cross-sectional or longitudinal. A cross-sectional modelling is chosen when the focus is upon international comparison whereas a time series modelling is chosen when it is a question of a national study. Rarely does one find a combined cross-sectional and longitudinal modelling by means of a pooling of the data. Maybe there is so much diversity in the findings simply because the same factors that are conducive to public sector growth over time do not also explain national differences.

Johan Lybeck has examined twelve well-known hypotheses about determinants of public sector expansion on the basis of both cross-sectional and longitudinal evidence and has failed to corroborate each of them in any strong sense. The rationale for focusing on time series modelling is given by the argument that major cross-sectional model approaches by Castles, Schmidt and Cameron have failed to identify general factors operating in all kinds of systems. It is believed that nation-specific data approaches may reveal more of the individual nation's institutional public spending background than is captured by means of general categories (Lybeck, 1986).

Much effort has been devoted to technical problems as the estimation of the kind of time series models involved presents serious methodological difficulties. Considering the fact that government growth may be measured in a variety of ways, it is no wonder that the employment of sophisticated econometric tools comes up with results that cannot be derived from a single theory. Although all national studies achieve rather impressive parameter estimations the findings diverge when compared. Can we be certain that some unknown factor like nation-specific institutions accounts for the striking way in which the national results differ? The basic distinction between institutional and non-institutional approaches is debatable, as it opens up the road for ad hoc explanations.

Perhaps the most common classification of government growth hypotheses is that between demand and supply side models. To the former category belong the hypotheses that focus on the expression of citizen needs and the preferences of politicians. In the latter category are the behaviour of bureaucrats and institutional production factors. The well-known median voter hypotheses stand somewhere in between as does the corporatist theme. What support is there for various demand and supply side models in the national studies (Lybeck and Henrekson, 1988)?

Demand and supply side models stem from two alternative conceptions of government in a representative democracy. The traditional democracy model regards government as a neutral and non-partisan vehicle for the voice of citizens – the *benevolent principal–agent* model. The new public choice approach views government as a potential source of distortion in the relationship between governed and governors where different special interest groups have a strategic position to promote their selfish interests, including those of the politicians and bureaucrats – the *economic being* model.

The economic being model factors have great explanatory relevance for the Swedish data, in particular those on the supply side. One may raise doubts about the general applicability of policy models as there is little support in Norwegian data for politico-economic or politico-institutional models. Finland confirms the median voter model of positive income elasticities for public programmes. Similarly, the data on France corroborates the median voter model although there is also empirical evidence for public choice models concerning the logic of suppliers. Wagner's law receives support in the Danish, Swiss, British and Austrian data, although various institutional or political supply side factors have to be added in all four cases. The Italian and Dutch cases are focused on the redistributive implications of public spending, pointing at the crucial role of strong interest groups attempting broad fragmented horizontal redistribution. The findings, however much they differ in each country, support the economic being model better than the benevolent principal–agent model (Lybeck and Henrekson, 1988).

The distinction between demand and supply side models does not necessarily entail that an equilibrium approach is chosen. The logic of public sector spending points in another direction, namely the use of a disequilibrium approach as there is no mechanism that instantly corrects for excess demand or supply. Including explicitly a revenue constraint on public spending means that excess demand or excess supply is counteracted somehow. Only French and German data display the importance of the revenue restriction in determining public spending, whilst the data on Great Britain show that expenditure controls are not easily introduced. An equilibrium approach would probably have to be something like a competing aspiration level strategy where equilibrating forces are modelled in terms of the interaction between actors with different interests.

There is now a substantial literature on the size of government in public policy, public finance or public choice perspectives. It is a highly informative source about the current state of the debate about how government budget-making drove out markets in advanced capitalist states. It is hard to come by radically new solutions to the basic problem in political economy: the state versus the market.

## CONCLUSION

Since policy analysis was recognized as a field of its own, there has been a search for a general theory of the policy process that could replace the actual proliferation of a number of different and special models. If there was ever some minimum agreement about the interpretation of the policy cycle – a Weberian conception of politics and administration as it were (Page, 1985) – we now face severe disagreement as how to model policy-making.

These various decision models score differently according to a number of metacriteria for model evaluation. In particular, there is a sharp gulf between the rationalist interpretation of the policy process – some rational choice model and the realist understanding of the actual conduct of policy-making – and a bounded rationality decision model, let alone a garbage can model.

Public policy-making may be approached as determined by structure, as for example in the demographic and incremental models. Or one may take an actor approach to policy-making emphasizing the intentional aspects involving ends and means (Parsons, 1968; Barry, 1971). Structure models appear to be too crude in the light of empirical evidence as well as in terms of the level of theoretical understanding aimed at. Introducing internal choice variables in terms of the actors' orientations increases empirical confirmation as well as theoretical coherence, but what kind of choice theory should one choose?

There seems to be a fundamental gulf between model simplicity and model realism. The realist models of policy-making suggest no limit to the amount of complexity and number of variables to be taken into account. On the other hand, the simple models of rational policy-making appear to be the only tools that give the policy analyst some direction as to where to look for explanations when policy-making deviates from model predictions.

It is hardly possible to argue that one of these four approaches to the policy process is superior to the others. They score differently according to the various metatheoretical criteria. The search for one true approach to the public policy process is a venture bound to fail. Model choice may be made in two fundamentally different ways. Either one may try to build a general model true of every policy cycle interpreted in terms of the making and implementation of decisions and rejecting various restrained models that have been falsified by the data. Or one may proceed in a relativist fashion operating with a number of restrictive models but stating the limits of their applicability clearly.

Yet there are more difficulties. The fate of public policies depends on both how the policy enacted is implemented and the nature of the organizations which are the target for policy implementation. In order to reach conclusions about the logic of policy-making we really should also include the implementation stage: what are the conditions for successful implementation? Attention has to be paid to implementation strategies as well as to the peculiar characteristics of the institutions that are involved in the implementation of policy, in addition to analysis of the policy-making stage.

Thus, understanding a policy process not only requires adequate theoretical modelling of the policy-making process, but also demands some good theories about policy implementation. Alas, they are hard to come by, as we shall see in the next chapter.

# 4

# IMPLEMENTATION MODELS

Implementation models were suggested in response to the neglect of the various stages of policy execution after the enactment of policies at the governmental level, the *missing link* as it was called. When using implementation models the basic problem is to design some institutional mechanisms by which implementation may work, if indeed implementation in the sense of goal achievement is at all workable.

Paul A. Sabatier, a pioneer in implementation analysis, raises some fundamental questions about the nature of implementation in a review of the present state of implementation theory (Sabatier, 1986). Although Sabatier's analysis of the two competing models of implementation – top-down versus bottom-up implementation – as well as his attempt to launch a third model – a kind of coalition model – is perceptive and challenging, it may be argued that it misses a more basic problem concerning the nature of public policy implementation.

It must be recognized that modelling the process of executing public policies – the implementation process – is different from evaluating the extent to which objectives have been accomplished – the implementation assessment. Surveying the plethora of implementation models may clarify some of the problems surrounding implementation analysis. It is based on the distinction between implementation as an outcome and implementation as a process. As long as the concept of implementation remains unexplained, any theory about the conditions for successful implementation will remain ambiguous.

## THE CONCEPT OF IMPLEMENTATION

The concept of implementation is characterized by a problematic structure. *Webster's Dictionary* states that 'implementation' means either the act of implementing or the state of having been implemented; it presents the following key words for 'implement':

> to carry out: accomplish, fulfil; to give practical effect to and ensure of actual fulfilment by concrete measures, to provide instruments or means of practical expression.

'To carry out something' or 'to accomplish something' may sound intelligible and require little explication. A formal definition might be:

(DF1) Implementation = F (Intention, Output, Outcome)

where implementation refers to the bringing about, by means of outputs, of outcomes that are congruent with the original intention(s). It is readily seen that 'implementation' has a double meaning: 'to give practical effect to' or execution on the one hand, and 'fulfil' or accomplishment on the other. A policy that is executed need not result in the accomplishment of its objectives.

Thus, we have a basic ambiguity in the notion of implementation: implementation as an end state or policy achievement, and implementation as a process or policy execution. The *Oxford English Dictionary* notes the same double meaning: 'to complete, perform; to fulfil'.

The performance of activities need not lead to the fulfilment of objectives. Implementation analysis could be considered a development of public administration whereby the execution of policies is expedited by the addition of evaluation research. Implementation analysis is not confined to what happens after political reforms have been enacted, because it goes beyond the focus on programme execution in public administration as it was traditionally conceived.

The concept of implementation implies assessment; it is made by the actors involved in the implementation process, and one basic task of the implementation analyst is to evaluate the implementation. Given the ends and means of the policy, implementation analysis cannot be confined to a statement of what happens afterwards. The analyst may use the tools of evaluation research in order to arrive at an implementation judgement of the extent of successful implementation, the first major focus in implementation analysis. Success or failure are not the only relevant properties of the implementation of public policies. The process of enforcing a policy has its own logic, which is the second major focus of the implementation analyst.

Aspects of the implementation process other than the accomplishment of the policy objectives that the analyst is interested in include: the strategies and tactics employed by various parties to the implementation game, the mechanism of delay as a decision parameter, the variety of motives among the participating actors, and the need for coalition building and fixing the game. Implementation requires more than a state of affairs in which there is a policy objective and an outcome (or several objectives and outcomes), since, in addition, the concept of implementation implies that these two entities – objective and outcome – satisfy two different relationships: the causal function and the accomplishment function.

Two ideas are fundamental to the concept of implementation: that the policy programme is the output that brings about the outcomes in such a way that the latter accomplish the objectives of the policy. Implementation assessment focuses on the operation of a public policy and its consequences. It includes three logically separate activities:

(a) clarification of the objectives involved (the goal function), (b) statement of the relationship between outputs and outcomes in terms of causal effectiveness (the causal function), and (c) clarification of the relation between objectives and outcomes in order to affirm the extent of goal achievement (the accomplishment function).

Each of the three tasks presents its own peculiar problems. Together they imply that it may be difficult to judge the effectiveness of implementation. The ends and means – the intentions – of policies are formulated and enacted by various kinds of actors in the political process. What is an end or a means is an intentional object to some actor, which means that any definition of implementation must specify the actors involved in the process. These actors may be divided into two sets, the formators and the implementors.

Implicit in implementation theory is the idea that the actors who decide on policy are different from the actors who are responsible for the implementation of policy. Though this is far from always the case, the implementation process is built up around an asymmetric relationship between the formators of policy and the implementors of policy. The formators may not be the initiators of policy; be that as it may, the theory of implementation assumes that public policy becomes a legitimate concern for implementors once it has been decided upon in formally defined ways. By developing the original implementation formula we are now at a stage where a more powerful and complex concept of implementation may be introduced:

(DF2) Implementation = F (Policy, Outcome, Formator,
    Implementor, Initiator, Time)

Suppose one asks whether a policy has been implemented. Then one needs information about the extent of congruence between policy objectives and outcomes, but that is not enough. In addition, there has to be a decision concerning the time span that may pass before an implementation judgement can be said to be neither premature nor belated. When is it appropriate to ask whether a programme's objectives have been realized? This is all relevant to the concept of implementation. When we move to the theory of implementation processes, conflicting views crop up. It is easier to introduce a formal concept of implementation than to model the evolving implementation process.

Whereas implementation as an outcome is rather unambiguous – to carry a policy into effect – the implementation process is a more complex phenomenon. Implementation processes involve coalitions, learning, political symbolism, implementation perspectives, as well as control. But this is not enough for the general claims that implementation is advocacy coalitions, is evolutionary learning or hierarchical control. Any kind of mechanism may be used in the implementation process, because of the loose connection between implementation as an outcome and implementation as a process.

## MODELLING PROCESSES OF IMPLEMENTATION

The status of so-called implementation models is precarious with regard to the standard public policy models (Dunsire, 1978). They are considered a necessary complement to policy models because, it is argued, these model only the decision-making process, assuming that the enactment of policy implies the execution of policy programmes as well as the implementation of policy objectives (Meter and Horn, 1975). Or, even worse, the policy models discussed above adhere to a naive assumption about public administration: namely that policies once decided upon will automatically achieve their objectives by means of the policy outputs as if implementation was something utterly simple and automatic.

The argument about *implementation deficit* implied a radical rejection of this hypothesis. Neglecting the implementation stage could not be considered worse than adhering to a naive theory about public administration and the behaviour of implementors.

Thus, implementation models constitute the missing link between policy decision-making on the one hand and policy execution and policy implementation on the other (Hargrove, 1975). The argument about the missing link may have appeared as a revelation to those who had realized that policy may have one appearance when enacted and a quite different one when put into practice. The basic problem was, however, to explain why this misfit tended to occur more than often – how are we to understand what happens after the formulation and formation of policy? To the extent that this hypothesis about a lack of congruence between policy objectives and policy outcomes is true, it amounted to a rather drastic criticism, if not straightforward rejection, of the standard policy models.

The basic policy models were accused of either neglecting the problematic phase in the policy process or adhering to a naive model of implementation: state the goals, derive the means, execute the programmes and find the outcomes. Beginning with the highly original Pressman and Wildavsky analysis in *Implementation* (1984), first published in 1973, a large literature poured out warnings against any public policy model that regarded implementation as simple or straightforward.

Every policy model was regarded as incomplete at best or deficient at worst because they lacked a theory about the mechanism of implementation – how programmes should be handled in order that stated objectives could be achieved in terms of positive outcomes. To identify this mechanism of implementation – the key to successful implementation – became the target of a number of new policy models focusing on what happens after the decision stage.

At the same time these new models were open to the same kind of criticism: they by-passed the initial phases of the policy process – that is, they were one-sided. The attempts to extend the implementation models to cover the entire policy cycle have hardly been successful. We are still stuck with a gulf between decision-making models and implementation models in the study of public policy (Sabatier, 1986).

The implementation models differ as to the nature of the mechanism to be employed in the monitoring of programmes: top-down models versus bottom-up models. A brief survey of the various implementation models follows.

## IMPLEMENTATION AS PERFECT ADMINISTRATION

Hood suggests a model of implementation that would 'produce perfect policy implementation' (1976: 6). Such a model would include a unitary administrative system with a single line of authority, enforcement of uniform rules or objectives, a set of clear and authoritative objectives implementable on the basis of perfect obedience or perfect administrative control, perfect coordination and perfect information within and between administrative units, absence of time pressure, unlimited material resources for tackling the problem and unambiguous overall objectives and perfect political acceptability of the policies pursued (Hood, 1976: 6–8).

The model of perfect administration is an ideal-type construct to discover the sources of implementation failure (Hood, 1976: 190–207). The model approaches implementation from the narrow focus of the characteristics of pure authority relations – hierarchy, obedience, control and perfect coordination – viewed as the mechanism for the accomplishment of successful implementation.

However, empirical work on implementation has resulted in a different finding: namely that mechanisms more symmetrical in nature, such as exchange and negotiation, are more germane to the implementation process than authority and its characteristics (Lipsky, 1980; Barrett and Fudge, 1981). These bargaining mechanisms for the implementation of policy are as important as structures of authority (Bardach, 1977; Pressman and Wildavsky, 1984: 87–124). It is questionable whether the model conditions listed really are conducive to perfect implementation; for example, the model conditions of this top-down version of implementation seldom apply due to intra- or inter-organizational complexity (Hanf and Scharpf, 1978).

## IMPLEMENTATION AS POLICY MANAGEMENT

A model of implementation may involve the search for guide-lines for successful implementation. In a 1979 article, 'The Conditions of Effective Implementation: A Guide to Accomplishing Policy Objectives', Sabatier and Mazmanian state:

The program is based on a sound theory relating changes in target group behaviour to the achievement to the desired end-state (objectives). The statute (or other basic policy decision) contains unambiguous policy directives and structures the implementation process so as to maximize the likelihood that target groups will perform as desired. The leaders of the implementing agencies possess substantial managerial and political skill and are committed to statutory goals.

These conditions may at first sight appear innocuous, but when one ponders about the availability of 'sound' causal hypotheses or clear ends and means as well as powerful management strategies, then the risk of circularity in the argument is evident: what works in the implementation process is what accomplishes implementation. Moreover, there are other equally demanding requirements.

The program is actively supported by organized constituency groups and by a few key legislators (or the chief executive) throughout the implementation process, with the courts being neutral or supportive. The relative priority of statutory objectives is not significantly undermined over time by the emergence of conflicting public policies or by changes in relevant socioeconomic conditions that undermine the statute's 'technical' theory or political support. (Sabatier and Mazmanian, 1979: 484–5)

These presumed sufficient conditions for successful implementation do identify crucial factors that affect policy accomplishment: technology, unambiguity of objectives, skill, support and consensus. However, the counter-argument is that this theory begs the question of what a 'sound' policy technology is. Moreover, what is 'substantial' policy skill and 'enough' policy support? And when is a policy 'significantly' undermined by conflict?

## IMPLEMENTATION AS EVOLUTION

Wildavsky has introduced the theory of a process of implementation as necessarily resulting not in implementation but in redefinition of objectives and reinterpretation of outcomes – that is, evolution. If implementation processes result in the redefinition of objectives and the reinterpretation of outcomes, then how could there be successful implementation? The evolutionary conception of implementation implies that implementation processes may not be neatly separated from stages of policy formulation, mingling objectives and outcomes. It also implies that implementation is endless: 'Implementation will always be evolutionary; it will inevitably reformulate as well as carry out policy' (Majone and Wildavsky, 1984: 116). This is an empirical argument that is open to refutation pending a major survey of programme accomplishments (see, for example, the analysis of the effects of social policy on British society in the post-war period in George and Wilding, 1984).

## IMPLEMENTATION AS LEARNING

Wildavsky has outlined yet another interesting interpretation of the nature of the implementation process (Browne and Wildavsky, 1984). Implementation is modelled as an endless learning process where the implementors through continuous search processes come up with improved goal functions and more reliable programme technologies. There is no natural end to the process of policy implementation because each stage means an improvement in relation to earlier stages where, over time, the original objectives are bound to become transformed and the initial means replaced.

The theory that implementation is learning may be regarded as an optimistic explanation of the hypothesis that implementation is evolution. The kind of implementation process conceived of in the various versions of a top-down approach – naive implementation, perfect administration, a hierarchical model, conditions for successful implementation – is considered suboptimal because of its assumption of a one-shot implementation process.

## IMPLEMENTATION AS STRUCTURE

The events constituting a process of implementation are typically approached as pieces forming a whole. How can one separate what is part of an implementation process and what is not (demarcation)? What are the basic components of a process of implementation (identification)? In 'Implementation Structures: A New Unit for Administrative Analysis', Hjern and Porter state: 'An implementation structure is comprised of subsets of members within organizations which view a programme as their primary (or an instrumentally important) interest' (1981: 216).

Obviously, an implementation structure consists of sets of actors, but which sets of actors constitute one and only one implementation structure? Is it enough that these actors are members of organizations and have a 'primary interest' in a programme? Is it not necessary for people who have a 'primary' interest in a policy also to wish or attempt to put it into effect?

The approach of an implementation structure follows from an emphasis on properties of processes of implementation other than those of the top-down perspective: organization complexity, self-selection of participants, multiplicity of goals and motives, local discretion. Hjern and Porter state:

> Implementation structures are not organizations. They are comprised of parts of many organizations; organizations are comprised of parts of many programmes. As analytic constructs, implementation structures are conceptualized to identify the units of purposive action which implement programmes. They are 'phenomenological administrative units', partly defined by their participating members. (1981: 222)

The description of implementation structures as comprising units that implement programmes is of little help as it is circular. Either an implementation structure is a construct – simply a 'unit for administrative analysis', or 'implementation structures are administrative entities' (Hjern and Porter, 1981: 219), but not both.

The concept of an implementation structure is relevant for the analysis of implementation processes, but one has to be aware of the fallacy of reification or misplaced concreteness. No wonder that implementation is described as difficult, as it is hard to find out how an implementation structure is to be demarcated and identified (Hjern and Hull, 1982).

## IMPLEMENTATION AS OUTCOME

Fudge and Barrett state that a theory of the implementation process follows from a particular concept of implementation. If implementation is not 'putting policy into effect', Fudge and Barrett state, then: 'The emphasis . . . shifts away from a master/subordinate relationship to one where policy-makers and implementers are more equal and the interaction between them becomes the focus for study' (1981: 258).

The concept of implementation and the concept of an implementation process should be kept analytically separate. Why could not organizational complexity or autonomy, just like exchange and negotiation, be conducive to, or compatible with, implementation as 'putting a policy into effect'? Similarly it could be the case that the perfect administration model may only achieve a state describable as 'getting something done'. To analyse what must obtain in order to apply the concept of implementation is different from producing a model as to how implementation – in particular, successful implementation – comes about.

## IMPLEMENTATION AS PERSPECTIVE

Walter Williams (1982) has argued strongly in favour of taking a special perspective as the starting point for policy execution. Is this so-called implementation perspective some kind of practical science of administration, a body of knowledge that policy-makers and implementors could draw upon as they approach the implementation of policies? For Williams, the implementation perspective is the perspective of the practitioners.

It does not follow from the fact that actors are participating in something which they label an 'implementation process' that implementation is really going on. As several implementation studies have testified, actors may execute policies believing that their actions eventually bring about implementation, but they may be wrong. In order to state the extent to which an implementation perspective meets with successful implementation there must be a different implementation perspective – that of the theoretician.

## IMPLEMENTATION AS BACKWARD MAPPING

The implementation process involves a number of participants – are some more important than others? Elmore (1978) argues convincingly that much of implementation analysis has focused upon those placed high up in the public authority structure, whereas implementation analysis actually demands that attention be focused upon those responsible for the production of outcomes on a day-to-day basis.

The crucial nexus in the implementation process is the behaviour of those who are placed most closely to the production of outputs – that is, those placed far down in the hierarchy (Lipsky, 1980). Elmore argues:

> Recall the logic of backward mapping outlined earlier: Begin with a concrete statement of the behaviour that creates the occasion for a policy intervention, describe a set of organizational operations that can be expected to affect that behaviour, describe the expected effect of those operations, and then describe for each level of the implementation process what effect one would expect that level to have on the target behaviour and what resources are required for that effect to occur. (1982: 28)

Even if a great deal of implementation analysis has focused single-mindedly on the formulator of policy and even if a naive assumption about the possibility of hierarchical control has plagued much of public administration – as Elmore states – it is hardly fruitful to reverse these exaggerations by making the implementor the sole crucial party to the implementation game.

It is not clear what is meant by a 'behaviour that creates the occasion for a policy intervention'; there is practically no limit to the number of instances of such behaviour that the scholar may find, but how are they to be selected if one cannot study them all?

The backward mapping perspective aims at reversing the tendency of implementation models to take a top-down approach, or, quoting Elmore: 'The advantage of beginning with a concrete behaviour and focussing on the delivery-level mechanism for affecting that behaviour is that it focusses attention on reciprocity and discretion' (Elmore, 1982: 28).

A necessary component of an implementation perspective is the enactment of a set of goals by some set of decision-makers. The goals of the policy formulator may be neither precise nor clear, and they may change over time or be in conflict with the goals of the implementor. Yet, without inclusion of the formulator and the goals enacted the implementation has no determinate focus. If there are no goals enacted, how could there be anything to be implemented?

# IMPLEMENTATION AS SYMBOLISM

Fudge and Barrett state that an implementation perspective cannot be taken for granted. Studies of implementation processes reveal not only that the implementors may resist change or approach both objectives and programmes in terms of their own interpretation, but also that the policy-makers may find it necessary or advantageous to neglect policy execution (Edelman, 1971).

The fact that a process of implementation exhibits political symbolism – by-passing a sincere effort at implementing a real policy – does not preclude the applicability of the concept of implementation; goals may be accomplished because they were intertwined with other goals, combined with pseudo-political behaviour as well as executed on the basis of extensive uncertainty among the participants. The extent to which every implementation process has more or fewer symbolic elements, and what the consequences are for the possibility of goal accomplishment, is an entirely empirical question.

# IMPLEMENTATION AS AMBIGUITY

Policy ambiguity may be less a strategic instrument manipulated by politicians at will than a necessary by-product of the political process (Baier et al., 1986). It is believed that implementation fails because bureaucracy is either not sufficiently able or too autonomous. However, the difficulty inherent in achieving successful implementation – namely the so-called implementation deficit – may reflect a far more serious threat to the idea of policy implementation. The policy process may be such as to make ambiguity systemic in all policies. Thus, policy implementation would fail not because of a gap between rational policy-making and imperfect policy implementation but due to the looseness of policy.

More radically, it is argued that policy cannot be separated from implementation, that, on the contrary, policy can only be identified in the process of implementation (Ham and Hill, 1984). If this were true, then the whole idea of a policy approach would be reducible to organizational analysis or the study of public administration. But is it really true that social reforms can never be conceived and outlined in a policy document? Again, if policy ambiguity were as prevalent as claimed, if policy were the resultant of implementation, then how could policy analysis improve policy-making (Meltsner, 1976)? Some policies are no doubt ambiguous, but do all policies have to be so?

# IMPLEMENTATION AS COALITION

Sabatier, once an adherent of a version of the top-down model of implementation, argues that implementation processes consist of so-called advocacy coalitions: 'actors from various public and private organizations who share a set of beliefs and who seek to realize their common goals over time' (Sabatier, 1986: 100). This new hybrid model is derived from two sources: the policy network framework (Richardson and Jordan, 1979; Dunleavy, 1985; Sharpe, 1985) and the hypothesis that implementation is basically learning (Browne and Wildavsky, 1984).

The new Sabatier theory seems to focus on the earlier stages of the implementation process. It may even be questioned whether it is not closer to a model of the general policy cycle, especially the policy enactment phase. Sabatier states: 'These outputs at the operational level mediated by a number of other factors (most notably, the validity of the causal underlying the program), result in a variety of impacts on targeted problem parameters, as well as side effects' (1986: 40). How can we be sure of this? Are we to deduce from this that any coalition of implementors – private and public – are bound to produce outputs that result in successful implementations? Maybe the effects on targets are dysfunctional?

The other component of the new theory of implementation is the emphasis on long-term learning in these advocacy coalitions. A distinction is made between the core and the secondary aspects of policy, where learning refers to the secondary aspects: 'While changes in the policy core are usually the result of external perturbations, changes in the secondary aspects of a governmental action program are often the result of policy-oriented learning by various coalitions or policy brokers' (Sabatier, 1986: 43).

If implementation is to be understood as a long-term process where policy coalitions interact and learn about programme technologies and programme outcomes, then perhaps implementation is everything? Why is there this need for more learning? Obviously, because implementation does not work. But is this always a function of a lack of learning which benevolent coalitions may undo? Simply having policy coalitions does not produce implementation, let alone successful implementation; too many actors or too many coalitions may block the implementation process. And how can we ever make beneficial assumptions about the probability that so-called policy-brokers will make peace between, and within, so-called policy coalitions?

## THE TWO IMPLEMENTATION PROBLEMS

There is no single model of policy execution that will guarantee policy accomplishment. Implementation theory has thus far been the search for some interaction pattern or way of structuring the process of implementation in such a manner as to achieve a high probability of policy accomplishment. This has resulted in a controversy between those who believe in control, planning and hierarchy on the one hand

and those who believe in spontaneity, learning and adaptation as implementation techniques on the other. A reorientation of implementation theory would be to inquire into how accountability is to be upheld in the implementation of policies and how much trust can be placed in policy implementors if they are still to be accountable.

The implementation models discussed above fall into two sets. On the one hand we have the top-down models which score high on simplicity and coherence but lack substantial evidence. On the other hand there is the set of bottom-up models which score high on realism and applicability. The difference between the two sets of models appears striking when it comes to practical or normative considerations. Whereas the top-down models emphasize responsibility, the bottom-up models underline trust. What is more important: departmental responsibility or trust in departmental autonomy?

The concept of implementation deals with the identification of a policy, a set of outcomes and the relationships between these two entities. The concept of an implementation process refers to how policies are carried out in an environment conducive to policy accomplishment or policy failure – what are usually referred to as stages of implementation (Mazmanian and Sabatier, 1983).

It does not follow that implementation exists just because it is possible to state what implementation would amount to if it came about. We could possess a clear and articulate concept of implementation but fail to identify processes of implementation. Actually, there are different arguments in the literature to the effect that implementation or successful implementation does not exist, because every process of implementation fails in its purpose.

If implementation is impossible or difficult, it is not because we lack an adequate concept of implementation but because the relationship between policy and action is such that processes of implementation have a number of properties that are not conducive to the occurrence of successful implementation.

According to Sabatier these models may be classified as either top-down or bottom-up models of implementation. Although this distinction is essential in theories of implementation, it is certainly not the only or fundamental demarcation line between alternative approaches. Nor is it obvious that the top-down and bottom-up models of implementation were developed in the historical sequence that Sabatier describes, as the importance of the Pressman and Wildavsky volume *Implementation* (1984; originally published 1973) is underestimated.

## RESPONSIBILITY AND TRUST

Obviously, an implementor gives practical effect to a policy by taking action in relation to the objectives of the policy. Hopefully, the implementor is sooner or later confronted with a set of outcomes that are positively relevant to the realization of the objectives. If these outcomes are congruent with the objectives, then there will be successful implementation. If the set of outcomes is related to the set of objectives in such a way that to each objective there is a corresponding outcome and vice versa – a one-to-one relationship – then we have policy accomplishment par preference. But this is only theory.

In actual practice objectives do not always find their outcomes, and there are outcomes that lack objectives. Outcomes have to be interpreted in terms of the objectives; one objective may be partly satisfied by several different outcomes, or it may be satisfied by one outcome but be in opposition to another. If a policy contains a number of goals – ends and means concerning various policy aspects – some of these goals may find their outcomes, whereas others may confront outcomes that are contrary to these objectives.

A judgement about implementation cannot be made mechanically. It depends on how the environment in which implementation takes place is interpreted. If a policy is only partly implementable from the very beginning, then maybe this fact should be added to the evaluation. Implementation analysis could require evaluation criteria that are not strictly intersubjective. Whether a goal has been achieved or not depends on how the goal and the outcomes are perceived by the actors involved in the implementation process. Whether there is policy success or policy failure depends on how the actors perceive the environment and judge the implementability of the policy or the means to be employed.

What is successful implementation to one group is failure to another because these groups perceive the ends, the means and the outcomes differently. There is no simple solution to these problems, and they all pertain to implementation as policy accomplishment or the extent to which objectives meet their outcomes independently of how the process of implementation is structured.

The first aspect of implementation is the relation between objectives and outcome – the responsibility side. The implementation of public policies takes place under an accountability norm which restricts the putting into effect of the public programmes. Political accountability and administrative as well as professional responsibility are impossible without the notion of implementation of public policy. If it is not possible to evaluate the extent to which objectives and outcomes match, then public accountability is meaningless. The fact that objectives sometimes do not find their outcomes or that outcomes sometimes cannot find their objectives does not imply that accountability is impossible. Implementation, according to this aspect, is simply the match between objectives and outcomes, perfect implementation being a perfect match as it were.

In whatever way implementation takes place, it is always valid to inquire into the extent to which objectives have been accomplished and the degree to which outcomes have occurred that work against the objectives. This is the basis for judging the accountability of implementors and the responsibility of politicians and officials. More and more it is argued in the literature that successful implementation does not exist, because no process of implementation is predictable.

Implementation is difficult because the relationship between policy and outcomes is such that processes of implementation result in uncertainty, ambiguity and confusion. If successful implementation is always impossible, then how about responsibility? The second aspect of implementation refers to the process of putting policies into effect – the trust side.

Implementation in a democratic system of government rests upon the public power entrusted to politicians and public officials, whether administrators or professionals. Politicians and officials are supposed to deliver on policies; this is the basic restriction on the degrees of freedom on decision-makers and implementors in relation to their principals, the citizens. How implementation is to be carried out is a task for the implementors, for which they are to be held accountable but where autonomy is vital. Without space for independent action the implementors cannot make use of their capacity to make judgements about what means are conducive to the ends and adapt in relation to environmental exigencies securing flexibility.

However, complete autonomy on the part of the implementors would mean a total absence of restrictions on their behaviour, so negating the fundamental accountability nature of the interaction between citizens and implementors. On the other hand, too many restrictions as a result of distrust in the implementors would jeopardize the possibility of successful implementation as it is impossible to outline once and for all a detailed plan as to how objectives are to be accomplished.

Trust is basic to the implementation process, but this does not dispense with the responsibility side of implementation. Top-down models over-emphasize the responsibility side, trying to nail down the inherent uncertainties of implementation processes in accordance with a firm plan or an outlined structure of control. Bottom-up models underline the trust side to much too high an extent in an attempt to safeguard as many degrees of freedom as possible to the implementor as a tool for handling the uncertainties by flexibility and learning. If responsibility is stressed unduly, then there will be too many restrictions on the implementors in the choice of alternative technologies for the accomplishment of objectives.

On the one hand, if trust is the sole basis of the activities of the implementors, then there will be too few restrictions on them, allowing even the replacement of the original objectives by new goals. An implementation process is a combination of responsibility and trust both in the relation between citizens and the public sector in general and in the relation between politicians and officials. Without the notion of implementation as policy accomplishment there is no basis for evaluating policies and holding politicians, administrators and professionals accountable.

On the other hand, implementation as policy execution rests upon trust or a certain degree of freedom for politicians and implementors to make choices about alternative means for the accomplishment of goals. There is no single model of policy execution that will guarantee policy accomplishment.

Implementation theory has searched for a process of implementation such that there will be policy accomplishment. There are those who believe in control, planning and hierarchy on the one hand, and those who believe in spontaneity, learning and adaptation as problem-solving techniques, on the other. Implementation theory could, however, inquire into how accountability may be combined with trust in the implementation process.

The logic of the dynamics of implementation forces the analysis to take different types of implementation processes into account: continuous versus step-wise implementation, repeated versus unique implementation, innovation implementation versus maintenance implementation, and short-span versus long-term implementation. Processes of implementation may not fit a simple notion of the implementation process as the unique continuous implementation of a social innovation in a short span of time. The distinction between continuous and step-wise implementation processes alerts the implementation analyst to the possibility of suboptimization.

A policy may comprise a number of subgoals which may only be implemented in a discrete fashion due to the interdependencies among the goals: once one subgoal has been implemented, another subgoal may be implemented, and so on. The time distinction draws attention to the fact that some programmes are commitments for long periods of time. The fact that such programmes require a substantial evolution over time does not necessarily imply that their objectives must change and that accountability is impossible; premature assessments about policy accomplishment are likely if the time dimension is neglected.

Programmes to be implemented are not all of one kind. Programmes may be approached differently depending on whether they are about to be initiated or are in the process of consolidation and maintenance. Consider the differences between conducting an implementation analysis of, on the one hand, a standard programme for the surveillance of traffic rules and, on the other, the unique programme of establishing a new university. The goals with regard to the former may be so apparent that they are trivial, while in the latter case they may be so complex that they contain goal conflicts and unrealistic goals. In the former case we have standard operating procedures which are oriented towards the maintenance of certain states whereas in the latter the programme offers innovation and social experiment.

It may be the case that a programme that calls for repeated maintenance implementation has to be evaluated differently from a programme that calls for major innovation, where the goals may be changed and the outputs revised. Also, it is pertinent to examine the point at which an innovative programme is redefined into a consolidating programme calling for an implementation analysis of how the accomplishments already made are being maintained.

The distinction between implementation as end state and as process is relevant when one is aware of the variety of implementation phenomena. Thus, the concept of implementation is suitable for the detection of goal changes, programme redefinition, discrepancies between innovation objectives and consolidation goals, short-term goals and long-term objectives – phenomena that, interpreted according to a conception of implementation as equivalent to evolution, learning, perspective or coalition, make accountability in implementation virtually impracticable.

## CONCLUSION

Attempts are now being made to integrate two of the major schools in implementation theory (Sabatier, 1986), which are highly relevant to tackling the fundamental problems of implementation in order to escape the stalemate between the top-down approach and the bottom-up approach. The solution offered is to make implementation almost indistinguishable from the general policy cycle and to identify implementation with the learning over time that takes place in groups that have an interest in policy-making.

Implementation, dictionaries tell us, is the accomplishment of objectives. There is no cause for controversy here. What is contested in theories about implementation is the nature of the implementation process. How are the public sector actors to go about successful implementation?

According to one line of argument there can be no successful implementation because the whole notion of implementation rests upon the idea of the classical public administration model which is not suitable for implementation problems in the era of big government.

Another line of argument suggests that implementation cannot take place because all policy processes constitute an unpredictable web of events as parts of an evolutionary process that refuses any specific goals or outcomes.

The third mode of reasoning is to focus on actual programmes and outcomes at the street level. Implementation is what takes place at the bottom, that is, implementation is the execution of policies, nothing more or less.

It is helpful to distinguish between implementation or successful implementation as an outcome, and the implementation process or how implementation comes about. There is no necessary link between implementation as an outcome and some special model of the implementation process – top-down, bottom-up or otherwise. Sometimes control and hierarchy may be conducive to successful implementation, sometimes exchange and interaction are crucial in implementation.

# 5

# MODELS OF PUBLIC REGULATION

The public sector may be identified in different ways, as stated in Chapter 1. The first conception dealt with the legal–rational interpretation of the public sector. Let us return to this classical concept of the state and the public sector. The public sector as a system of state-introduced laws and regulations of conduct in both public and private organizations as well as households has not figured as much as the resource allocation or resource redistribution approaches. When the state or the system of national and local governments are viewed as a set of institutions with their own employees, then the public sector is highly visible. But when the state is considered as the creator of normative systems – regulations – then it is far more difficult to identify the vast system of laws and directives – the *invisible state* – that govern all kinds of behaviour. Regulations are not of one kind. Why is the state so active in providing legislation that directs conduct in various spheres of human activity?

## TYPES OF PUBLIC REGULATIONS

One may distinguish between two fundamental kinds of public regulation. First, there is the old type of economic regulation that involves entry conditions as well as price controls. The theory of natural monopoly has been regarded as providing the reasons for the establishment of institutions that result in legal monopolies, as argued in the theory of public utilities (Eatwell et al., 1987). It remains to assess whether there really is some justification for economic regulations.

Secondly, a large set of product regulations stipulate how various kinds of goods are to be both produced and delivered. They may involve directives that prohibit the use of certain dangerous materials or the sales of products that are potentially harmful to the consumer. According to the research into the occurrence of public regulations, product regulations outnumber economic ones, although there are difficult problems inherent in the calculation of the number of laws and directives in a society (see Derthick and Quirk, 1985).

It is often stated that the invisible state is huge – what aspects of life, private or public, are not the target for some type of regulation? Public regulation may be oriented towards national or local governments themselves, private organizations (firms or those that are non-profit-making), banks and the financial markets, the relationships between public authorities and citizens or the interaction between persons in the private sector, processes of production, employment and provision as well as the behaviour of courts and legal institutions.

How exactly one measures the degree of regulation in a sector of society is far from clear, but there is a general consensus that modern society is overregulated and is in need of regulatory reform, such as deregulation of markets – in the case of various transport systems for example (trucking and air flights, etc.). However, it has proved very difficult to halt the process of increasing regulation (Mitnick, 1980; Wilson, 1980; Noll and Owen, 1983; Weiss and Klass, 1986). This applies in particular to product regulations, whereas the regulatory reform movement in various manifestations has been more successful in removing or deregulating economic regulations concerning market structure and price determination.

The foundation for public regulation has been laid by welfare economics and its theories about externalities and economies of scale (Chapter 1). The reasoning for economic regulations is to be found in the theory of natural monopoly in relation to economies of scale and economies of scope in production (Berg and Tschirhart, 1988; Sherman, 1989). When there are considerable economies of scale or scope in the production of goods that require large fixed costs – so-called sunk costs – there tends to be market failure (Chapters 1 and 8). Product regulations are motivated by the occurrence of external effects that do not show up in the market price and thus have to be internalized by means of, for example, a tax that equates marginal cost with social cost or marginal value with social value (Spulber, 1989).

The regulatory reform movement usually focuses on the public regulation of production and markets in the private sector. These regulations bring two kinds of costs that in the end will have to be picked up by the consumer or citizens. Direct costs tend to be small as it is not very costly to operate a regulatory commission, but indirect costs can be very high as regulations may give rise to inefficiencies in both production and consumption. However, the need for regulatory reform of the public sector itself is no less apparent if one examines the system of public regulations from an efficiency standpoint. Local governments tend to be constrained by a number of state directives in the form of laws or conditions entailed in programme transfers from national government to local governments. The same also applies to the structure of state authorities at various levels, where the bureaucratic principles of subordination could result in a lack of flexibility and of adaptive capacity at lower levels of state hierarchies.

## NORMATIVE REGULATION MODEL

The case for public regulation of market allocation is stated most succinctly in the theory of monopoly. The standard monopoly situation arises when there are economies of scale or economies of scope in production. When there exist economies of scale, the phenomenon of subadditivity arises, meaning that the cost of one firm producing a set of goods is lower than the joint costs of several firms producing the same output. Economies of scope refers to the multiproduct case where one firm may produce a set of various products less expensively than if there were a whole set of firms producing the same output. A.E. Kahn in *The Economics of Regulation* argues that public regulation is required when:

> a natural monopoly is an industry in which the economies of scale – that is, the tendency for average cost to decrease the larger the producing firm – are continuous up to a point that one company supplies the entire demand . . . their costs will be lower if they consist in a single supplier. (1988: 123–4, 11)

A position of natural monopoly invites state activities as there is too little output at too high a cost (Figure 5.1). Maximizing social welfare, the state may decide to transform the natural monopoly into a legal monopoly, determining both output and price.

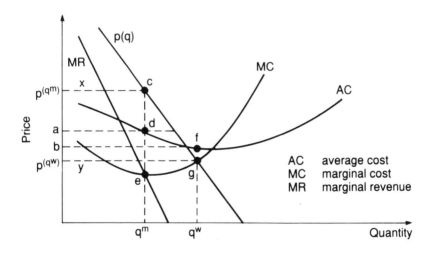

Figure 5.1 *Monopolies, prices and quantities*

Thus, by setting the price equal to marginal cost, output will rise from $q^m$ to $q^w$ and consumer surplus increase to include the deadweight loss in monopoly allocation, that is, the area ceg. At this level of output the firm, however, suffers a loss since average cost continues to fall, meaning that marginal cost will be higher than average cost at the level of output. Regulating price and determining output is not sufficient in public regulation introducing a legal monopoly by means of barriers to entry. The cost to the firm must also be covered somehow, either by means of a deviation from the efficient price equating marginal cost with demand or by means of a financial contribution that covers the loss at marginal cost price setting.

This is all economic theory, stating a case for public intervention in terms of a welfare maximization framework. It tacitly assumes not only rational behaviour on the part of the two parties in the interaction, the regulator and those regulated; in addition, there is the innocent assumption that both parties act sincerely and in the interest of the public or the consumers. Public regulation is based upon the notion of a benevolent sovereign taking the necessary steps to increase consumer welfare by means of authority, working in the public interest. But what happens once this crucial public interest hypothesis is relaxed, and bounded rationality, opportunist behaviour and strategic decision-making in order to enhance self-interest enter the model of public regulation?

The new models of regulation start from assumptions about the interacting parties that do not prejudge the question of how close the outcome will be to the welfare economics ideal. Modelling the behaviour of the regulators and the regulated on the basis of the standard economic-being assumption, the Chicago school produced a whole set of new ideas about how the invisible state could be modelled (see George Stigler's edited volume *Chicago Studies in Political Economy*, 1988).

## POSITIVE REGULATION MODELS

The standard regulation models from textbook economics suggest a number of solutions to the problem of allocating goods and services in a monopoly market. Although there is no single best solution, regulation theory arrives at a number of proposals for decreasing the efficiency losses and for increasing consumer surplus. However, regulation theory assumes somewhat naively that all these improvements will be automatically implemented, once they become known to the actors in the regulation game. Here is the starting point for so-called positive regulation theory, which models the real life behaviour of the regulators and those regulated. There is a set of different positive theories modelling the regulation game on the basis of the assumptions of the economic being.

Positive regulation models are highly policy relevant, because what matters in the conduct of public policy is real life possibilities and not ideal solutions. The practicality of a large invisible state regulating both the private and the public sectors depends on the extent to which institutions may be created that together with the motivation structure of the actors involved in the regulation game afford mechanisms that contribute to the implementation of desirable but realistic end states.

As Vickers and Yarrow show in their *Privatization: An Economic Analysis* (1989), the whole issue of regulation strategies is of crucial importance in making decisions about the private and public sector demarcation in privatization questions. The selling-off of public enterprises has to be based on a sound policy about market structure, competition and demand. Often public enterprises at national government level or public utilities at local government level offer services characterized by low elasticity of demand. This may well call for a regulation approach in order to undo negative effects of privatization such as monopoly behaviour. Again, we come back to the basic problem with the invisible state: can regulation policies be made workable?

## THE CAPTURE MODEL

Stigler in *The Citizen and the State* (1975) questioned how one could be sure that public regulation works in the public interest. It is not enough to specify what the optimum solution is in public regulation of monopoly, as we also need a theory about the motivation that would lead both regulators and those regulated to implement the solution identified as in the public interest. If one assumes that both regulators and those regulated act in accordance with their own self-interests, then why would the optimum solution be the strategy in a regulation game?

The capture model states the opposite, namely that one may expect the regulators and those regulated to end up in a common strategy after playing the regulation game a couple of times. Both would agree on a regulation policy that would remain stable over time, with maximization of their joint interests in stable and predictable outcomes. The outcome would tend towards the natural monopoly solution involving substantial dead-weight losses and huge monopoly profits. How could the regulator force those regulated away from their best position, when there is asymmetric information that works to the benefit of those regulated? Who knows the exact shape of the cost curves in an industry? What about elasticity of demand? If one resorts to so-called Ramsey prices recognizing that marginal cost price setting will not work, then who could calculate the optimum Ramsey prices?

Determining output and price by means of regulation is a difficult task, as the regulator can only use indicators that are at best fairly reliable tools but at worst carry simply straightforward erroneous information. The regulator is dependent upon those regulated to provide them with basic information, as they act within the confines of bounded rationality. There is no guarantee that there will not be opportunist behaviour and strategic steps in the interaction process between those regulated and the regulators. In order to minimize these disruptive tendencies it may be to the advantage of the regulators to settle for less than optimum solutions to output and price determination. To quote Stigler:

> Until the logic of political life is developed, reformers will be ill-equipped to use the state for their reforms, and victims of the pervasive use of the state's support of special groups will be helpless to protect themselves. Economists should quickly establish the licence to practice on the rational theory of political behavior. (1975: 132–4)

Williamson (1975) identified a number of difficulties in economic contracting which apply to the regulation game, where the state entrusts an agency or board with the task of controlling a set of private firms. The Williamson difficulties – bounded rationality, small numbers problem, opportunist strategies – appear both in the relationship between the government and the regulating board and in the interaction between the regulator and the regulated firms. Public regulation typically takes the form of a concession introducing legal monopoly rights – barriers to entry – for the firms in exchange for public influence over basic economic parameters such as quantity supplied and unit price charged. In order to handle the difficulties which tend to show up in any kind of economic contracting Williamson argued that hierarchy instead of voluntary exchange was to be preferred.

Hierarchy replacing voluntary exchange in industrial organization opened up a new way of viewing the firm structure along lines suggested by Ronald Coase's 'The Nature of the Firm' (1937). In order to minimize transaction costs inherent in the voluntary exchange approach the firm would employ authority instead of contracting to reach its objectives. Vertical integration may be a sound way to proceed in economic organization (Williamson, 1986) and the modern corporation (Mueller, 1986), but it will not aid the search for *first-best* (Pareto-optimal) solutions involved in public regulation.

The capture model implies that the special interests of both the regulator and the regulated will dominate over the public interest. Moreover, it also predicts that the special interests of these two groups will converge towards some stable solution not far removed from the monopoly solution. The regulators are simply swamped by those regulated as the latter have a systematic information advantage over the former and because the former lack any credible motivation to reverse asymmetric information in order to reach outcomes that the latter would resist.

Public regulation in its various modes – price control, subsidies, output specification, public utility status, public authority – invites opportunistic behaviour on the part of those regulated. Since all cost calculations are made by the regulated firm or bureau, it can always ask for prices that will cover its costs. A legal monopoly removes all traces of competitive price setting, thus the regulators would have to look very closely at the costs for which the regulated ask compensation. But how is such an information base to be assembled, when there is asymmetric information built into the very interaction between the regulators and those regulated? Why would the regulators really start looking into a sector of the economy that is regulated to such an extent that they could disclose and prohibit all kinds of opportunism? Both the information problem and the motivation problem militate against the transformation of so-called natural monopolies into legal monopolies, because the second-best solutions suggested by regulation theory are very difficult to implement in the public sector. Controlling price and quantity is not easily achieved when there is a monopoly or a strong price leader among a set of oligopolists.

Actually, government may have better options than the remedy of legal monopolies suggested in the normative theory of monopoly. What is crucial in a market is not the sheer number of actors, but the degree of real or potential contestation between these. A market could be fiercely competitive with only two major actors. And a market could even be competitive with only one actor as long as there was the potential of market entry by another actor. What matters is contestability. This means that government could use the public sector to enhance contestation in various sectors of the economy instead of shutting competition out by means of the introduction of legal monopolies. In terms of infrastructure, where the public sector tends to be very much active in various institutions, this would mean the search for competitive forms of supply such as bidding, contracting, franchise, the separation between transmission, production and distribution in electricity and railway systems. Much of what looks like a natural monopoly, such as electricity distribution, could be turned into competitive supply simply by allowing various actors to rent one and the same transmission system. Even public provision could become competitive by such strategies: for example, by inviting several actors to bid for the use of the railway track system. The government should enhance entry conditions into a sector and not close it off by means of a legal monopoly as, for example, in telecommunications.

Empirical tests of the capture model have resulted in mixed evidence. Some economists claim that the dead-weight loss remains high even though there is public regulation of a sector such as various infrastructures. They also state that the regulatory scheme is ineffective, meaning that the existence of a regulatory body has no impact on price and quantity (Stigler, 1988). Some political scientists as well as economists deny both these assertions, arguing that public regulation could make a difference (Wilson, 1980). Of the two types of public regulation, it seems as if economic regulation, that is, entry closure by means of a legal monopoly, performs worse than simply product regulation in the evaluation of public regulatory institutions.

The capture model may be generalized into a general principal–agent framework that models the interaction difficulties when two parties contract for a considerable time period and the nature of the contract remains underspecified due to contingencies, strategies and randomness. Let us outline some of the characteristics of the principal–agent approach which apply to public regulation.

## PRINCIPAL–AGENT PROBLEMS IN REGULATION

Public regulation, or the specification of rules for conduct in the private sector, involves the problems typical of economic relationships within the private sector. At the heart of public regulation is the ambition of the principal to *monitor* the efforts of the agents in terms of a set of goals decided upon corresponding to the private sector contract. Whenever there are considerable transaction costs due to the nature of the economic interaction between two parties as well as the coordination difficulties involved in collective action, then principal–agent problems arise.

The principal–agent problem of designing an agreement or system of contracts that motivate the agent to act in the interests of the principal as well as of monitoring the behaviour of the agent in relation to the agreement is not confined to private insurance institutions, to which the principal–agent model was first applied. Principal–agent difficulties are constitutive of public sector institutions, policy-making as well as public regulation.

To employ a principal–agent framework for the analysis of government action involves a clear rejection of the notion of the public interest as the motivational basis in the public sector. The only interests that exist within a principal–agent framework of public policy-making and public regulation are those that belong to either the principal or the agents. The interests of principals and agents would include selfish, altruistic, personal or social interests, as there is no scope for the public interest as the driving force of the public sector. In the principal–agent framework the activities of the agent are determined by both the effort of the agent and an unobservable random factor.

Making the agent in the political body serve the wishes of the population results in all the difficulties of having an agent serve the principal. Typical of democracies is the distance between the electing body and government, which gives rise to all the kinds of principal–agent interactions encountered in the analysis of the private sector (Ross, 1973; Ricketts, 1987). In elections the population as the principal interacts with parties and politicians, which results in uncertainty about what action the principal wishes the agent to take as well as problems with regard to how the action of the agent could be costlessly monitored.

The public choice school suggests a number of models of the inter-action between voters and politicians, identifying the basic problem of how one group is to survey the activities of another group where the interaction is characterized by fundamental fuzziness, lack of observ-ability, bounded rationality and asymmetric strategic moves (Mueller, 1989). How is the relation between electorate and politicians to be handled given the transaction costs of deciding and implementing public policies within an institutional setting where there is ambiguity concerning the rewards of the agent with regard to the desired actions to be taken as well as with regard to the causal link between actions and the environment?

Asymmetrical information, moral hazard and adverse selection enter the basic political contract between the electorate and the politicians. First, there is ambiguity as to whether the actions taken by the agent are the correct ones or the desired ones given the state of the environ-ment as well as to when it is acceptable for the principal to call for alternative courses of action by the agent. Politicians may argue that the actions desired by the principal were not feasible under the given circumstances, or that the only ones feasible in the given circumstances were the ones taken by the agent. Or politicians may argue that the divergence of the desired outcomes from the actual results did not involve any breaking of the election contract.

There is bound to be *moral hazard* about what actions are to be engaged in given the election promises. Moreover, there exist oppor-tunities for self-seeking politicians to interpret the terms of the political contract in terms of their own wishes and to engage in irresponsible behaviour symbolism, meaning that there is a danger for *adverse selec-tion* among politicians.

Policy-making involves more than deciding on a policy or the ends and means of a programme, as the important implementation stage also needs to be taken into account, that is, the activities of public administrators, professionals and regulating agencies. The implemen-tation stage gives rise to the typical double principal–agent problem in the public sector, referred to sometimes as the classical but invalid politics versus administration distinction. Politicians in government have to implement the election contract, however vague it may be, by means of a structure of bureaux and a set of regulatory policies.

Enactment of policies means that government becomes the principal and the bureaux and the agencies become the agents. Thus, in the execution of policies and regulations government faces the same principal–agent problems as discussed above: asymmetric information, moral hazard and adverse selection. The conclusion of the capture model of public regulation is that in economic regulation the regulated firms will be much stronger than the regulating agency, which in its turn will be in a strategically advantageous position in relation to the government.

Which interests are to be served in public regulation is thus an outcome of many factors in a long process of interaction. To maximize consumer welfare is only a very general catch-phrase that may occur in the loose election contract but requires specification when regulating agencies start to implement regulatory policies. There is no guarantee that the subsequent definition of the interests to be served in a regulatory framework may not drift towards narrow special interests, first and foremost the self-interests of the regulating firms and the regulatory agencies.

Pinning down the overall notion of efficiency in regulation maximizing consumer surplus and output is very difficult in all the myopia and inertia that characterizes the reality of the activities of regulators and regulated. Who can decide what price is justifiable and what output level is optimal? All regulatory schemes tend towards the use of indicators by the regulators in monitoring the activities of the regulated firms which are anything but precise and clear-cut (Berg and Tschirhart, 1988; Sherman, 1989). The tendency of public regulation to move away from the ideal framework of the monopoly model is stated most succinctly in a special public choice model that will now be analysed, thus concluding this chapter on public regulation.

## THE RENT-SEEKING MODEL

The public interest regulation model is based on the idea of saving consumers from the dead-weight loss in monopoly allocation. How large these costs are to the economy has been a matter of dispute. The capture theory applied to the public interest framework proposed that any regulatory scheme that failed in its purpose would itself bring about a considerable dead-weight loss to the economy as it transformed a natural monopoly into a legal one. The problem then to pursue was how the entire costs of both monopoly and regulation should be estimated (Posner, 1974, 1988; Rowley et al., 1988).

Public interest theory argued the case for regulation with reference to decreasing average cost and so-called sunk costs. The combination of huge investments with little cost in augmenting the provision of services to another consumer meant that there were natural barriers to entry which it would be economically unsound not to respect. Thus, there was no sense in promoting the standard model of competitive markets as only one firm could afford to take on the sunk costs in the long run. However, it was argued that there is no such thing as a natural monopoly, as what counts is contestability and not merely the number of supplying firms. And contestability could be achieved even when there was only one firm operating, as long as the state did not

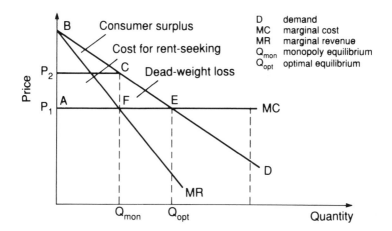

Figure 5.2 *Rent-seeking model*

introduce a legal monopoly destroying any degree of contestability. Contestability only required potential entry, which could exist even when there was only one firm operating (Demsetz, 1988; Peltzman, 1988).

The case against public regulation was strengthened by Tullock (1965) when he suggested the theory of rent-seeking as a general model of private entrepreneurs trying to solicit favours from government in the form of legal concessions that created barriers to entry benefiting the entrepreneur. As a positive theory about monopoly behaviour the rent-seeking model pointed out that the social costs would be larger than the dead-weight loss, because the entrepreneur had to spend resources in order to get the concession (Figure 5.2).

According to standard monopoly theory a part of the potential consumer welfare in competitive allocation – $P_1$, $P_2$, C and F – would end up as profits for the producer. However, the rent-seeking model implies that even these resources may be wasted, because there would surely be competition in some form or other for receiving the government favour. In the extreme all the gains to the producer from the allocation of the monopoly good or service would be diverted into expenses in order to get the favour, meaning that legal monopolies could be even more expensive socially than monopoly allocation without government interference.

Actually, the rent-seeking model could be generalized to any situation where government restricts entry or creates barriers to entry (Buchanan et al., 1980; Tollison, 1982). All government policies, allocative, redistributive or regulative, have implications for the amount of competition in the private sector. In so far as policies result in a favourable treatment of a firm, organization or group of

Table 5.1  *Benefits and costs of public policies*

|  |  | Costs | |
|---|---|---|---|
|  |  | Dispersed | Concentrated |
| **Benefits** | Dispersed | I | II |
|  | Concentrated | III | IV |

entrepreneurs, there are bound to be efforts on the parts of various groups to seize these for their own sake. All such manoeuvres carry costs that add no value to the economy as rent-seeking is simply a zero-sum game. Rent-seeking on a massive scale is engaged in by so-called distributional coalitions (Olson, 1982) resulting in a web of institutional sclerosis. The costs of rent-seeking have been estimated in various ways (Mueller, 1989).

The rent-seeking model may be looked upon as an application of the more general theory that there is a tendency towards an asymmetric distribution of costs and benefits in big government. Each public programme results in benefits as well as costs for certain groups of varying size. The crux of the matter is whether the group that benefits overlaps with the groups that have to pay the costs of the programme (Table 5.1).

The model about asymmetrical costs and benefits claims that it is typical of several public programmes that they tend to concentrate the benefits in favour of special interest groups while forcing the broad majority of people to take on the costs of the programmes. The positive regulation theories argue that economic regulation could very well belong to type III in the table. Those being regulated have a strategic advantage over and above the regulators as a result of asymmetric information about the costs and benefits of regulatory schemes.

## SECOND-BEST SOLUTIONS

The debate about the role of government for the governance of public utilities reflects the uncertainty about defining the means and ends of public policy when there is market failure. The optimistic theory of public regulation – the so-called Harvard school – argues that the state can undo the negative outcomes of monopolistic behaviour: too little output at too high a cost. The so-called Chicago school delivers the counter-argument that transforming a natural monopoly into a legal monopoly is bound to result in policy failure.

What we have here is related to the debate about so-called second-best solutions, those one might try to implement when so-called first-best solutions fail (Nath, 1969: 48–55). Thus, there may exist some solutions to the problem of deciding by government interference a quantity and a price that approximate the optimal solution at marginal value equal to marginal costs. When there are significant economies of scale in the supply of infrastructure, then it is also the case that marginal cost price-setting involves a loss to the producer, as average costs will not be covered.

Perhaps government should subsidize the supply of an optimal quantity by means of lump-sum subsidies or by allowing the firm to set a price that covers all the costs, so-called Ramsey prices? However, Lipsey and Lancaster discovered as early as 1956 that second-best solutions to the allocation problem may require that all the conditions for economic efficiency are broken. Once one of the conditions for Pareto-optimality is violated, it could very well be the case that economic efficiency is enhanced by not implementing the remaining conditions for Pareto-optimality – the second-best theorem (Lipsey and Lancaster, 1956).

Thus, if government is to regulate the firm until it somehow implements the optimal quantity at the optimal price, it may only bring out new forms of inefficiencies. The problem of regulation basically concerns the scope and strength of opportunistic behaviour following the presence of asymmetric information to the advantage of the firm or the public utility. If the state tried to balance asymmetric information, then it would face huge transaction costs. The reason that second-best solutions are difficult to define and implement is simply that there is a substantial transaction cost that the producer places on the government, if it attempts to reduce the surplus profit or economic rent of the firm.

Another approach to the public regulation of utilities could be to turn to a bidding process, where alternative producers offer bids on the running of the infrastructure. There would then be incentives for the various producers to augment the consumer surplus and reduce the dead-weight loss, because none of them can predict what bids others will make. However, such a procedure could not undo all the negative consequences of not achieving marginal cost pricing, particularly if there is tacit cooperation between the regulators and those regulated after the competition for the monopoly contract.

The naive theory of public regulation that governments may easily promote the public interest by simply deciding quantities and prices is hardly a realistic one. Systems of public regulation must be incentive compatible, meaning that they must employ techniques for control that are not in opposition to the basic incentives of the actors in the regulated system. Thus, only such systems of regulation that make it in the self-interest of the parties to reduce their opportunistic behaviour and reveal their asymmetric information about the kinds of costs involved should be implemented.

Policies aiming at moving the allocation of goods and services in some sectors fail to reach the ideal conditions of economic efficiency because the assumptions about interests and institutions are too blunt. Pareto-optimality in consumption on the demand side of the economy and Pareto-optimality in production on the supply side, as well as arrival at overall Pareto-optimality equating marginal value with marginal cost, remains an ideal-type model. The politics of economic policy-making does not bring out the tools for strictly and successfully implementing economic efficiency by analysing the occurrence of market failure (Grant and Nath, 1984), which the debate between the Harvard school and Chicago school confirms with regard to the regulation branch of government.

## CONCLUSION

The public sector is an abstract concept. It may be unpacked into a variety of dimensions. Most visible is government when it employs people to produce goods and services. Least visible is government when it regulates behaviour in the private sector. To the distinction between public resource allocation and public resource redistribution we have to add a third very important category: public regulation.

The state as command, the legislator, has not been given the attention it deserves in the analysis of the public sector. It has been almost neglected in comparison with all the approaches to public resource allocation and redistribution. This is all the more strange as classic political theory around the early 1900s emphasized the model of the state as creating and maintaining rules in society. To theorists like Jellinek, Austin, Weber and Kelsen the legal order and the state were inextricably bound together.

However, in the models of public regulation the problems of the invisible state have been analysed. There exists a deep gulf between normative and positive models of economic regulation where recently special interest group theory and the public choice school have modelled regulatory behaviour in a way that is very different from public interest theory. It opens up the route towards a theory of the public sector as an institutional web of directives – laws and regulations – that may harbour the interests of various groups, not to say special interests.

One type of regulation that has not been dealt with at length here is product regulations. Their effects on the economy can, however, be modelled in the standard way as costs that either make supply more expensive or tighten demand; in addition, there may also be effects on trade depending on how imports and exports affect the product that is regulated. This does not mean that product regulation is trivial.

Quite the contrary, it remains to be explained why product regulation is very popular, with the amount of such regulations increasing all the time. It seems to be the case that the demand for product regulations is not fixed but a function of the dominating culture in society. Product regulations stem from deliberations about risks and opportunities in economic life where a reconsideration of the risks to be taken may lead to new product regulations simply because the evaluation has become more risk-averse.

Models of public regulation raise questions about institutions that fail to achieve first-best solutions. What is at stake here is the tendency of actors under various regulatory schemes to restrict quantity produced and charge too high prices. Could government find and implement second-best solutions that are close to the optimal quantity and price? Under public policy, monopolies imply allocative solutions that fall to the left of the optimal solution, whereas a Niskanen budget-maximizing bureau seeks allocative solutions to the right of the first-best solution. Whereas a legal monopoly could result in too little output at too high a price, the Niskanen bureau allocates too much of public services at a cost that is higher than their value. Thus, the Niskanen bureau is not a true monopolist, although it is the sole provider (Figures 2.1 and 5.2).

Finally, one may try to combine public regulation with public production as when the so-called natural monopolies are organized as public corporations, inside or outside the public sector, and are also the targets of public regulation as, for example, postal services. Such public corporations are typically heavily staffed and thus highly visible.

The two types of branches of government dealt with so far – public resource allocation and public regulation – raise questions about leadership in the public sector. The implementation of policies as well as the conduct of regulatory behaviour requires public managers. Thus, we need to look at the logic of management and leadership in the public sector below the level of government.

# 6

# PUBLIC MANAGEMENT, LEADERSHIP AND PRIVATIZATION

Policy-making and implementation are certainly important activities in the public sector. Yet, all the institutions that inhabit the public sector have to be run on a daily basis and take care of the mundane matters: how is this to be done? A common question in the international literature is what is public management (Kooiman and Eliassen, 1987; Metcalfe and Richards, 1987)? If it is not the traditional public administration principles once again (see Introduction), or traditional public goods provision in the public finance model, then what is it? In a large public sector leadership becomes an essential function, but what does 'leadership' mean in public institutions?

Public sector expansion has occurred in most nations during this century. The mixed economy model, acclaimed as the OECD model for the future relations between the public and private sectors, has stabilized at a mature level of about 50 per cent of total resources with roughly 50 per cent going to public consumption and investments and the other 50 per cent constituting transfer payments, including a high service on the state debt in the average country entering the twenty-four nations in the OECD.

The seminal process of public sector expansion in the advanced economies is over, the size of government reaching a steady state at a high level of the total resources in these societies. However, the basic problem remains to be solved: how is the public sector to be run? When such vast resources are allocated by means of the government budget, then there is bound to be a search for models of public management. Proper decision processes have to be identified, implementation structures devised and the boundaries to the private sector delineated.

Thus, we face the simple question: what are the characteristics of public management? There are two firm beliefs about how to handle the day-to-day and routine operations of public institutions. The first thesis states that there is a science of public administration delivering clear and precise operating procedures. Whereas management would be appropriate for private institutions, in particular profit-maximization ones, administration according to the traditional public administration maxims would be the model for handling public sector institutions.

The second thesis claims that an operational code for public institutions would have to devise management and leadership principles that are fundamentally different from those that are employed in the private sector, that is, private leaders' management maxims and discretion according to some kind of profit-maximization objective (see Dunsire and Hood, 1989). What are the arguments for and against these two theses about managing institutions in the public sector?

To some the concept of management enters the broader concept of administration, though it is far from clear what type of administration management is. Such a per genus proximum and differentia specifica approach cannot inform us about the concept of management, because the concept of administration contains a semantic predicament not very different from that of the concept of management. Dunsire in *Administration* (1973) lists fourteen meanings of 'administration' – which one(s) are relevant to the specification of the concept of management? If the semantic predicament of the word 'bureaucracy' is one of rather extreme ambiguity and terminological controversy, and if broader terms are of little help, then we certainly have a problem when testing different assertions about the nature of management behaviour.

Whereas there used to be much certainty about the advantages of expanding budget allocation in relation to market allocation, there is now considerable hesitance about how public organizations are to be managed: which model is the adequate one for managing such vast human and capital resources? Let us first take a look at various models suggested in the literature and then move on to discuss if and to what extent public leadership is distinctly different from private leadership.

## PUBLIC MANAGEMENT AS PUBLIC ADMINISTRATION

It used to be believed that the science of public administration could deliver the principles for how public agencies and bureaux should conduct their operation – see the classical formulation of this position in textbooks like *Public Administration* (1950) by Simon, Smithburg and Thompson (Willoughby, 1927; Waldo, 1948, 1971; Hyneman, 1950; Thompson, 1964; Charlesworth, 1968; Marini, 1971; Benveniste, 1972). However, to clarify what public management is by resorting to the public administration approach may not be the most viable option, although Charles T. Goodsell in *The Case for Bureaucracy* (1983) reaffirms the public administration approach by reinterpreting some of its maxims.

As long as the public sector was small there was more or less practical adherence to the traditional model of public administration as interpreted by, for example, Woodrow Wilson (1887) or Max Weber (1978). However, in an era of big government the principles of the science of public administration neither describe the structure and operations of the various layers of the public sector adequately nor offer clever guidance to the solution of practical policy problems (Hood, 1990; Hill, 1992).

Basically, the public administration approach identified characteristics that were more or less firmly institutionalized in government structures, the state and local governments. Thus, the system of public law emphasized rules and the close adherence to procedures in administrative processes. Public decision-making focused on the elements of the public sector identified as so-called *cases* that were to be handled in accordance with standardized procedures, including legal rules. Cases had a logic of their own constituting the administrative process: initiation, preparation, decision, implementation. The aim of rigid rules was to guarantee legality and equal treatment under the law.

The public employee was identified as a bureaucrat. The employment contract was based on the philosophy of public management as devotion to the public interest. The salary was sometimes low but the public employee had tenure, though he/she was forbidden to strike. There were clear rules of promotion, mainly based on seniority, and the tasks of the bureaucrat were defined on the basis of objective criteria mainly derived from the legal sciences. Public administration was hierarchical, responsibility resting with top management, as well as characterized by a high degree of division of labour limiting the activity of the various public employees to narrow functions.

The definition of the public employee was orientated towards the concepts of responsibility and duty. So-called official duty applied to all public employees, in the state as well as in local government, with a few minor exceptions (clerks, caretakers). It penalized the intentional or unintentional making of errors in public service.

Official duty according to a penal code could be complemented by a disciplinary responsibility practised internally at each public authority as well as by a fiscal liability for damages done by the employee when in public service. Not only was the making of errors in service most often penalized but also minor offences could result in warning, suspension, removal or a salary deduction by means of the disciplinary responsibility. The liability for damages resulting from errors in service often rested with the public employee. Given the emphasis on duty and responsibility the orientation to rules became a prime occupation in public administration.

To administer a system of rules was easy as long as government was small. Within the public sector there could be a system of rules governing the operations of the state authorities as well as within the local government sector. On the one hand the administrative system would comprise general rules for the exercise of public authority and the handling of issues. On the other hand each public authority would have a special document laid down for it which specified its functions and structure.

Local governments – the municipalities and the county councils –

tended to be small and their operations could be guided by means of state instructions in the form of a general local government law but also in terms of special legislation for the carrying out of functions commissioned by the national government, which would state the obligations of the local governments, possibly in return for state grants. In addition, court rulings could limit their autonomy.

At the same time as public administration was structured in accordance with Weberian notions, the supposition was that bureaucracy would be mingled with political leadership recruited by means of representative democratic principles. The interrelationship between bureaucracy and democracy was to be handled by means of the traditional politics/administration separation assigning political leadership the task of formulating decisions and the bureaucracy with the task of executing these (Page, 1985).

As long as government was small, public management was defined as basically administration, the exercise of public authority in accordance with a fixed system of rules. The emphasis was on administrative action, formal decision-making and implementation according to established procedures. It all revolved around the concept of an administrative issue to be treated in a manner that maximized the goals of predictability and legal justice.

However, once government started to grow with service functions becoming more important than administrative functions, then the relevance of public administration came under strain. How is big government to be managed? Moreover, with public sector expansion and increasing complexity came the critique of public administration, already present to some extent in Herbert Simon's *Administrative Behavior* (1947) and Paul Appleby's *Policy and Administration* (1949).

## THE PUBLIC ADMINISTRATION MODEL AND ECONOMICS

According to mainstream organizational theory the Weberian or Woodrow Wilson model of public administration suits an environment which is stable and a decision-making situation which involves clear ends and safe means (Thompson, 1967; Mintzberg, 1979, 1983). This applies first and foremost to that part of the public sector that allocates so-called public goods. When it is a question of the delivery of services, then these model assumptions do not apply. Means–end chains in the welfare state do not satisfy the Weberian requirements. And big government is not solely the allocation of public goods but the allocation of semi-public or private goods and services.

Classical public goods comprise indivisibles like law and order, defence and general administration. When government was small they made up almost one half of public consumption; nowadays they are quite small items in big government allocating divisibles.

Just as the discipline of public administration offered a single solution as to how to manage public power – the ideal-type Weberian model of bureaucracy – the discipline of economics complemented classical public administration theory by claiming that it had a unique solution to how large the public sector should be – the public finance model.

## PUBLIC MANAGEMENT AS PUBLIC FINANCE

There are natural limits to public management according to the basic theory of the market. Economic theory predicts from efficiency considerations that the state will concentrate on the allocation of a special set of goods and services – public goods. And the size of the state will be determined on the basis of welfare deliberations by means of an examination of consumer preferences: the Wicksell unanimity rule or the Lindahl so-called tax prices. Just as the Weberian model of public management would lead to rationality in management procedures, the public finance model would be conducive to a rational size of the public sector. Acknowledging the necessity of public management – market failures in the face of externalities and economies of scale – there were natural restrictions on the size of the state to be derived from the concept of efficiency (Buchanan, 1967).

The seminal process of public sector expansion in the so-called capitalist countries has made the public finance model obsolete. The concept of public goods has no explanatory power whatsoever in relation to the budgetary activities of governments, whether national or local.

The concept of public goods explains only some 10 per cent of the items in the average OECD state budget, which accounts for the allocation of one-third of the resources of the country. Yet, theories once deemed powerful die slowly. In the authoritative interpretation of the public finance tradition by Musgrave and Musgrave (1980) it is argued that public management is a rational complement to market allocation. Whatever else the budget comprises besides public goods refers to income redistribution, which is a function of justice. Public management is either public goods allocation based on given and revealed preferences or it is income redistribution changing the premises for the operation of the markets and budgets alike.

However, the addition of transfer items to public management does not save the model, because the distinction between efficiency and justice is not useful in public management. Much public resource allocation is income redistribution. Government employs public management to provide every citizen with the same goods or services at the same cost not because it is efficient but because it is just. And several of the items in the budget concern goods and services which citizens do not demand or which have a reversed impact on the

distribution of incomes. The economic model of public management –
the public finance tradition – may be as theoretically attractive as the
Weberian ideal-type model of bureaucracy, but it is equally outdated.

## DECLINE OF THE PUBLIC ADMINISTRATION FRAMEWORK

The traditional models of public management – the Weberian
bureaucracy model and the public finance model – imply that government should be small and organized in accordance with clear rules
that promote predictability and legality. But government is no longer
small and big government cannot be operated in accordance with a
rule-oriented system of behaviour – traditional public administration.
Several administrative reforms of the post-war period have diminished
the relevance of the traditional public administration model as the
instrument for handling the public sector.

The public sector today is a highly complex system for allocating
resources and it is embedded in a changing environment, meaning
that flexibility adds to complexity to make management a real problem.
Not only is government big but its borders are not easily identified
(Hanf and Scharpf, 1978; Hood and Schuppert, 1987).

Beside the standard budget operations at various levels of government – national, regional and local – there are substantial resources
allocated by public bodies outside normal budgetary procedures. Not
only are there publicly owned joint stock companies or public
authorities paid for by means of charges, but considerable sums of
money are allocated outside the state budget as well as by local
government companies. Nobody really knows how large the public
sector is in the average OECD country (Rose, 1984), although it
matters to everyday citizens (Rose, 1989).

The gist of the public sector reforms may be described by means of
the distinction between rules and goals. Various attempts have been
made to play down the importance of adherence to rules and underline the ends of public activities. Ask not what you may do but why
it is done in the first place. Of importance is not whether a decision
or an action is in accordance with some paragraph in some system of
law, but the function that it promotes or the ends served. At the same
time the intention – ends and means – in the public sector tends to
be ambiguous (Wildavsky, 1979).

Whereas rules used to be the characteristic medium for governing the
public sector – defined as narrow restrictions on the choice of technologies for the enhancement of goals – all the reforms – budgetary
reform, legal reforms and decentralization – now point in the same
direction: public management is the fulfilment of goals that are vital for
the welfare of the citizens, not the careful observation of procedures.

The transition from rule governance to goal governance manifested itself in the public sector first in budgetary procedures, the transformation of an itemized budget into a programme budget. It took several years to make that transition in the state budget beginning in the 1960s whereas the process was somewhat more rapid in local government budgeting starting in the 1970s. Ambitions were high, but practice largely confirmed the theoretical critique of rational tools for budget-making (Wildavsky, 1986, 1988). A lot of work went into the redescription of activities, yet the budgetary process stayed the same in its focus on real costs, not goals. A second stage in the strategy for innovation in several countries was the resort to framework legislation.

The third stage complementing the introduction of programme budgeting and framework legislation was the decentralization trend which often covered a number of activities in Western Europe: relocation of authorities from the metropolitan area; transfer of activities from the state to local governments; movement of decision-making competence downwards within the state; restructuring local governments in order to strengthen the power of this tier of government, in particular at the implementation stage; the introduction of private management techniques into the running of public institutions.

The fundamental reorientation of the governance of the public sector of several rich countries amounts to a de facto acknowledgement of the irrelevance of traditional public administration. Rules may be handled by administrative personnel whereas goals must be accomplished by professionals. This is the missing distinction in the Weberian model.

Big government does not entail a huge number of administrators; instead it implies a wide variety of professional groups that carry out their functions on the basis of professional expertise. They need to know what they are going to do, not how they are going to go about doing it, because the logic of operations is derived not from statute but from knowledge defined by means of professional criteria. The entrance into government service of large numbers of professionals has had a fundamental impact on the nature of the public servant, the status of public trade unions as well as the nature of managing public organizations.

## PUBLIC MANAGEMENT AS PLANNING

Big government means that professionals will have to be relied on in the provision of goods and services. What matters is less the careful observation of rules by administrators when handling issues than the efficient production of goods and services. How is the public sector to be governed in an age of professional assertiveness? By planning – but what does 'planning' mean (Wildavsky, 1973)?

It has been suggested that planning is the solution. Thus, in the 1970s public management turned into planning in many countries. At all levels there was to be planning: local government planning at the bottom, regional planning at the intermediate level and national planning at the top – both one-year and five-year. Great ambitions were displayed aiming at total planning of each sector of policy-making on a short-term as well as long-term basis, but performance was mixed, if not completely disappointing. By means of comprehensive programme planning the fundamental operations in the public sector would be defined to be implemented by professionals.

The theory of planning is based on the so-called Barone theorem (Chapter 1). It argues that there are two fundamental allocation mechanisms, the budget of the planning ministry and the market of the private sector. Furthermore, the Barone theorem claims that both mechanisms may fulfil the standard conditions for efficiency in resource allocation on the consumer side, the production side as well as total social efficiency, meaning that marginal value equals marginal costs for the allocation of every good and service.

However, the theorem is only theory. It lacks any institutional theory of how the general conditions of optimality are to be implemented by an existing planning system. And there is no existing planning system that may implement the Barone solution.

Planners do not possess the knowledge necessary for the specification of all the Barone equations relating resources to production opportunities and goods and services to needs. And planners or implementors do not possess the motivation necessary to fulfil the conditions for the Barone model, because incentives are lacking in the planned economy.

To arrive at some workable planning system planners tried indicative planning on a large-scale basis, trying to predict more than to control future events. However, the environment of big government is much too turbulent for planning to work. The lesson was that planning is not the model with which to govern the public sector.

First, the errors in prediction were large and repetitive. Secondly, time and again day-to-day circumstances forced decision-makers to make exceptions to the plans enacted. Both kinds of deviations from the plan had the same impact on planning, lessening enthusiasm. Today, there is less talk about planning and more emphasis on designing organizations that are flexible and can adapt when conditions or circumstances change: resilience. Public institutions should be more like tents than castles (Hedberg et al., 1976; Starbuck, 1976).

The planning ambitions fitted well with the attempts at programme budgeting and framework legislation. Planning, if at all possible, requires top-heavy public authorities. However, it is more questionable whether planning as the general model for public management suits a system of decentralized organizations. Perhaps, then, if planning as a mechanism for resource allocation does not work, public management should be structured as quasi-private management?

## PUBLIC MANAGEMENT AS QUASI-PRIVATE MANAGEMENT

In several countries a demand for more privatization has met with understanding from the political authorities who at the same time often maintain that welfare services should be allocated in an equal way to all citizens independently of their purchasing power.

In the 1980s the private sector in the health care system was strengthened in some countries as a result of a dissatisfaction with complexity, size and bureaucracy in the public sector. A demand for more variety in health care provision as well as for a return to the old system of a more personal relationship between patients and practitioners has offset a number of attempts at privatization, including the establishment of small-scale health care centres, more private practitioners, the combination of both public and private service and the opening up of new private hospitals.

The welfare state ideology emphasizing standardization and the maxim of equal services at equal costs is no longer as dominant as it used to be when the welfare state grew rapidly and steadily. The market values of consumer sovereignty, efficiency and productivity and variety in supply have been recognized by central and regional planning bodies. During the 1980s many municipalities and county councils turned to the privatization option as one alternative to manage their share of the mounting costs for some programmes.

Several local governments manage a number of capital assets. Whether in their own administration or in the form of local joint stock companies, the municipalities are responsible for huge capital investments in various kinds of infrastructure, buildings and machinery. As part of a general quest for greater efficiency and productivity in the public sector municipalities and county councils have begun to search for strategies to improve on their capital management.

Public capital management has traditionally been mainly oriented towards legal rules protecting against embezzlement, speculation and diversion of funds from assigned functions. The value of their capital assets has traditionally not been decided by market prices and its use has not generally been tied to any user charges determined by market techniques. Several local governments have initiated new capital management strategies in order to make use of their capital assets according to their market value.

## PUBLIC MANAGEMENT AS PRIVATIZATION

Public management has traditionally meant that government and its agencies and boards themselves supply a large number of goods and services in order to meet the demand for health, education, social care, drinking water, waste disposal, energy and infrastructure, for example.

Most of the provision of infrastructure goods and welfare services has been handled by national or local governments setting up production units, defining production technologies and offering these services virtually free of charge. The question is, however, should governments really always be the actual producers of these goods and services? One alternative to local government production of goods and services is the employment of private contractors in accordance with a bidding process where market forces would be revealed. Although the provision is public the production would be private. In several countries both national and local governments have become more interested in privatization or quasi-privatization in the form of the use of contractors.

Often contracting as an alternative to self-production has been resorted to more due to lack of personnel than out of ideological or efficiency motives. Since contracting is mainly employed in relation to technical services, it is not very likely that it constitutes the main alternative to improving public management. True, there will be a trend towards privatization in the public sector, but it will appear in different forms, to be discussed later on. Privatization is a complex concept involving a whole menu of alternative strategies.

## PUBLIC MANAGEMENT AS DISILLUSIONMENT

Before one starts to outline a model of public management that would fit the realities of big government in an uncertain environment it is necessary to raise a more fundamental question: is adequate public management at all feasible? Recent findings in policy studies and implementation analysis as well as in organizational theory imply that goals are systematically ambiguous and means inherently unreliable in the governance of public organizations (March and Olsen, 1976; Pressman and Wildavsky, 1984; Hogwood and Peters, 1985).

Policy studies have shown that comprehensive rational decision-making no longer works. It is simply not possible to reach all the outcomes aimed at by means of large-scale political decision-making. Public institutions have a life of their own which does not lend itself to grand-scale reform. Adaptation has to come by means of techniques other than comprehensive political reform on the basis of large-scale central investigations. Planning implementation steering has become more and more difficult.

Comprehensive policy-making is no longer a viable model for public management in the public sector. If the rational decision model is not an alternative, if not even the model of bounded rationality works, then maybe we have to conclude that public management in a large public sector implies that solutions look for problems, leadership is a matter of luck and participation fluid.

Although the occurrence of garbage can processes in decision-

making and implementation constitutes a real threat in a large public
sector, the irrational model is an undesirable one. The prospects for
public management are not that gloomy. Perhaps the grave challenge
to public management in some countries comes not from policy
randomness or implementation chaos but simply from a lack of
productivity. Large public sectors in ten OECD countries tend to suffer
from so-called Baumol's disease. Quite contrary to the private sector,
there may be negative productivity growth over a period of decades.

## PUBLIC MANAGEMENT AS EVALUATION

Data about the public sector indicate substantial cost variations
between various similar public organizations when standardized
measures are employed. These cost differentials are to be found both
at the macro-level and at the micro-level. Why? Different production
conditions? Different service quality standards? Or inefficiency? Again,
administrative costs may vary by a factor of 2 or 3 between bureaux
and authorities, meaning that the more expensive ones could learn
from those with small-sized administrative staffs how to improve on
their operations by comparisons.

Moreover, competition may be introduced into the public sector
without resorting to massive privatization, simply by finding out how
organizations differ in their outputs and inputs and why. The development of the overall practical management philosophy concerning the
public sector has in many countries taken the course of a movement
from an ex ante perspective to an ex post perspective. After the
Second World War governments stated that planning was the key to
the adequate employment of the vast resources in the public sector.
However, in the 1980s the new management philosophy declared that
evaluation and performance measurement are the proper means of
governing public authorities or bureaux.

The orientation away from ex ante public management in the form
of various kinds of planning techniques towards ex post management
necessitates that activities in the public sector are capable of some kind
of measurement. The evaluation approach requires a set of criteria
with which to analyse the output and outcomes of public institutions.
They include not only the standard effectiveness and efficiency
indicators, but also indicators that are less amenable to quantification:
consumer and employee satisfaction, predictability of legal procedures
and flexibility (Chapter 9). Let us end with some reflections on the
thesis that the private and public sectors are fundamentally distinct in
terms of the logic of steering activities.

## LEADERSHIP

In the early 1980s there was a call for more leadership and management within the public sector. This contrasts rather sharply with the demand for participation so typical of the 1970s. No doubt the search for more leadership in the public sector is related to the fiscal crisis of the state that has evolved since about 1975. It may also be regarded as a reflection of an attempt to introduce more private sector principles into the public sector. Leadership in private organizations is often seen as less ambiguous and controversial than leadership in public management.

We shall argue that there is such a distinction to be made but that it is one of degree rather than one of kind. Moreover, it is vital to observe that leadership in the public and the private sectors has different pros and cons. Comparing public and private leadership necessitates stating the advantages and disadvantages of both.

## ORGANIZATIONAL BEINGS

Modern society has turned its citizens into organizational beings, it is often claimed. And the complex network of organizations raises heavy demands on the management function in particular and on leadership in general (Selznick, 1957). Organizations, whether public or private, are human-made institutions which may be schematized, singling out certain common features. An organization has a design – a formal constitution – that outlines its purposes, structures and functions. Organizations have objectives that are pursued by means of various activities that more or less correspond to the formal outline of the institution. Values or goals matter to organizations, but institutional performance is also heavily dependent on knowledge of the means to be employed to promote the ends – an organizational technology.

If leaders are to determine the preferences of their organizations, then it is up to organizational management to arrive at feasible and, it is hoped, efficient technologies. Organizations strive for predictability, minimizing the uncertainty that stems from internal as well as external sources. To enhance stability, organizations pattern their life by means of institutionalizing a structure in an organizational context. In the end organizational survival is a function of institutional legitimacy, and organizational viability depends on the evaluation of organizational performance of the consumers or clients that the organization is to serve. These parameters are common to every organization though they may differ fundamentally on the various modes of each of these concepts (Pfiffner and Sherwood, 1960; Blau, 1974; Mintzberg, 1979, 1983).

Public organizations tend to differ from private organizations on these basic organizational properties. What are the implications for the leadership function in public and private management?

## DESIGN

Both public and private organizations attempt to structure their internal situation by means of formal design, an organizational charter stating the structure and functions of the various elements of the organization. Such documents may be more or less in contact with organizational realities. What matters in both public and private management is the informal organization which gets things done (Bernard, 1938). However, in both types of organizations there is a clear understanding of who the principal is, which groups handle overall decision-making and which groups are involved in implementation.

### Principal

There is a clear difference between public and private organizations as far as the nature of the principal is concerned. In public organizations the principal is the political body, the government or the people – depending on the constitution. Public organizations have an unmistakable political element in that the organization is an arm of the public or the government, whether national, regional or local. In a private organization the principal consists of the people who have a personal interest in the organization – a group of shareholders or a set of members. As long as the organization benefits their interests they are willing to support it.

Whereas public organizations tend to have an obligatory character, making participation in the board of the organization a duty towards the public, interest involvement in private organization is on a voluntary basis. Public organizations have a different value context as they are oriented towards the promotion of the common interest, at least in theory.

Private interest contra public interest, voluntary association versus compulsory association makes a difference. Public management has a different time commitment from private management that significantly conditions the exercise of leadership. Public leadership builds on past commitments and organizational annihilation is no option for most public organizations in times of hardship, whereas organizational extinction constitutes a proper method for ending private management difficulties. Private leadership stands and falls with the commitment of those interested in supporting the organization with monetary or non-monetary resources, but public leadership may employ authority in order to uphold the organization, forcing citizens to support it.

It makes a difference to govern citizens on the one hand and to promote the interests of shareholders or union members on the other. The state cannot go bankrupt or dissolve itself, it is not just another organization (Sharpe, 1985). The political element in public management has a number of implications for the conduct of the leadership function. It broadens the focus of public management towards the vague notion of public interest and away from a narrow specific interest orientation.

The public interest conception as an attitude has profound implications for leadership styles in public management. It is conducive to the fostering and institutionalization of a special ethics – the ethics of 'Beruf' in the Weberian sense (Parsons, 1947). It appears in the behaviour and attitudes of administrators as well as professionals and it tends to be upheld by various mechanisms of control.

However, the public interest hypothesis is not without limitations in public management nor is there a complete lack of an orientation towards an ethics of duty in private management. Public choice theory has called attention to the extent to which public leaders are motivated by a private objective function (Breton, 1974). The difference in this respect between public and private leadership is one of degree, not of kind, as public leaders tend to pay attention to their personal or organizational interests just as private organizations do – budget-maximizing bureaucrats (Niskanen, 1971) or growth-oriented bureaux (Downs, 1967).

Moreover, private leadership has to take other considerations into account besides simply narrow, selfish interests. Yet, the difference between the nature of the principal has a profound impact on the conduct of public and private management.

### Decision-making

Typical of the distinction between public and private leadership is the difference in the composition of the public and private boards. Whereas the private boards tend to be a strict reflection of the interest composition of the principal defined by means of some voting procedure, the composition of the public boards tends to follow other guide-lines. Public boards may be recruited from within the organization on a merit basis, or they may combine representation for various interests defined in terms of political criteria with professional participation. The difference is one of degree not of kind.

Private organizations may include a professional leadership element besides the interest participation, and public organizations may be set up in a way that resembles some kind of interest participation. Even when public leadership in bureaux is recruited on the basis of some representational formula including the recognition of various interests, it is still maintained, at least in principle, that first and foremost, the bureau has to consider wider interests than the participating groups' own demands. Private leadership finds it difficult to argue for a separation between the interests of the organization and the interests of the groups represented on the board of trustees.

## Implementation

There tends to be a difference between public and private organizations with regard to implementation in so far as it is more difficult to create effective implementation structures in public organizations (Pressman and Wildavsky, 1984). Implementation structures work at the base level across organizational divisions and territories. These divisions tend to be much firmer in public organizations than in private ones.

The design of an organization outlines basic elements of an institution: principal, decision-makers and implementation structures. The public nature of organizations leads management to emphasize the formal design to a much higher extent than in private organizations (Crozier, 1964). The formal organization in public organization is a way to resolve ambiguities and create stability, but it may be a source of confusion and conflicts as well as rigidity. In private organizations these designs are less detailed and govern the way the organization actually works to a lesser extent. This difference is reflected in the objective function of these two types of organizations.

## OBJECTIVES

It is often stated that private management differs from public management as it has one single over-riding goal – profit maximization. Public management on the other hand would be characterized by a multiplicity of goals. From this difference it would follow that goal conflicts would be more likely in public organizations than in private ones.

The standard image of the difference between public and private management in terms of objectives has been criticized with the argument that private management also faces multi-objective goal functions. It is simply not the case that profit maximization is the single over-arching goal or that this very objective is clearly interpretable (March and Simon, 1958). However, there is some basis for the alleged difference.

Public organizations tend to have goals that are difficult to quantify, meaning that it is often hard to measure outcomes (Wildavsky, 1979). The purpose of a public organization is to provide something in a 'good' way, in a 'proper' way, or in an 'efficient' manner, but what is meant by these objectives? There is simply no uniform currency available that may be used to evaluate the objectives. Whereas there is such a goal (profit) and such a measure (money) in private organizations, there is nothing similar in public organizations. This does not mean that private organizations have no goals except profit maximization (Simon, 1957) or that public organizations cannot identify any objectives at all. There is a difference in degree, however, as to how easy it is to measure programme objectives.

It is often stated that public organizations have two over-riding objectives: efficiency or productivity versus due process and legality, and it is claimed that these objectives are in conflict with each other. However, it must be remembered that private organizations have the same goal conflict. Private organizations also have to act within certain rules for appropriate behaviour. And it is not always the case that a decision that comes out of a due process must be less efficient than a decision that pays less attention to legality.

It is true, though, that public management has to pay far more attention to due process and legality than do private organizations. As a matter of fact, one argument for certain types of public organizations is that they are needed in order to keep up the respect for due process and legality in private organizations. There would be less legality and just procedure in private management were it not for the fact that public organizations emphasize these objectives.

The difference between private and public management is not that one type of organization pursues one goal and the other several goals but that there is a difficulty with the objectives of public organizations, their lack of a quantitative measure – their qualitative nature. This makes it extremely difficult to evaluate the benefits from the public provision of goods and services other than simply referring to the costs of the activities. Leadership requires sources of legitimation other than a reference to the costs incurred, but how is the demand for the public provision of goods and services to be revealed in a rational way (Brown and Jackson, 1978; Bruin, 1991)?

Public leadership sets itself certain tasks and has a set of resources with which to fulfil these tasks. Certain outcomes are accomplished, but who can tell what efficiency or productivity implies (Etzioni, 1964)? What is good health care? What is a proper provision of roads and communications? There is the difficult problem of effectiveness: have the goals been achieved? Perhaps the achievement of these goals is impossible because the goals are ambiguous or unattainable.

Then there is the problem of productivity: how much of the resources should be used to reach a certain service level? But if the service quality goal has been set too high, then there may be no limit to the amount of resources to be allocated. And who can say what a proper service quality level amounts to? There are unlimited needs and who could say that some should be satisfied while others should not?

The difficult thing about public objectives is their qualitative nature. It is simply too easy to raise the demand for the quality of a public service without any consideration of costs. This is different in private organizations where the input and the output of the organization are measured by the same standard. Leadership in public management is difficult, not because there are many goals but because they are highly qualitative.

## EVALUATION

The qualitative nature of the objective function has implications for the evaluation of leadership in public management. Evaluation in private organizations may take place in terms of figures, in a close look at the relationship between resources and outcomes in accordance with some criterion of satisfaction (Cyert and March, 1963). Evaluation in public organizations tends to be far less clear-cut as evaluative criteria differ and public management cannot rely only on monetary figures. Evaluation could take the form of peer review or be conducted in the form of a legal procedure where higher organizations reconsider the case about the legality of activities. Or evaluation may come out of the deliberations of some committee about the achievements of the organization which may be open to doubt and conflict as notions of effectiveness or productivity tend to be ambiguous.

Legal evaluation looms large in public management to an extent that has no equivalent in private management. The emphasis on legal revision and control implies that rules have to be stated clearly and behaviour documented. Legal revision may involve the legal system or some special court system. It may be administrative or professional. It may be financial or goal-oriented.

Effectiveness evaluation or productivity analysis tend to become complicated in public management. Some goals may be almost impossible to measure or the trade-off against other goals may make cost-benefit analysis easily refutable. Or efficiency notions may simply be irrelevant as the service is based on other conceptions (Mishan, 1981). The fuzzy process of evaluation in public management creates a problem for the leadership function. On the one hand, when evaluation is so difficult in public organizations it is more problematic to exercise a leadership role as it is not clear what to expect from various personnel nor how to replace them if necessary. On the other hand, it creates less pressure on the leadership function itself as it does not have to face continuous and severe evaluation.

Evaluation tends to become problematic in public organizations (Wildavsky, 1979). This does not mean that evaluation is simple in private organizations as it may be difficult to pin down what an acceptable level of profit-making amounts to. But there is nothing similar to the elaborate procedures for review and control typical of public organizations. These elaborate control procedures undoubtedly set limits to the operation of leadership in public management.

## OPENNESS OF PROCEDURES

Leadership in public organizations cannot be conducted secretly. Typical of public leadership is the orientation to openness of processes. Although some public organizations are permitted to hide their operations behind a veil of secrecy, it is characteristic of public management that leaders have to state publicly their decisions and let the public have open access to written documents. Typical of public organizations is the close scrutiny of leadership by means of various mechanisms: open debates, written decisions, open appointment processes, stated criteria for decision-making and recruitment, clear-cut appeal processes. This creates an atmosphere for the conduct of leadership that is different from private leadership, where secrecy is very much part of the conduct of operations.

Information tends to be more strategic in private leadership than in public leadership. It is not only that the norms differ as the public ethos of management underlines the transmission of unbiased information, whereas the principles of private management imply that it is necessary to consider information strategically in order to safeguard other goals. Realities are also different in public and private management, although this should not be exaggerated. Since the transmission of open and reliable information is of value in itself in public management, a number of rules have been institutionalized to protect this value.

It is required that there be an open consideration of matters relating to each decision as well as that citizens have a real opportunity to take part in the arguments employed in the decision process. Private management operates differently as protecting information is a basic value. However, in the public budgetary process we find a strategic play of information and in certain circumstances it is considered absolutely vital that sincere and comprehensive information is conveyed by private leadership.

## RULES

The strong emphasis on openness is conducive to the institutionaliza-tion of a number of rules concerning the conduct of public manage-ment. Clear-cut definitions of various situations structure processes in a predictable fashion. Matters have to be addressed in certain ways, decided on in a particular fashion and implemented in specified manners. There are rules for the entire process of public management: recruitment, hiring and firing of staff, salaries, workload, decision structures and implementation stages. These rules are laid down in formal documents and supervised by special institutions and they act as constraints in terms of a code of conduct.

Some rules define what is typically public: impartiality, neutrality, predictability. There can be no doubt that the institutionalization of these rules is sometimes questionable, but it is also the case that their strong presence sets public management apart from private manage-ment, where such a set of rules does not carry the same weight. These rules are sometimes considered unnecessary constraints on public leadership.

Public management, it is argued, should be relieved of several rules, in particular those which hinder the effective accomplishment of objectives. However, a distinction must be made between those rules which simply mean unnecessary red tape and those rules which define what is public about public management.

## PREDICTABILITY

Public management, like all kinds of management, searches for stability. Leadership in public organizations faces the need to adapt to an uncertain world where problems change and solutions become obsolete. The organization is confronted with a constant stream of stimuli from the environment with which the leadership has to cope. Public and private management tend to operate differently in relation to uncertainty. Whereas private management tries to adopt a flexible position (Hedberg et al., 1976), public management emphasizes incrementalism (Wildavsky, 1984) in order to hedge off the turbulence.

Public management tends to be incremental, meaning that it regularly defines a programme base where there will be few changes. Although policy shift-points may certainly occur to and fro, it is often the case that stability is achieved by the protection of the base, making small adaptations at the margin. Private management copes with uncertainty by resilience, whereas public management handles risk by holding on to past or fundamental commitments (Braybrooke and Lindblom, 1963).

The incrementalist approach to public decision-making emphasizes the regularity in public management. It seems to be a basic fact that private management cannot count upon the same stability in rates of expansion or retardation. However, it should be pointed out that the incrementalist approach to the public sector has been criticized as it neglects the occurrence of so-called shift-points, or more than marginal policy changes. It may be true that most policy reforms are changes of already existing programmes, but this does not mean that major change is impossible (see Hogwood and Peters, 1983).

## TECHNOLOGY

Public management is dependent on technology to the same extent as private management (Thompson, 1967). Leaders in the public sector cannot govern their institutions without a firm knowledge of the technology available to implement their objectives. Yet, there is a severe technology problem, because reliable knowledge about means–end relationships is scarce. Hypotheses about the relation between the input of resources and outcomes are far from certain (Rose, 1984).

There is a risk of garbage can processes in public leadership, meaning that ends are ambiguous and means unreliable. How can leaders in public management assure themselves of access to reliable information about programme performance and programme outcomes? It may be argued that the risk of garbage can processes is greater in public management than in private, because participation tends to be more fluid, the goals more uncertain and diffuse and the cause and effect relationships more unpredictable.

Higher education organizations have been mentioned as examples of institutions plagued by frequent garbage can processes (Enderud, 1977). Top-down management, whether at the national level in the form of comprehensive university reform or at the local level in the nature of coordination above the basic units of academia, seems to involve a high probability of failure as ends and means are far from clear or reliable (Clark, 1983).

However, it has been argued on empirical grounds that the applicability of the garbage can model is more limited in relation to higher education institutions than envisaged (Trow, 1984, 1985), as even these types of organizations have to act within the restriction of a rationality norm in order to cope with the exigencies of their environment like any other kind of organization (Thompson, 1967). More and more public leaders tend to increase their knowledge about public programme technology, but it must be underlined that the information basis of certain programmes is plagued by much uncertainty.

## ADMINISTRATION AND PROFESSIONALISM

Both private and public leadership face the need for a combination of administrative and professional knowledge in order to guide the organization to the production of outputs. Both types of management have to reconcile administrative authority with professional authority (Parsons, 1947). It may be argued that the tension between these two types of authority is more acute within public organizations than within private ones.

The public character of the organization makes leadership sensitive to administrative procedures which hamper the exercise of professional authority. Professional authority fosters an environment that is different from that of administrative efficiency. Yet public management is much dependent on professional expertise (Benveniste, 1972).

Public leadership in management functions may be exercised by administrative personnel or professionals and it may not be easy to draw the boundary line where administrative authority is to reign and where professional authority is to be decisive (Dunsire, 1973). Whereas professional competence may be reconciled with overall management objectives by means of the distinction between line and staff in private organizations, no such separation is generally applicable in public management. The tension between administrative routine and professional requirements is endemic in public management.

The rule-oriented nature of public management tends to increase the administrative part of the undertaking. The well-known size hypothesis – that the relative size of the administrative component of an organization falls with increasing organizational size (Starbuck, 1965) – appears to receive support in empirical studies on the private sector, but how about the public sector? The applicability of the size hypothesis to the relative size of the administrative component in public organizations has been questioned in the model of bureau growth (Downs, 1967).

On the other hand, the findings from studies of social insurance institutions (Blau and Schoenherr, 1971) and academic institutions (Blau, 1973) seem to support the hypothesis of a general tendency towards an administrative economy of scale (Blau, 1974). However, it may be questioned whether, when a public sector organization becomes very large, it displays the opposite tendency – bureaucratization in the sense that the administrative component tends to grow at the expense of other components in public organizations. Public management has an unmistakable administrative emphasis.

## ORGANIZATIONAL STRUCTURE

Leadership in public management must recognize the need for coordination with other organizations. Characteristic of public management is the interdependence between different organizations in various ways (Hanf and Scharpf, 1978; Milward, 1982; Hjern and Hull, 1984). The inter-organizational dependencies have no doubt increased in complex, modern society with its numerous public policies.

The conduct of public management is no longer something simple which requires only the laying down of clear principles by central government based on full knowledge about the ends and means of public action. And inter-organizational dependency, between national, regional and local government, as well as between public and private institutions, makes control and predictability in public management structures difficult (Pressman and Wildavsky, 1984; Scharpf et al., 1975; Jones, 1980; Barrett and Fudge, 1981; Rhodes, 1981).

The theory of a control deficit in public management implies that there are limits to hierarchy in public management structures. However, the theory of inter-organizational dependency also opens up the possibility that public leadership may compensate for the control gap by designing and implementing policies in cooperation with private leadership, making policy-making predictable in terms of policy networks or iron circles (Richardson and Jordan, 1979; Jordan, 1990; Rhodes, 1990).

Responsibility patterns tend to be different in public and private management. Hierarchical patterns tend to be defined on a more detailed basis in public management, higher-level organizations governing lower-level organizations in several aspects of their behaviour. Centralization is prevalent in public management whereas in private management decentralization may be combined with a demand for complete responsibility as measured by quantitative indicators.

In public leadership there tend to be defined modes of operation for the exercise of governance and control which restrict the behaviour of public leaders, whereas in private management outcomes are stressed more than procedures. Thus, we find in public management an intricate system of superordination and subordination, a mixture of rules combining autonomy with heteronomy, and an intricate system of directives through which higher leadership relates to lower leadership (Peabody and Rourke, 1965; Sharkansky, 1979).

According to one theory – contingency theory (Pugh et al., 1969) – all kinds of organizations face similar structural laws. There is a finite set of ways of structuring organizations in relation to a fixed set of contingency factors like age and size of the organization, the nature of the technical system it operates, the type of environment it faces and the nature of power relations in the organization. The basic types of structure – the simple structure, the machine bureaucracy, the professional bureaucracy, the adhocracy – suit some constellations of contingency factors but not others (Mintzberg, 1979).

It is often argued that public management mostly resembles the machine bureaucracy. However, the expansion of the public sector has meant that we have to recognize more variety among public management structures. In any case, whatever the type of the organization, it tends to exhibit some basic structural arrangement in relation to its context. This similarity hypothesis has been questioned by public administration specialists who argue that government is different.

## CONSUMERS AND CLIENTS

Private leadership is sensitive to consumer demands in a way that public leadership is not. The market-oriented nature of private leadership implies that consumers have the exit option when they are not satisfied with the performance of enterprises (Hirschman, 1970). Private leadership is basically dependent on an exchange relationship to the consumer where there is reciprocity as long as there are elements of competition.

Public leadership relates to the consumer on a different basis, that is, authority. The tools of governing are different in public management. Since public management often has monopoly traits, the consumer has only the voice option which tends to be much weaker than exit. Public leadership may count on the contribution of the consumer simply by using the tax authority which reflects the non-voluntary nature of much of public management. On the other hand, the more protective nature of public leadership makes it suitable for the allocation of goods and services where sudden changes in consumer demand are less relevant.

The quasi-monopoly characteristics of public management make a difference for the conduct of leadership as there is a concentration on long-term planning and the continuation of programmes whereas private leadership is sensitive to short-term changes in consumer demands adapting to sudden changes. The difference is one of degree as private leadership also concentrates on long-term engagements and public leadership is sensitive to changes in citizen wishes.

## LEADERSHIP STYLES

Leadership is not radically different in public and private organizations, but there are a number of differences in emphasis which together result in two models of leadership style – the public and the private. Let us try to list a few of these systematically.

### Innovation

It is often argued that private and public leaders differ in terms of their capacity to innovate. In public management leaders are slow to innovate, emphasizing established procedures and holding on to traditional modes of operation – red tape. On the other hand, it has been argued that this is not necessarily so. In an empirical analysis of two public agencies using the case study method, Peter Blau (1955) showed that employment security and autonomy in bureaux are conducive to a positive attitude towards organizational change as well as towards social change in general. Public leaders may care for their clients, know much about the programme technology as well as improving performance. However, there is in general a stronger emphasis on innovation in the private sector, as change is necessary for survival.

### Motivation

According to the classical theory of public administration, public leaders differ from private leaders in terms of motivation: the public interest orientation is what sets public leaders apart. According to public choice theory there is no such distinction between public and private leaders. They are both motivated by the goal of maximization of a private objective function. This leads both to emphasize growth as organizational expansion is conducive to the achievement of their private objectives. Public leaders may tend to push their objectives so much that there will be wasteful bureaucratic growth. However, the private ambitions of bureaucrats may be employed for public purposes given a proper mechanism for the private reward of public virtues (Jonsson, 1985).

## Stability

Public leadership is generally speaking less sensitive to environmental changes than private leadership. This does not mean that leaders in public management can count on life-long service in the same function. They have to cope with the vagaries of political change as well as relate to the changing demands of the environment (see the analysis in Kaufman, 1985). They act on trust just as private leaders, but there is generally speaking more scope for public leaders than for private leaders in relation to their principals. Public bureaucracies are seldom completely abolished and public managers are seldom replaced. Several positions as managers are tenured, meaning that they can be replaced only after a court procedure.

## Power

Leaders in public management have to combine a number of skills in order to maintain a powerful position. They have to be able to relate to politicians in order to convince them of their need for more resources and the relevance of their institutions. They face a number of demands for participation from various interests and they must nurture the professional competence of their own organization. Successful leaders in public management may create a large amount of discretion for themselves.

It has been argued that the drive for independence is typical of public management. Yet, it seems clear that leaders in public management may also be the victims of strong pressures for influence on their organizations. It may be difficult to reconcile various claims – professional or administrative – within the organization. The organization may become too dependent on special interests thus becoming interlocked in a corporatist pattern (Olsen, 1983).

## Entrepreneurship

Leadership in private management is based on the notion of entrepreneurship: to reach objectives by the selection of the effective means under appropriate norms of ethics, rationality and maximization. Leadership in public management is founded on the principle of administration: to arrive at some predictable output in terms of defined decision criteria. The difference between entrepreneurship and administration should not be exaggerated, yet it is inherent in the distinction between private and public management and sets the tone of leadership in the various spheres. Both private and public leadership combine entrepreneurship and administration, but the overall balance is different.

## DIVIDED SOCIETY

Modern society is by and large divided into two sectors – the private and the public – and governed in accordance with different principles of administration. Will this dualism persist? It is argued that the future development of society will see a mix of bureaucracy and market that partly transcends this traditional distinction.

Even if the trend towards the emergence of a third sector – non-profit-making organizations – is no longer as strong as it used to be, there is some truth in the prediction that the structuring of leadership and management in private and public organizations tends to converge. More and more public organizations emphasize service, playing down authority as the basic mode for relating to their customers. And private organizations recognize objectives other than simple profit maximization (Williamson, 1975, 1986; Mueller, 1986).

Leadership in public and private organizations has become alert to the need for maintaining alliances with other institutions and securing support from various groups of citizens affirming the legitimacy of the organization. In this process of promoting the legitimacy of the organization, public and private organizations tend to rest upon support from each other. Thus, at the same time as differences between the management of private and public organizations have lessened, these organizations have tended to cooperate in a world of uncertainties in order to maintain their existence by forming inter-dependencies.

One prediction about the future states that we shall see even more inter-organizational dependency and interlocking (Schmitter, 1983). A quite different prediction is that the reaction towards excessive public sector growth will result in privatization and a sharper demarcation between the public and the private.

## PRIVATIZATION

The increasing attraction of privatization as a set of strategies for reforming the public sector stems from a dissatisfaction with the traditional organizational structure of the public sector. It is argued that the bureau model originating in the Weberian approach to bureaucracy faces severe problems of leadership as well as efficiency. However, privatization of big government in the welfare states may involve very different things (Savas, 1982, 1987; Hanke, 1987; Pirie, 1988).

Privatization involves both ends and means. The means of privatization stretch from replacing public ownership with private ownership to the introduction of private management techniques into the public sector. Although much interest has focused on spectacular examples of the first kind of strategy, as, for example, in the sale of huge public enterprises (Vickers and Yarrow, 1989), it may be argued that the most extensive type of privatization is the search for internal reform within the public sector under the influence of private management models.

What are the goals of privatization? The first and immediate goal is efficiency. The basic argument is that the traditional organization of public provision of goods and services on a grand scale lacks mechanisms that enhance effectiveness and productivity. On the demand side of the public household taxes play a large role in sending signals about how much people are prepared to pay, but taxes do not tie benefits and costs together at the level of the individual consumer. On the supply side bureaux provide goods and services virtually without any competition, thus having a kind of monopoly position. Therefore, the lack of charges for the consumption of each item as well as of competition between producers is seen as a major obstacle to efficiency in the public sector (Table 6.1).

Table 6.1 *Two alternative organizational models*

|  |  | Supply | |
|---|---|---|---|
|  |  | Bureau model | Competitive model |
| **Demand** | Taxes | I | II |
|  | Charges | III | IV |

The traditional model of organizing the public sector – taxes in combination with a sole provider (type I) – may be reformed by inserting more charges or more competition (type IV). Actually, privatization and its alternative modes concerns the step out of box I towards box IV, as there are several means of accomplishing such a transformation towards more choice and competition.

The second and more general aim behind privatization is to use the private sector and its mechanisms to a larger extent, because there is a fundamental recognition of the weakness of big government. When discussing privatization and its various options it is vital to focus not only on what benefits the public sector may give, but also on the risk of policy mistakes or programme malfunctioning. Thus, *exit* is considered more effective than *voice* when a citizen is dissatisfied with some goods or services (Hirschman, 1970). By privatizing public service the relevance of the exit option is increased as a tool for citizen grievance.

The means of privatization consist of a battery of alternative ways to emphasize choice on the demand side and competition on the supply side. These include: (1) the substitution of taxes by charges; (2) the use of contracting on the basis of bidding by several suppliers, private or public; (3) the lease of public assets to private entrepreneurs providing services; (4) the transfer from public ownership to private ownership of, for example, public enterprises or public utilities; (5) the employment of private management techniques within bureaux, such as new systems for budget-making and evaluation as well as the introduction of private incentive mechanisms; (6) the creation of competition within the public sector by means of systematic cost comparisons and efficiency criteria.

The concept of privatization is ambiguous, as it may imply severe reductions in the size of the public sector and a drastic shrinkage of public ownership of key industries. However, it may also stand for a broad and rather loose effort at reforming the provision of goods and services in the public sector on the basis of market values such as choice and competition. This ambiguity accounts for the fact that the demand for privatization meets with different reactions and is carried on with varying zeal (Vickers and Wright, 1988).

In the crisis of the welfare state during the 1980s privatization became a catch-phrase for a number of different strategies for public sector reform. Most attention was undoubtedly focused on the sell-off of some large public enterprises allocating infrastructure. But perhaps more important in a long-term perspective was the diffusion of market values over the public sector in the sense that principles derived from the private sector became more relevant for the operation of public programmes in general and public enterprises in particular. Thus, new management techniques were imported requiring the calculation of unit costs, depreciation schemes and profitability of invested capital. Somehow the public sector started to place a higher priority on pecuniary aspects than previously, although the social values remained important.

## CONCLUSION

It is true that in a mixed economy, according to the model of the 'bargaining society' (Johansen, 1979), it may be difficult to distinguish clearly between public and private leadership. Each appears to work with a multiplicity of goals, facing a complex environment where several interests look for participation and many rules restrict behaviour. However, public and private leadership differ along two dimensions which reflect fundamental differences between public and private management still in force in the mixed economy.

First, the goal orientation of public leaders tends to differ from that of private leaders. Whereas private leaders attempt to maximize or satisfy a private objective function, public leaders have to face the notion of public interest. From this notion, however vague it may be,

Table 6.2  *Public and private leadership*

**Environment**

|  | | Stable | Unstable |
|---|---|---|---|
| | Public interest | I | II |
| **Orientation** | Private interests | III | IV |

follow certain consequences for their motivation – the ethics of *Beruf*. Secondly, public leaders work in a more stable environment than private leaders. They are not unaffected by hazardous events, sudden changes or long-term transformations but they can rely upon the existence of a base that tends to remain rather fixed over time. This can be represented by a 2×2 table (Table 6.2). The traditional image of public leaders is type I whereas the standard portrait of private leaders is type IV. There is more to the distinction between private and public leaders than these two stereotypes, but the difference in degree between private and public leadership relates to the difference between types I and IV.

Although, in general, public management models are replacing the traditional public administrator role, the latter remains relevant for certain aspects of the public sector. The focus on rules stems from the concept of the state as a *Rechtsstaat*. Whenever public authority is exercised over individuals, justice and fairness demand that specific procedures are followed in due process. Administrative law holds a strong position within public administration because it regulates how cases are to be handled in state and local government. Constitutional and administrative law are important ingredients in neo-institutionalism.

We need to take a closer look at the concept of interests as emphasized by the public choice school and the concept of institutions as underlined in the new institutionalism. Interests would constitute the motivation of actors whereas institutions would create part of the environment for the conduct of public sector activities. The next two chapters discuss these concepts.

# 7

# THE PUBLIC CHOICE APPROACH

We have referred to the public choice framework several times in the earlier chapters. Here, we look more closely at the foundation of the public choice approach, at its methodological assumptions often appear dauntingly problematic. Would the conduct of social inquiry along its lines imply special methodological difficulties?

The distinction between the *is* and the *ought* may be employed as a demarcation line between two types of social science theories: strictly theoretical-empirical ones on the one hand and normative ones on the other. Although not all theories fall neatly within one or the other of these categories, the distinction may be used as a tool for pointing out implicit or explicit normative elements in theories which claim to be strictly neutral or objective from a scientific point of view. We will employ this demarcation line in the way Max Weber (1949) conceived of it in order to analyse the epistemology of the emerging public choice approach.

It is argued that the public choice framework for the analysis of public sector decision-making and implementation is deficient in terms of the distinction between science and values. Is this accusation warranted? Although we need not claim that normative theory is inherently 'unscientific' or that the statement of an ideology is a 'meaningless' undertaking, we must remain clear about the implications of the demarcation between the *is* and the *ought*.

## PUBLIC CHOICE AND THE VIRGINIA SCHOOL

It is not difficult to find in the Virginia school of public choice highly critical statements about the nature of politics and the essence of bureaucracy. It is not only argued that political behaviour sometimes displays deficiencies of various types pointed out in normal scientific discourse; nor is it only claimed that the lives of bureaux are sometimes despicable, a theme often repeated in the sociology of formal organizations. Much more is implied in the Virginia version of the public choice approach:

> The basic structure of property rights is now threatened more seriously than at any period in the two-century history of the United States. . . . But there is more to it. We may be witnessing the disintegration of our effective constitutional rights, regardless of the prattle about 'the constitution' as seen by our judicial tyrants from their own visions of the entrails of their sacrificial beats. (Buchanan, 1977: 93)

Maybe James Buchanan would defend such a general statement about the misfortunes of modern political life in the welfare state by claiming that it is a piece of neutral observation. However, it is not difficult to find the *action* emphasis in Buchanan:

> 'Government failure' against standard efficiency norms may be demonstrated, analytically and empirically, but I see no basis for the faith that such demonstrations will magically produce institutional reform. I come back to constitutional revolution as the only attractive alternative to the scenario that we have seen bent to act out. In the decade ahead, we shall approach the bicentenary of the constitution itself. Can this occasion spur the dialogue that must precede action? (Buchanan, 1978: 368)

If one asks why revolutionary action is of such utmost importance, then the answer could not possibly be simply a neutral and objective analysis of the public sector, but would have to include some normative theory of the state. Thus, Buchanan moves from public choice analysis to the quest for public choice activities.

In Gordon Tullock we find the same generalizations about the unhappy state of politics. Every bureau is a burden for society:

> We are saddled with a large and basically inefficient bureaucracy. Improved efficiency in this sector could, looking at the matter economically, raise our national income and improve our rate of growth. Politically, it could both increase the degree of control the citizen, qua voter, has over many fields of our national life and enlarge his personal freedom. (Tullock, 1965: 221)

Among other scholars tied to the Virginia school of public choice we find the same vehement rejection of present day democracy, not least the usual majoritarian decision technique:

> The expansion in the powers of government – particularly the federal government – and the accompanying erosion of wealth and liberty is not the result of incompetent public officials motivated by evil intentions. Rather the core of the problem emanates from the incentives that ordinary people confront within the prevailing system of majoritarian government. (Gwartney and Wagner, 1988: 54)

The Virginia school argues that the public sector is suffering from inherent systemic failure in terms of policy-making and policy implementation. Political failure is more severe than market failure. The action implication is that the public sector must be rolled back by means of a new political revolution leading to constitutional contracts limiting the power of the state – the Leviathan of the twentieth century (Tullock, 1970; Buchanan, 1975a, 1977; Brennan and Buchanan, 1980).

What we are talking about here is the Virginia interpretation of advanced societies with a liberal democratic constitution, leading to a fully fledged rejection of the welfare state. What is science and what is ideology in the Virginia interpretation? In the Virginia version of the public choice approach there is an explicit normative theory about how these societies ought to be changed. Does the same hold for the public choice approach in general? Since we as social scientists should distinguish between the neutral and objective analysis of the public choice domain and the normative evaluation of what public choice ought to be taken, it seems vital to discern whether the confusion of the *is* and the *ought* is of necessity true of public choice theory in general.

## PUBLIC CHOICE AND THE PUBLIC CHOICE APPROACH

The domain of public choice is quite distinct from the variety of approaches to the analysis of this domain. There is a large variety of frameworks for the understanding of public sector decision-making and implementation, one subset of which constitutes the so-called public choice school. However, within the so-called public choice school there is scope for a number of various approaches, one of which is the Virginia school.

It is often argued against the public choice approach that it is not unbiased in the sense of scientific neutrality. It scores low on objectivity as it is inherently oriented towards market values. It is critical of the state and welfare spending simply because it favours market allocation and market values for ideologically right-wing reasons. This criticism is a serious one and it requires explicit consideration, particularly from those who argue that the public choice approach is a new set of innovative scientific models (McLean, 1987; Dunleavy, 1991). How is this claim about the fundamentally biased nature of the public choice approach to be countered?

There are two options: either one accepts the accusation but argues that every approach is bound to be biased one way or the other, or one rebuts the criticism. The accusation of scientific subjectivity and a lack of scientific neutrality is hardly correct with regard to the general public choice approach, although one may find in the Virginia interpretation of public choice strong ingredients of an explicit right-wing ideology.

## ETHICAL NEUTRALITY AND SCIENTIFIC OBJECTIVITY

The notions of ethical neutrality and scientific objectivity are regulative concepts. They are meaningful even if there exist no texts that fulfil the criteria of neutrality or objectivity. Like the notion of truth they are important to the conduct of scientific inquiry, because they provide us with criteria with which to evaluate arguments. Just as one cannot show that a theory is true once and for all but may detect that a theory is false, so one may use the criteria of neutrality and objectivity to point out the occurrence of biases in arguments, although it may be impossible to vindicate an argument in terms of its neutrality and objectivity.

Some argue that ethical neutrality and scientific objectivity do not matter in scientific discourse. The logic of scientific discovery is complete anarchy, meaning that anything goes as long as it works (Feyerabend, 1975). Others claim that the criteria of ethical neutrality and scientific objectivity are unfeasible, because it is impossible for a theory to be unbiased as it is bound to be value-ingrained (Myrdal, 1970). Neither position appears to be convincing. It seems difficult to dispense with the distinction between the context of discovery and the context of justification (Scheffler, 1967b), as scientific arguments do claim a justification which is beyond mere personal factors.

Although it certainly is true that social science concepts often are value-loaded (Myrdal, 1961), this in itself does not prove that neutrality or objectivity is impossible in principle (Nagel, 1961). Actually, the continuous detection of bias in social science theories does indicate that ethical neutrality and scientific objectivity are important and valid concepts. Stating that an approach like the public choice perspective is biased is a serious challenge that needs to be considered not simply by answering that every approach is subjective.

The case for ethical neutrality or scientific objectivity may be based on either a thin or a thick epistemological theory. A *thick* defence of these regulative notions would take us into basic issues in meta-ethical argument about the status of values or bring up fundamental epistemic problems about the relationship between perspective and object. A *thin* defence of the notions of ethical neutrality and scientific objectivity is all that is needed here, because it is enough to start from an assumption that truth and value are different and that objectivity is distinct from subjectivity – that is, the classical Weberian position (Weber, 1923). Scientific inquiry is somehow different from ethics or political ideology – a difference that has to do with ethical neutrality and objectivity in research.

Thus, we have two distinctions, one between the public choice approach in general and other public sector perspectives on the one hand, and another one between scientific objectivity and subjectivity on the other hand. These distinctions may be combined (Table 7.1).

Table 7.1  *Public choice and scientific neutrality*

|  | Public choice approach | Other public sector approaches |
|---|---|---|
| Scientific objectivity | I | II |
| Scientific subjectivity | III | IV |

The accusation directed towards the public choice approach is that it by *necessity* ends up in combination III, whereas other approaches to the analysis of the public sector may end up in combination II. In order to evaluate this statement we must take a close look at the basic elements of the public choice epistemology.

## WHAT IS THE PUBLIC CHOICE APPROACH?

In order to deal with the objection that the public choice approach is biased – a right-wing perspective on the public sector as it were – we need to identify the entire enterprise in a way that makes the accusation of an implicit ideological bias an open question. If we start from the identification of the public choice approach as the science of political failure (Buchanan, 1988), then there is indeed a risk that the bias is already there from the start. Claiming that politics as a mechanism for handling practical social problems is bound to result in disaster is after all a commitment in classical liberal ideology as well as in neo-conservatism. Why would public choice necessarily refer to political failure and not to one single case of political success?

The public choice approach is undoubtedly oriented towards the understanding of the domain of public choice, that is, politics and bureaucracy. As D. Mueller states in his authoritative interpretation:

> Public choice can be defined as the economics of nonmarket decisionmaking, or simply the application of economics to political science. The subject matter of public choice is the same as that of political science: the theory of the state, voting rules, voter behavior, party politics, the bureaucracy, and so on. The methodology of public choice is that of economics, however. (1979: 1)

The Mueller identification is not only exceptionally clear but also ethically neutral. It does not imply that public choice is the science of the public sector as misfortune. At the same time it carries no commitment to some naive model of politics as the straightforward achievement of objectives in an efficient manner.

The combination of politics with economic method is usually singled out as characteristic of public choice. In *The Political Economy of Public Choice* R. Sugden arrives at a slightly different identification by means of a more complex route. He states:

> I attempt to integrate two broad themes in economic theory: traditional Paretian welfare economics . . . and the theory of social choice . . . . Both of these bodies of theory, I shall suggest, are to be understood as analyses of the logic of value judgements that may be made about public choice . . . they analyse the logic of arguments that can be put forward to justify particular public decisions, or to justify particular procedures for taking public decisions. (Sugden, 1981: ix)

Evidently, welfare economics is narrower than the economic method itself and social choice is broader than politics and bureaucracy. The emphasis on value judgements and justification is misleading as it somehow places moral argument at the heart of the public choice approach. Such an identification would make the problem of ethical neutrality troublesome from the beginning. The Mueller description of the focus and method of public choice is to be preferred.

If public choice is the economic method applied to the analysis of the public sector, then which are the basic epistemological commitments? Two fundamental notions lie at the foundation of all layers of public choice models: methodological individualism and the homo economicus model (Buchanan, 1975, 1984; Mueller, 1979, 1989; Sugden, 1981; Tullock, 1988). Thus we arrive at two principles:

1  Public sector actors behave as if they maximize their own interests.
2  All social entities are fundamentally sets of individual actors.

These two methodological themes have been discussed in a substantial literature, but here it suffices to focus on whether they entail a problem in relation to scientific objectivity when they are employed in modelling behaviour in the public sector domain. Is it true that methodological individualism and the homo economicus model implicitly entail a right-wing ideological bias?

## THE BEHAVIOUR POSTULATE

The doctrine of methodological individualism in the social sciences requires that the fundamental units of analysis be identified as individual actors and that various aggregates be regarded as somehow reducible to actors and their properties (Hayek, 1955). Buchanan states: 'The basic units are choosing units, acting, behaving persons rather than organic units such as parties, provinces, or nations' (1984: 13). Buchanan combines the doctrine of methodological individualism with the typical economic being assumption: 'persons seek to maximize their own utilities, and . . . their own narrowly defined economic well-being is an important component of these utilities' (1984: 13).

Buchanan explicitly recognizes that the tie between methodological individualism and the self-interest axiom is not a necessary relationship, but it lays the foundation for the peculiar public choice perspective of looking at the public sector and all its aggregates in terms of individual choice on a par with market behaviour. There must be a fundamental symmetry between public action and private action, which entails that the burden of proof is with those who argue that entirely different models of individuals apply in the political and economic realms of behaviour (Buchanan, 1984: 13–14).

By combining the doctrine of methodological individualism with the model of self-interest-maximizing behaviour we face the most basic problems concerning the structure of the public sector and the motivation of public action. Are political parties or bureaux or nation-states nothing but sums of persons? Is social choice simply a function of self-interest? Granted that the basic motive is self-interest, why does it have to be only economic interests? What about the role of public interests or ideology?

As Tullock has recently argued, these serious problems have to be faced within the framework of public choice analysis and should not be resolved by means of simple fiat placing the burden of argument with those who question these implications (1988: 158–70). The reductionist bias in the public choice approach locating all behaviour motivation with singular individuals whatever their role or position and underlining narrow economic self-interests as the decisive incentive is bound to result in difficulties when it comes to the understanding of the public sector and its complexity.

However, what may be lost in descriptive realism is gained in analytical power. By employing the standard assumptions of economic method powerful implications may be derived from a strong theoretical core. Deductive strength is gained at the expense of descriptive accuracy (Friedman, 1953). Let us look at each of the two components separately, first the self-interest maxim and then methodological individualism. It is not these two assumptions per se that create the problem of value bias with regard to the public choice approach. Only if we add other assumptions do we end up in the Virginia right-wing corner.

## INTEREST MAXIMIZATION

In a fundamental methodological sense all political action is behaviour by individuals. In politics, persons tend to be members of various formal organizations, be these political parties, interest groups or public institutions. And with membership in large-scale organizations as the basis for political action individuals become spokespersons for the ideology that formal organizations employ to state their rationale. Now, if individuals are the basic units in the public sector, does it follow that the organizations involved in public action are just sets of individual persons? Buchanan seems to take such a stance, for example, in the debate about social justice in society: 'As is the case with efficiency, persons are not likely to express interests in abstract distributional ideals for the society in general when in political decisions. They are likely, instead, to seek to further their own well-defined interests' (1988: 11).

Politicians in a wide sense including not simply political party people but also the representatives of organized groups do make statements about distributional justice and do argue such notions as the reason for various policy demands. Such abstract distributional ideologies may focus on different definitions of justice as need, desert or rights (Miller, 1976). As a matter of simple facts it is not correct to deny that political argument is to a large extent about such contesting distributional ideals. However, one may argue that such abstract notions simply reflect narrow self-centred interests, but whose interests? Why does it have to be the 'well-defined interests' of individual persons?

Let me call this theory about public motivation the 'simplicity theory'. It assumes that public action may be fully accounted for in terms of the well-defined economic self-interests of individuals. There are two fundamental problems involved here. On the one hand there is the enormous difficulty tied to the doctrine of selfishness as the basic motivational force of persons. On the other hand, we have the collective action problem, meaning that public wishes are somehow a function of the aggregation of individual wishes about not only their self-interests but also social states in general. Why would the public choice approach have to commit itself to the simplicity theory? It faces tremendous difficulties with regard to the distinctions between selfishness and altruism on the one hand and between economic and other interests on the other hand, as well as in relation to the institutional context of preference aggregation.

If we start from the traditional separation between decision-making and implementation in public choice (Doel, 1979), we may pin-point the profound difficulties of the simplicity theory. When persons argue publicly for a policy position, whether in elections or in Parliament, are they promoting their own well-defined economic interests? Presumably, they argue for policy options that are social in the sense that their implementation would concern everyone, not just the person arguing the case. If so, are we not forced to make a distinction between self-centred interests and public interests or some similar kind of separation between private interests and social interests?

Or take the case of a bureaucrat or a professional doing service in a public programme. When they act in the implementation of policies, are they ipso facto pursuing the well-defined economic interests of their own? Or if they put a lot of effort into improving existing technologies, would they do that only because their own economic interests are at stake?

Some public choice scholars not only recognize the validity of these distinctions, but they also claim they are vital in the analysis of the domain of public choice. Let us quote Michael Laver: 'the two general families of evaluation criteria that I shall be using relate to the direct consumption of costs and benefits by the person making the evaluation and to her vicarious interest in the consumption of others' (1986: 58). The distinction that Laver aims at is traditionally expressed by means of the selfishness–altruism distinction. Any person would thus have two types of evaluations: selfish and vicarious. However, both types of interests are personal in the sense of accruing to the person in question. Yet there is a need for a second distinction, between consumer-controlled actions and spillover effects (Laver, 1986: 65ff.).

Thus, besides the two types of private or personal interests – selfish ones and vicarious or altruistic ones – we must take into account interests related to the existence of social costs and benefits. If so, how can we argue that individuals in public choice settings act on the basis of their own well-defined economic interests? What does it really mean?

The identification of vicarious interests in combination with social costs and benefits may appear as a restriction on the applicability of the public choice approach to the understanding of the domain of public choice. If it is true, as Mueller states, that: 'The basic behavioral postulate of public choice, as for economics, is that man is an egoistic, rational, utility maximizer' (1989: 2), then there are only two alternatives. Either one must accept that the public choice approach lacks fundamental concepts for entities that are important in politics or one has to redefine the methodology of economics so that it takes into account the variety of interests or preferences.

In his *Selfishness, Altruism and Rationality* H. Margolis argues for the second solution, although he notes that the scope of the economic model was never strictly limited to competitive market behaviour: 'important areas of economics do not have any simple relation to the empirical study of prices and quantities in markets, and among these are a number of topics (welfare economics, decision theory, public goods) with obvious relevance to broader questions of social choice' (1982: 10). Yet, in order to extend the economic method to the analysis of the domain of public choice Margolis states that we need to add new entities besides the utility-maximizing individual. To quote: 'we have good reason to expect that a viable formal theory of politics needs to extend the traditional model of rational choice in at least three ways: provision of a central role for public goods; explicit treatment of altruistic motivation; and explicit treatment of the role of persuasion' (1982: 13).

The maximization axiom results in difficulties, because it is not clear which interests are being maximized by public sector officials. By combining the distinctions introduced above we arrive at Table 7.2.

Table 7.2   *Types of interests*

|           | Personal | Social |
|-----------|:--------:|:------:|
| Selfish   | I        | II     |
| Vicarious | III      | IV     |

The behaviour axiom of the public choice approach may be interpreted in a narrow fashion meaning that it focuses only on combination I; however, it may also be interpreted in a broader way to cover all the various combinations as long as they somehow relate to the utility of the actor. The main alternative to the simplicity theory would be to reexamine the structure of preferences, interests or utility. When persons act publicly, why do we have to assume that they pursue either their own interests (selfishness) or the interests of others (altruism)? Why could not one be a means to the other?

Obviously, public behaviour is strongly oriented in terms of social goals, whether they take the form of altruistic motivations or the target is social cost or collective benefit. When a premier or a president runs the country or when a parliamentarian promotes a piece of legislation or when a bureaucrat administers a system of rules or when a citizen takes a stand on the issue of nuclear power, then they all pay attention to interests that are broader than their own well-defined interests.

Policy options may be argued because they are believed to enhance abstract liberty or power of institutions or groups which in turn the various actors have selfish or altruistic evaluations of. Be that as it may, the doctrine that individuals somehow maximize some utility function consisting of their own evaluations does not imply that they necessarily seek their own well-defined economic interests in every activity. The self-interest axiom cannot be applied without qualifications.

## METHODOLOGICAL INDIVIDUALISM

When the simplicity theory of human motivation is combined with a strong version of the doctrine of methodological individualism, then the difficulties become pronounced. Methodological individualism is the theory that social aggregates of whatever form – mere groups or huge formal organizations – are in reality nothing but sets of human beings (Nagel, 1961). Thus, the properties of social aggregates are reducible to the properties of individuals. The reductionist hypothesis about the construction of social reality has caused much debate about the nature of wholes. If we accept the starting point that there could be no other actors than human beings, must we then also negate the possibility that human organization resulting in organized collective action can result in emergent properties that are not reducible to individual beings?

The problem of holism versus reductionism becomes acute as we enter the domain of public choice. Here a large number of participants in the arena of policy-making and policy implementation are organized collectivities of various kinds: institutions, parties, interest organizations and so forth. What about their motivation? What is it that drives these formal organizations to act and do certain things in the public arena?

The simplicity theory in combination with a strong version of methodological individualism would imply that the individuals who occupy the crucial positions in the domain of public choice watch their own well-defined economic interests (Breton, 1974). Thus, public officials seek reelection and private remuneration (Downs, 1957); bureaucrats act in order to maximize their salary, power and prestige (Niskanen, 1971). This is not denying that such interests may play a vital role in politics and bureaucracies. What is wrong is the extreme simplification which omits an important element: group interests. When organizations – political parties, interest groups, citizen movements – take action, then more than the well-defined economic interests of individuals are at stake.

Collective action, which is a very prominent feature in the domain of public choice, is about group interests. And collective interests may range from the very selfish narrow interests of small lobby groups to widely shared public interests. Such public interests in peace, prosperity, fairness and equal treatment under the law may be promoted in the public sector by means of public choice activities. The theory of rent-seeking behaviour is a recognition of the fact that broad social interests may be enhanced by large collectivities (Buchanan et al., 1980; Tollison, 1982; Rowley et al., 1988).

The typical motivation assumption in the public choice perspective creates difficulties when public sector behaviour is to be analyzed. Yet, it may be defended by the argument that there are limits to the explanatory power of any assumptions. It is important to be aware of how far the self-interest assumption works when explaining public action. Whether it works well depends on whether there are other assumptions that may allow for the same amount of integration of knowledge in this area. That it cannot explain everything is not the same as saying that it fails to explain anything. Moreover, the self-interest axiom is not a normative proposition with the meaning that actors in the public sector should only pay attention to their own well-defined interests. In order to move to normative public choice theory we need additional assumptions.

## THE WICKSELL STATE IDEOLOGY

The Virginia version of the public choice approach is not just a positive theory about the public sector based on the two fundamental assumptions of utility maximization and methodological individualism. Crucial in the Virginia interpretation is a normative theory about the state that is straightforward right-wing ideology of a neo-liberal kind or what used to be called Manchester liberalism. It is vehemently opposed to the welfare state and its justification in externalities and equity. The foundation of the normative approach was laid by the elements of a state theory proposed in 1896 by Knut Wicksell in 'A New Principle of Just Taxation' (1967), in which he launched his special decision rule for policy-making: the unanimity rule. Buchanan has employed the unanimity rule as the basis for a contractarian theory of the state. Considering the fact that the Wicksell idea hardly had any practical consequences this is no small accomplishment.

Buchanan argues that his neo-liberal theory of the state is at the heart of the public choice approach. This is erroneous. The public choice approach has no special link to any normative theory of the state – its proper size or appropriate programme structure. The insistence on a distinction between the *is* and the *ought* is not meant as part of any positivistic philosophy of science. It is interesting, meaningful and valid to undertake both positive and normative analysis of the public sector. However, the public choice approach as a scientific framework cannot possibly be logically committed to the values that the Virginia school wishes to promote (Buchanan, 1984).

The Wicksell state theory derived from considerations of efficiency in taxation and argued a strong case for a quid pro quo rule on an individual basis. Efficiency demands that each citizen can balance the value and cost of a particular item on the state budget at the marginal. Equating marginal value with marginal cost may be accomplished by means of the benefit approach to taxation as long as we do not face public goods. In relation to the free-rider problem the only mechanism that will guarantee optimal taxation for public goods provision is the unanimity rule or the individual veto principle in a legislative context (Musgrave and Peacock, 1967).

Buchanan (1987) employs the Wicksellian decision principle to derive two normative rules that he considers constitutive of the public choice approach: politics as exchange, and economic constitutionalism or contractarianism as the basis of public policy-making. Yet, these two normative principles are very different from the two basic assumptions of the public choice approach listed above; they are different, because they orient the entire analysis of the public sector in a right-wing ideological direction with logical necessity. Thus, we have two new principles:

3  Political interaction is to be based on voluntary exchange.
4  Politics as voluntary exchange requires the making of an economic constitution that is to guide the relationship between the state and the individual.

It is obvious that the basic assumptions of the public choice approach – (1) and (2) above (p. 155) – do not imply or contain the fundamental principles of the Wicksellian state ideology. This is not to say that one could not adhere to all four axioms without contradiction; the point is only that the axioms be kept separate as (1) and (2) refer to the *is* whereas (3) and (4) deal with the *ought*.

## POLITICS AS EXCHANGE

The axiom of politics as exchange means that every public policy must be based on the consent of all citizens, as unanimity is the criterion by which policy is judged to be in the interest of the citizen. This is certainly a very optimistic interpretation of the nature of politics as legitimated by the interests of citizens. However, this is not positive theory but an ethical theory of the state. In the public choice domain, which the public choice approach is aimed at understanding, politics reveals itself in a number of different ways, from coercion over corporate interests formed at the expense of consumer interests to the few cases where broad citizen interests rule.

The unanimity rule introduced by Wicksell may be given two different interpretations. On the one hand we have the positivist interpretation, that politics is exchange between individuals in a setting of political institutions. Politics is not about the definition and implementation of the common good – some ultimate principle that stands above the interests of individual: 'In the absence of individual interest, there is no interest' (Buchanan, 1987: 338). Public choice analysis means the unpacking of such notions into the interests of the participating individuals. But if it is admitted that politics is not about the common good, then what prevents a public choice approach from modelling politics as coercion or the exploitation of some interests by other interests? Why is politics as symmetrical as market exchange? Buchanan would answer:

> The observed presence of coercive elements in the activity of the state seems difficult to reconcile with the model of voluntary exchange among individuals. We may, however, ask: Coercion to what purpose? Why must individuals subject themselves to the coercion inherent in collective action? The answer is evident. Individuals acquiesce in the coercion of the state, of politics, only if the ultimate constitutional 'exchange' furthers their interests. (1987: 338)

This is a confusion of the *is* and the *ought*. Individuals acquiesce in coercive politics because to do otherwise is not in accordance with liberal political values. This will not suffice as a foundation for a public choice analysis of politics as long as the purpose is scientific neutrality and objectivity.

On the other hand we have the normative interpretation, that only those policies which meet with unanimous consent from individual citizens can be called just. But why is this so? That unanimity is the criterion for social justice is obvious in the Wicksell tradition, but why? Wicksell states: 'It would seem to be a blatant injustice if someone should be forced to contribute toward the costs of some activity which does not further his interests or may even be diametrically opposed to them' (1967: 89).

If one accepts the unanimity criterion for efficiency and justice, then naturally Wicksell's conclusion follows. But why do we have to do that? We are here in the realm of ethical argument where there are contending views about what social justice requires. If Wicksell's position is the only reasonable one, then we would have to dispense with all kinds of welfare programmes that cannot be derived from unanimous consent – which one would be thus derivable one may ask? This is of course Buchanan's conclusion from applying the Wicksell justice or efficiency rule to the existing welfare state. This is not scientific analysis. It is normative theory, neither more nor less. One should also bear in mind that Wicksell did make a distinction between political justice or efficiency as unanimity and social justice in an ethical sense. The latter could certainly demand that some vested interests be removed in the name of social justice whether or not there be unanimous consent.

## CONSTITUTIONAL ECONOMICS

The normative framework in the Virginia public choice interpretation becomes very visible in the theory of economic constitutionalism. The theory of normative public policy concerns the rules of the political decision-making process which could meet with unanimity. Buchanan states: 'Existing constitutions, or structures or rules, are the subject of critical scrutiny. The conjectural question becomes: Could these rules have emerged from agreement by participants in an authentic constitutional convention?' (1987: 341). Since there exists no system of constitutional revisions on a permanent basis one could only speculate about what citizens would agree to were they in a constitutional setting. Thus, the idea of a constitutional economics is not an analysis of reality but a mechanism for the expression of political criticism.

Not only is the notion of constitutional economics normative, it is also part of a highly restricted normative theory about politics. It not only cautions the public choice scholar against evaluating existing politico-economic institutions but it also forbids all evaluative approaches except the unanimity rule. According to Buchanan, we are not allowed to employ ethical criteria to evaluate the state:

> There is no criterion through which policy may be directly evaluated. An indirect evaluation may be based on some measure of the degree to which the political process facilitates the translation of expressed individual preferences into observed political outcomes. The focus of evaluative attention becomes the process itself, as contrasted with end-state or outcome patterns. (1987: 339)

The distinction that Buchanan refers to – outcome criteria or process criteria – is well-known in ethical argument, but why should a public choice scholar have to accept the solution that Buchanan prefers? There is no scientific basis whatsoever for the claim that we cannot evaluate policies by means of utilitarian or Rawlsian criteria. A debate about grounds for the evaluation of politico-economic regimes is certainly not meaningless and the arguments pro and contra various solutions can be scrutinized. The public choice approach as such cannot commit itself to any one special ethical doctrine about social justice or a proper economic constitution, simply because the fundamental problem involved here is the choice of ultimate values, a question which the social sciences cannot resolve by means of their special methodology (Brecht, 1959).

## CONCLUSION

The public choice approach has been attacked for not being scientifically neutral and objective. It has been argued that its epistemological core includes the acceptance of political values that correctly belong to a special ideology. Thus, the emergent public choice school would mix the *is* and the *ought* to the same extent as the earlier prevailing political economy, that is, the set of Marxist approaches. Admitting that it is often difficult to distinguish the *is* and the *ought* and that social science theories often are biased, it is still vital to maintain the concepts of scientific neutrality and objectivity as Weber interpreted them. It must be possible to employ the public choice approach for the understanding of the public choice domain without advocating some political ideology.

Public choice theories should stand on their own supported by means of the ordinary canons employed in the conduct of scientific inquiry. The two peculiar assumptions in the public choice approach – methodological individualism and the self-interest motivation – afford necessary and sufficient identification criteria. Ethical assumptions need not be resorted to. This is not to deny that ethical argument is important or that public choice scholars could possibly engage in both scientific and ethical activities, adding, for example, politics as exchange and a very special conception of constitutional economics to the typical public choice assumptions. However, it would clarify epistemological matters if the scientific framework were separated explicitly from the ethical framework. You do not have to adhere to the political values that the Virginia public choice school propagates in order to conduct serious public choice analysis of the public choice domain.

The basic assumption in the public choice approach, the self-interest maximization hypothesis, should best be conceived as simply an assumption and not an axiom. Its potential depends on the number of interesting implications that can be derived from it when it is applied to Downsian politicians and bureaucrats à la Niskanen. Tullock stated it in the following way:

> It is my opinion that most human beings are (except within their families) to a very large extent interested in fairly narrow selfish goals. . . . The point

I am making is simply that the resources they are willing to invest in these goals are customarily very much less than the amount they are willing to invest to reach straightforward selfish goals. (1970: 33)

The self-interest assumption does not rule out altruistic behaviour in the public sector; and it does not have to be confined to a set of very narrow personal materialistic interests. Finally, it may help to explain behaviour that is duty-oriented, because such behaviour may be a means to self-interest ends.

The public choice approach underlines one basic component in social life, namely the interests of the persons who form groups and make up organizations. Actually, the concept of self-interest as it is used in this approach includes a variety of motivational elements: wishes, needs, preferences and demands. And it covers both narrow egoistic and materialistic interests and broad collective interests of groups and organizations. Not denying the existence of altruistic interests the public choice school rejects the notion of an objective public interest. However, interests often collide or compete with each other, which calls for rules about how individual interests are to be coordinated. The new institutionalism is the social science approach that most strongly underlines this second fundamental component in social life: institutions.

Basic to the public choice approach is the *quid pro quo* assumption. It means that citizens provide rulers or the state with resources and power for which they expect a return of goods and services as well as laws regulating society that matches what they are giving up.

# 8

# THE NEW INSTITUTIONALISM

The institutionalist paradigm has grown stronger in the past two decades. Its revival is a reaction to various reductionist perspectives that attempt to explain how political organizations work by means of non-political factors. Institutions in general and political ones in particular have a logic of their own the understanding of which requires alternatives to the reductionist approaches explaining politics in terms only of preferences (economic beings) or social structure (sociological beings). The new institutionalism comes in two very different versions, the first one originating in organization theory and the second one emerging within the new institutional economics.

One basic theme in the neo-institutionalist literature is the recognition that 'institutions do matter'. Broadly conceived, institutions are the humanly created constraints on the interaction between individuals (North, 1990b). They are the rules and norms resulting in formal or informal rights and obligations which facilitate exchange by allowing people to form stable and fairly reliable expectations about the actions of others.

There is disagreement among the neo-institutionalists about what social phenomena are to be called 'institutions'. Matthews (1986) distinguishes between four approaches: institutions as property rights, as conventions, as types of contracts and specifically as contracts about authority or governance structures like the firm. Williamson (1985: 15) states: 'Firms, markets and relational contracting are important economic institutions', whereas North (1990b) stresses the importance of distinguishing conceptually between the rules of the game (institutions) and the strategies (organization) the players in the social game find it advantageous to adopt (1990b: 5). Firms are also seen as a type of organization, evolving within an institutional framework. Organizations may, in the view of North, act as agents of institutional change, although mainly of an incremental kind.

The basic problem here is whether the new institutionalism can be applied to the public sector, allowing us to look at it with a different perspective. How can we make sense of the new institutionalist theories about interests and institutions if we are primarily interested in the public sector? Could neo-institutionalist concepts be employed in modelling the public sector?

## POLITICS, ECONOMICS AND INTERESTS

Political science and economics are not as remote from each other as believed; it used to be taught in the lecture hall that politics was about power and its modes whereas economics dealt with money in the forms of resource allocation and redistribution. *Staatswissenschaft* should analyse the public institutions and *Wirtschaft* the private ones. The old version of political economy never made these distinctions as it looked upon society as both a polity and an economy (Palgrave, 1894, Vol. III); Adam Smith stated: 'Political economy, considered as a branch of the science of the statesman or legislator, proposes two distinct objectives: first, to provide a plentiful revenue or subsistence for the people, or more properly to enable them to provide such a revenue or subsistence for themselves; and, secondly, to supply the state or commonwealth with a revenue sufficient for the public services' (1962, Vol. I: 375).

Any radical separation between politics and economics is unjustified, because it neglects the fact that both these social sciences study the same phenomena, namely institutions and interests; it is certainly not the case either that selfish interests only show up in market institutions or that public institutions only focus on power and never on money. Why could not the public interest, if indeed there really exists such a species in the world of social systems, disclose itself in both private and public institutions? Why should power be little evident in market institutions or money less predominant in public institutions? The new political economy rejects the conceptual distinctions between politics and economics, because they do not do justice to the closeness between the two (Eatwell et al., 1987, Vol. III: 900–10); the public sector, just as the market, offers rules for the interaction between persons and institutions that interrelate, coordinate or aggregate the interests individuals bring to social life, that is, preferences, demands or wants, values and beliefs.

One prevailing mode of conducting political research is to try to pin down the interests that people or various groups bring to political institutions in an effort to further these by various state activities. This framework for the analysis of politics and public life, separating the rules and procedures of political life from the world of egoistic, altruistic, personal and collective interests with which public institutions work, has a long standing in both political science and economics (Truman, 1951).

A problem in the analysis of the public sector is how to strike a balance between interest theory and the new institutionalism, that is, between wants, needs and preferences on the one hand and rules, procedures and institutions on the other hand. The welfare economics approach to the institutions and interests in the public sector involved hypotheses the neo-institutionalist approach questions, in particular the theory of market failure as the foundation for a rational theory of the state in an advanced economy (Schotter, 1985).

Traditional welfare economics stated that various kinds of market failure in themselves constituted sufficient conditions for the making and implementation of public policies. The new institutionalism argues that public institutions are not neutral in relation to the policies that they host. Public institutions matter, it is claimed by both the major contrary interpretations within the new institutionalism, namely the sociological version of institutions as more than the sum of their parts (holist version) and the economic version of institutions as rational responses to individual interests and their aggregation into collective action (atomistic version).

## MARKET FAILURE AND NON-MARKET FAILURE

Market or politics is the classical problem in political economy, be it the old brand focusing on resource allocation and income distribution, with Adam Smith, David Ricardo or Karl Marx, or the new brand dealing with the interaction between the polity and the economy, with, for example, Gordon Tullock, James Buchanan, Mancur Olson and Bruno Frey. How are we to choose between markets and the state? The traditional theory of market failures tried to offer systematic criteria for this crucial institutional choice problem (Mishan, 1981).

There are four types of market failures, or situations where the allocation mechanisms of the market cannot be used to allocate resources. These may be either technical or economic failures in the sense of physical unfeasibility in general or inefficiency more specifically. The four kinds of market failures are: (1) externalities, positive or negative; (2) economies of scale; (3) information imperfection; (4) justice in the distribution of income and wealth.

Market failure theory argued that the demand and supply of public programmes including resource allocation, income redistribution and public regulation could be derived from citizens' preferences with regard to categories (1) to (4) without any institutional assumptions. Charles Wolf in *Markets or Governments* (1988) identifies the following two basic functions in welfare economics.

The demand for public programmes would be an aggregation of the demand for each single public programme, which would be affected by the number of externalities in various markets (X), the extent of monopoly in the private sector (M), the information imperfection (I), the need for public goods (G), the perception of inequalities (E), the tax rate (R) and the unit cost for a public programme (P). Factors X, M, I, G and E would increase the demand for public programmes whereas factors R and P would decrease it, all other things being equal. This is a most general model for determining the demand side of the public household.

A general supply model would include the factors that enter the supply function of single public programmes to be aggregated into a total supply of public programmes. These factors include: how accurately a public programme may be measured (V), the extent of monopoly in the public programme (m), how clear the technological relation between input and output is for a programme (T), the unit cost (P), the tax rate (X) and national income (Y).

In these two models a number of conditions for public sector activities are identified, but each of them is conducive to difficulties. Looking at the demand side there is the tendency for too high a demand with regard to both the number and comprehensiveness of public programmes. Different factors in combination drive up demand for public programmes: an emphasis on market failures from groups that directly benefit from these programmes, the competition between political élites leading to an underestimation of the costs and an overestimation of the benefits, as well as the basic divergence between consumption and payment.

These imperfections on the demand side result in information deficiencies that are conducive to micro- and macro-failures. Micro-imperfection means that benefits and costs are not tied together, which in its turn implies a fundamental asymmetry in that benefits tend to be concentrated in small, strongly organized groups whereas costs are diffused among the silent majority. Macro-imperfection occurs when a political majority employs the public budget for redistributive purposes, favouring themselves at the expense of the minority. These two demand side imperfections drive up both the number and size of public programmes far beyond what is rational.

On the supply side of the public sector there are several factors that increase the public budget: the systemic difficulties in identifying and measuring outputs, the use of public monopolies, uncertainty in the production technology as well as the non-existence of natural evaluation criteria (Wolf, 1988: 35–99).

Combining these types of imperfections there is a high likelihood of politics (non-market) failure, including: (1) the disjunction between costs and revenues; (2) redundant and rising costs; (3) internalities or costs derived from the presence of private groups in public programmes; (4) externalities or costs for others derived from public programmes; (5) distributional inequities caused by public programmes.

The existence of failures on both the demand and supply side of the public sector implies that public sector equilibria will be indeterminate, yet the equilibrium quantity would tend to be too high (Figure 8.1).

The public sector equilibrium $Y_e$ would occur too far to the right in the figure, because only full information could reduce the impact of the imperfections that drive up demand and supply. In opposition to the standard market failure theory of welfare economics new models

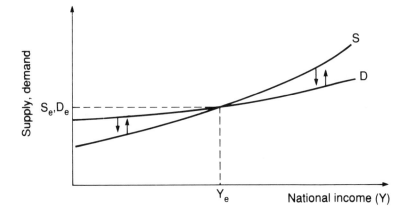

Figure 8.1  *Hypothetical non-market demand and supply functions*

were suggested that recognized the impact of institutional factors on citizens' preferences for public programmes as well as their impact on the aggregation process resulting in demand and supply curves for public programmes.

## SOCIOLOGICAL INSTITUTIONALISM

Two of the leading scholars of the institutionalist approach are James G. March and Johan P. Olsen (March and Olsen, 1984; March, 1988; Olsen, 1988). What, more specifically, defines their neo-institutionalism? Common sense teaches us that interests and institutions are separate entities in social reality. *Rediscovering Institutions* by March and Olsen (1989) presents a contrary argument. First, they claim that we cannot separate the set of interests from the set of institutions; secondly, they state that institutions come before interests in all kinds of positive or negative social interaction.

March and Olsen present a case for revitalizing the old institutionalism that, we were once told, had mutilated political research for such a long time (Eulau, 1963). By confining the conduct of inquiry to history and case studies institutionalism was accused of localism and particularism; by emphasizing formal rules it had neglected real life behaviour and its lawlike regularities. The crucial question is whether the new institutionalism can be brought over into the 1990s, surviving the criticism by the behavioural and comparative approaches in the 1960s (Powell and DiMaggio, 1991).

There are two difficulties with the idea that institutions matter in the public sector. First, how do we single out political institutions in the general set of institutions? Acknowledging the existence of political, economic, social and cultural institutions, the typical features of political institutions are described in the following way: 'A political order sets a framework for conflict resolution and steering. It defines the most important bodies of governing, how they arise and change, how they interrelate as well as how they relate to the individual citizens' (Olsen, 1988: 22).

Obviously, political institutions constitute the political order. However, there are several mechanisms for conflict resolution and coordination in a society. Is every one part of the political order? The new institutionalism responds that the concept of the state is crucial in designating those institutions that are political and it regards the revival of state theory as an institutionalist trend (Skocpol, 1979, 1985; Dunleavy and O'Leary, 1987).

However, if the institutionalist approach requires a concept of the state, then what is the state? The traditional approach to the state greatly emphasizes that what is special about the state – sovereignty, centralization, force – is not the fact that it is composed of institutions per se, but that state institutions in general are very particular. Claiming that institutionalism focuses on the state is hardly adequate, because equating public sector institutions with the state leaves us with a new set of unresolved problems.

Institutionalism faces a dilemma: it needs to differentiate between various kinds of institution – political, economic, social – but when it employs the concept of the state to do this it is pushed back to the difficult problem of defining the state so that this key concept consists of specific properties of political institutions. Secondly, we need to know what institutions are in general. Is an institution a set of behaviour or a set of rules or maybe both? And would any set of behaviour or rules qualify as an institution? Olsen states:

> Institutions dispose of authority and power, but also of collective wisdom and ethics. They provide physical, cognitive and moral frames for joint action; capacity for intervention; conceptual lenses for observation; agenda, memory, rights and duties as well as conceptions of justice; and symbols you may identify yourself with. (1988: 35)

There is a tone of enthusiasm if not admiration in the characterization of an institution by the new institutionalists (March, 1988). Yet we must ask if institutions may not also be wicked, violent and unjust. It seems as if institutions could be what has been described as organizations: collective action, legitimacy and symbolism.

According to March and Olsen, institutions shape individual actors; institutions are what organized human activity is all about. How do we show that these institutionalist claims are true, that institutions are more important than individuals?

The new institutionalism claims not only that institutions exist in social reality. The new theory also implies claims about how institutionalist phenomena are to be approached and explained. Institutionalist epistemology involves two components, one negative and one positive.

The negative argument is a rejection of two prevailing modes for the explanation of organizational phenomena, the contextual framework and the actor approach where politics is looked upon as a by-product of non-political factors. The explanations would be either contextual, thus resting with social structure, or reductionist in the sense of individually oriented (Olsen, 1988: 35).

A number of approaches are dispensed with by the negative argument: behaviouralism, political sociology, rational and social choice, public choice and so on. They all share the erroneous assumption that political phenomena like public institutions may be accounted for by means of non-political factors. This negative argument is based on an empirical proposition that is open to falsification. In order to prove its point institutionalism must convincingly show that there is no and can be no theory of public sector institutions that achieves a high degree of explained variance by relating institutional properties to social factors or individual choice variables. It may be the case that some contextual and individual choice frameworks work better than others and that one could conceive of some theoretical innovation that led to some adequate contextual or individual theory.

The positive argument offers a suggestion as to what should count instead. Neo-institutionalism suggests that one should look at: (a) physical structure; (b) demographic structure; (c) historical development; (d) personal networks; (e) temporal structure (decision points in time) (Olsen, 1988: 37).

Institutions may be analysed as: (1) normative orders; (2) cognitive orders; (3) symbolic orders. But what about the action aspect of institutions? Are institutions primarily norms, belief-systems or symbolism? And do they comprise action phenomena, meaning that collective activity takes place and leads to social outcomes? Just as the old institutionalism over-emphasized the formal aspect of organized collective action, so there is a corresponding risk with the new institutionalism.

The theory about institutional change that institutionalism sets forward is interesting for the policy perspective. It argues that change processes in institutions are inherently of a political nature. There is again a negative and a positive side of the argument. Negatively, the new institutionalism rejects the idea of organizational design, which more specifically means that organizations can never be restructured according to formulas by means of policy fiat and that the notion of effective organizational adaptability to environmental needs is an illusion.

The positive side of the argument about institutional dynamics is the notion that organizational change is a contested process involving accidental outcomes and random activity, meaning that results cannot be predicted and change cannot be controlled by fiat. The new institutionalism explains how social dynamics are affected by institutions (Olsen, 1988: 44).

The theory of organizational change which underlines sluggishness, resistance to change, randomness, surprise and unintentionality seems to be highly relevant in an age of big government. Whether it is necessarily tied to ontological and epistemological institutionalism is doubtful to say the least. Certainly, it is highly relevant to the understanding of policy processes in countries which have traditionally relied on top-down implementation as well as on planning models.

The new institutionalism is not only a framework for the analysis of what was neglected in the prevailing political science approaches, but it is also a theory about a new phenomenon: the negotiation society. Why do we need a new institutionalist paradigm in the social sciences? Not because institutions are as real as individuals and not because institutions could not possibly be understood in terms of environmental adaptation or individual rational action, but simply because recent developments have made them more prevalent, salient and powerful.

The new institutionalism amounts to a new theory of the state: the interpretation of the welfare state, the role and structure of the public sector and the future of its affluent society. What kind of state is feasible in a capitalist democracy? Olsen presents four model alternatives: the sovereign state, the moral state community, the classical liberal state and the segmented state.

The sustained process of public sector growth since the end of the Second World War has meant that the segmented negotiation state has become the prevalent model. The segmented state is different from the sovereign state as there is no single centre of control and there are no uniform channels of authority, meaning that parliamentary power has been reduced.

The segmented state is distinct from the state as a moral community, because the interaction takes place between organized interests and not individual citizens and it is determined by the logic of collective action and not by moral appeal. The segmented state is widely divergent from the guardian state as market processes are continuously interfered with by negotiations between monopolists and oligopolists within both the public and private sector. The era of big government is also the time of weak government, the devolution of power and authority on to public and private organizations.

The 1980s witnessed a reappraisal of the state models, their pros and cons. The established segmented state model has been criticized by those who adhere to the other models. The adherents of the sovereignty model want to see more democratic decision-making in representative assemblies as well as more political leadership; those who speak for the guardian state wish to replace budget allocation with market allocation; and the believers in the community model look for morally attractive ways of life which promote individual rights and ecological balance.

Here is the nub of the new institutionalist argument: whatever the outcomes will be in the contestation between the alternative models of the state, whatever compromise may be struck between the implications of these models, the understanding of what goes on can only be enhanced by an institutionalist approach, because what is at stake is nothing less than the kind of institutions people would choose had they been able to do so constitutionally. The new institutionalism, like the new cultural theory, is a response to the need to be able to discuss the elementary forms of political institutions without a methodological rigour that would restrict the scope and depth of the debate.

Sociological neo-institutionalism harbours three basic ideas: (1) that institutions constitute the important entities in social systems (ontology); (2) that institutional phenomena require a special social science methodology (epistemology); and (3) that institutions determine interests (metaphysics).

Semantic considerations must loom large since the denotation of 'institution' is said to be so important in social life; however, only the implicit meaning or some of the references of the key term are hinted at. As examples of political institutions March and Olsen mention the state, the legal order and the legislature or a parliamentary assembly; yet would not these social systems consist of sets of various institutions? No doubt, the future of the promising new political institutionalism will depend on how much progress is made in identifying the theoretical and empirical meaning of 'institution'. 'Institution' denotes not only rules but also technologies and cultures; how are we existentially to distinguish between an institution of a social system and the behaviour that is oriented in terms of its rules, technology and culture?

What is original is not the ontological hypothesis that institutions matter very much in social life; the methodological idea that institutions require a distinct epistemology, namely interpretative hermeneutics, has not been proposed in such a succinct way before. There is both a positive and a negative argument involved here. The negative one claims that much of the analysis of public institutions has been reductionist. Both of the prevailing approaches to politics and administration, the systems perspective (social structure) as well as the rational choice perspective (individual preferences), fail to recognize that public institutions are a specimen sui generis.

The positive argument states that institutions in general and public ones in particular must be understood in terms of how they solve a fundamental problem in the social sciences: what makes social life orderly and social systems workable? The neo-classical decision-making model employs economic being assumptions explaining social order as the outcome of purely rational self-interest maximization whereas the sociological model points to structural forces that stabilize individual behaviour.

With these explanations of the possibility of social order failing, March and Olsen claim that phenomena like rules, laws and norms make social systems possible. And they cannot be reduced to the interest concept or the social structure notion. What sets institutions apart from interests is that as rules in a social system these entities constitute meaningful phenomena in the sense that what is crucial about their existence is how their rules are interpreted by the participating actors. Institutional rules constrain behaviour because they suggest the reasons and not the causes for action.

Thus, the standard social science concepts of causality and reduction to self-interest or sociological functionalism have to be replaced by hermeneutic concepts. Understanding the so-called *Sinn* of the rules of a social system immediately provides the rationale for action in it. No reduction takes place making public institutions autonomous actors. But how can we explain or predict behaviour in public institutions without resorting to the concepts of interest?

Institutions come before interests; institutions shape the wishes and wants of individual persons, their preferences. Already this position is risky, but March and Olsen move to the doctrine of holism (Nagel, 1961), that is, that public institutions constitute a social reality that involves more than simply the acting persons. The emergent properties of institutions as organized social systems give the public institutions a life of their own, a destiny that even the social researcher finds it difficult to unravel.

Institutions are more than an important part of the common sense behaviour equation of rules plus interests, as they shape or even determine individual preferences or interests. There is little difficulty with thesis (1) that public institutions are as important as individual interests or preferences; nor would there be much hesitancy in accepting the plausibility of thesis (2), that the hermeneutic methodology can shed light on institutions; but thesis (3), that institutions determine interests, is really difficult to adopt.

March and Olsen support thesis (3) by arguing that the impossibility of aggregating individual interests to a group decision in such a manner that the institutional rules of aggregation do not matter – so-called *path independence* – shows that institutions and interests cannot be logically separated. As a matter of fact there are several collective choice situations where the outcome is not only a function of the participating individuals' interests but also the institution that happens to be employed (Riker, 1982).

However, the conclusion does not follow from the premises about interaction between institutions and interests. Quite the opposite is true, because what makes the design of institutions such a vital political concern is that they may affect the outcome in collective decision-making concerning the interests of persons and groups. It is the very fact that social outcomes depend not only upon the interests involved in confrontation and collaboration but also upon the institution through which interaction takes place which makes it so essential to distinguish conceptually between the institutions of a social system on the one hand and the individual preferences or group interests that motivate people in the system on the other.

## ECONOMIC NEO-INSTITUTIONALISM

The new economic theory of the state – new institutional economics or neo-institutional economics – argues that political institutions may be chosen rationally by means of deliberations about which rules are appropriate for the patterns of interaction in society. Instead of treating institutions as given, the institutionalist approach in economics attempts to endogenize what has traditionally been regarded as exogenous. Various stands in modern economics prefigure the development of a theory of institutions that is highly relevant to the interpretation of the public sector (Hodgson, 1988; Bromley, 1989; Heap, 1989; Eggertson, 1990).

The new institutional economics of Oliver Williamson has resulted in an original theory of the firm (Williamson, 1986) as well as insights into the contemporary institution of capitalism (Williamson, 1985). The neo-institutional economics of Coase, Demsetz, De Allesi, Alchian and Cheung emphasize the implications of (a) information costs, (b) transaction costs and (c) property rights constraints in the competition among contractual arrangements from which government may choose. In order to arrive at a general theory of the interaction between interests and institutions in the public sector we have to move to the principal–agent framework derived partly from the public choice school and partly from the application of the neo-classical paradigm to non-traditional topics (Stiglitz, 1987).

### Transaction costs

The new institutionalism in economics focuses on the role of the state in defining the basics of contractual arrangements, which depend on existing technologies and natural endowments. As technologies or endowments change, a process is initiated towards new contracts in which the state may play a profound role in minimizing transaction costs by institutional innovation. The prevailing structure of interests not only enter public institutions as the building blocks of public decision-making and implementation. Interests also affect the derivation of public institutions prior to ongoing policy-making. Institutional arrangements in the public sector may constitute so-called structure-induced equilibria which may be changed rationally, contrary to what the sociological version of institutionalism implies (Shepsle and Weingast, 1981).

In a well-known article, 'The Problem of Social Cost' (1960), Coase argued that allocative outcomes will tend towards efficiency, if transaction costs are negligible. In fact, there are several arguments which have been referred to as the Coase theorem (Veljanovski, 1982), but it generally implies that efficiency in allocation does not require public policy as it could be more advantageous to minimize the transaction costs: for example, by creating or clarifying property rights. Developing this argument, the state could be interpreted as a rational device for handling transaction costs (North, 1981, 1990a,b). Taken to its conclusion the economic theory of public institutions would end up in economic constitutionalism (Buchanan, 1986).

There is an emphasis on the problems of exchange and the importance of transaction costs for analyzing social outcomes and institutions in virtually all the literature within neo-institutionalism. Its models depart from neo-classical economic models, which assume that the costs of transacting when engaging in exchange are zero. Coase's demonstration was of great importance: only in a world of zero transaction costs would the initial assignment of property rights not affect the resource allocation in the economy, although it may have distributional consequences. Formulated more generally, when the cost of transacting is zero, institutions (systems of property rights) do not affect outcomes (the resource allocation in society). The implication is that the neo-classical economic model, indeed any model which does not recognize the importance of transaction costs, will fail to pay adequate attention to the existence of institutions. In the words of Williamson: 'the transactions cost approach [to the economic institutions of capitalism] maintains that these institutions have the main purpose and effect of economizing on transaction costs' (1985: 1).

As a matter of fact, this basic hypothesis may be equally or even more relevant for political institutions because the issues brought on to the public agenda tend to be social problems with high transaction costs involved, issues which could not be resolved by private contracting.

Neo-classical economic theory describes the interaction of given utility-maximizing individuals in a determinate institutional structure (Matthews, 1986: 903). Individual choice and action is based upon stable preferences and a rational consideration of alternatives and their consequences where the alternative yielding the highest level of expected utility is chosen. The process of choice takes place within one given institutional structure of fully defined and enforced property rights. Some authors, like Williamson, have gone further by introducing the concept of bounded rationality in an alternative model of individual choice. Williamson's (1975) conception of the term 'bounded rationality' is more or less the same as Herbert Simon's. It refers to the limited capability of people to have information about all alternatives and consequences, to process that information, and to communicate within the limits of language. With this model of choice, which is markedly different from the rational, Williamson addresses the same questions with which neo-institutional authors work – how does an institution emerge?

It should be pointed out that the concept of transaction costs is not a very clear one. It remains as a kind of residual: all the expenses made in order to reach a contract, whether they be personal or social. Could one measure the reduction in transaction costs by moving from a system of individual contracts to a hierarchy like the firm or the bureau? What should be included when government is said to have minimized transaction costs by reforming an institution like property rights or local government structure?

## Levels of analysis

Neo-institutional economics starts from the recognition that an individual may pursue his/her interests more effectively by making an effort to change the institutional constraints he or she faces rather than simply adapting to the institutional structure as if it was unsusceptible to change. The producer operating within the constraints of perfect competition may try to collude with others or seek favourable regulation by the government in order to avoid threatening competition which would reduce profit margins. Thus, the problem of the choice of institutions arises, which has political implications.

Three levels of analysis may be identified (Eggertson, 1990). The most important distinction between these levels is the distinction between level one and the other two levels. *At the first level*, the emphasis is on outcomes and how they are determined by the institutional structure in combination with the individuals' preferences. Institutions are exogenous in this analysis. Economic outcomes depend on the structure of property rights and the organization of exchange in society in addition to individual preferences. Political outcomes from political bodies, for example, a legislature, depend on the established rules and norms of the legislature as well as the representatives' preferences.

If one is searching for a parallel within politics, studies of decision-making in legislatures and public bureaux would be a candidate. The outcome is the decision: the institution or the political rules in force, together with the interests of politicians and/or bureaucrats determine what decision is made. Another parallel is the 'does politics matter?' literature, where the question is whether public policy is influenced by political party preferences.

*At the second level,* institutions become the focus of the analysis. The structure of the institutions which on the first level influences the pursuit of interests emerges as the outcome of interaction between individuals (or groups) pursuing their interests. At both level two and three the analysis deals with the explanation of the institutional structure, and not the effect of that structure on outcomes. In short, institutions are endogenous.

Here we find the body of the literature on the theory of the firm. Within a given structure of property rights and political rules, different ways of organizing exchange appear (Coase, 1988; Alchian and Demsetz, 1972; Williamson, 1975; Clarke and McGuiness, 1987). The models of economic organization and principal–agent models may be extended to legislatures and public bureaux – that is, to organizations involved in defining, deciding and enforcing the formal rules of society. This approach emphasizes that problems of exchange and control may be as relevant for legislatures and public bureaux as they have proved to be for markets and firms (Moe, 1984; Weingast, 1989).

The analysis on level two is concerned with how actors regulate the mechanisms of transactions between themselves, but without making an attempt to change the basic political and economic rules in society. The analysis of economic organization can be extended to the public sector here as well. It is important to distinguish between institutional changes which are mainly due to decisions made by political bodies with the formal authority to make such decisions on the part of society, and changes that to a lesser extent require or are due to such decisions. That not all institutions are dependent on political decisions is clear when informal constraints like societal norms are considered.

*At the third level,* the system of property rights, the state and public institutions, including the rules for authority, agenda control and decision-making, are to be explained. North (1990b) divides these formal rules into three categories: political rules (authority, agenda control and decision), economic rules (property rights) and individual contracts. The study of political and economic rules takes place on the third level of analysis, where studying economic rules requires a model of the state, the basic political rules in action, as well as the interests involved. The study of political rules, meanwhile, requires an interest group model of politics even though politicians would be the main actors. The study of contracts, on the other hand, takes place on the second level of analysis as the emphasis is on private actors seeking solutions to contractual problems within a fairly constant set of political and economic rules. Examples of the type of institutions focused on include: systems of property rights (Demsetz, 1967; Furubotn and Pejovich, 1972), types of contracts including firm governance (Williamson, 1975, 1986) and the structure and practices of political bodies (Weingast and Marshall, 1988; North, 1990a).

When transaction costs are positive, the costs of reaching an agreement on, for example, the optimal level of pollution/abatement will prevent the achievement of a solution which maximizes joint gain through the frictionless process of reallocating resources described above. The frictionless process rests on a few additional assumptions: property rights fully defined over all valuable margins, information about the relevant cost curves available at no cost to the parties and an absence of income effects. Consequently, outcomes become dependent on the initial allocation of rights.

The validity of the Coase theorem depends crucially on whether the costs due to strategic action are recognized under the heading transaction costs. This concept has an ambiguous content, especially in relation to the frequent usage of the term. Within a defined system of property rights it may be conceived as the costs involved in the transfer of sets of property rights. More generally, it is most often conceived as the costs involved in establishing, monitoring and enforcing a contract. The costs of establishing a contract include the costs of searching for contractual partners, acquiring information and negotiating. The effect of positive transaction costs is to make institutions matter. This conclusion is – it should be emphasized – of general relevance no matter whether one studies actors within the private or public sector.

Williamson (1975, 1986) looks upon the firm in a comparative institutional framework as an institutional arrangement that under certain circumstances is the most transaction cost efficient way of organizing exchange, although the basic question is under what circumstances a firm should organize an exchange, internally or through the market respectively. Governance structures should be assigned to transactions with the aim of reducing the cost of transacting.

Williamson points out two human factors and two environmental factors which combined help to explain the relative higher cost of writing and enforcing contracts in the market compared to internal organization. The human factors are bounded rationality and opportunism whereas the environmental factors include uncertainty and the small numbers problem.

*Bounded rationality* refers to the limited ability of individuals to receive/process information and to communicate it. Individuals are not capable of handling large amounts of information, making it difficult to foresee all contingencies in a complex and changing environment. *Opportunism* refers to self-interest-seeking through deliberate manipulation of information about attributes of the object of exchange as well as own preferences and intentions. *Uncertainty* should perhaps rather be termed 'complexity': the environment is complex and changing. *Small numbers problem* refers to the fact that only a few actors participate in the exchange.

The combination of bounded rationality with uncertainty means that writing contracts that cover all contingencies that may occur over a long period of time is impossible. Any attempt to approach the goal of rational decision-making will tend to be very costly. The market solution to this coordination problem would be an incomplete long-term contract or recurrent short-term contracts.

However, both these alternatives are subject to the problems that may appear when opportunism is paired with the small numbers condition. This last condition ensures that competitive pressures do not eliminate the potential gain of opportunistic action. Incomplete contracts may leave room for behaviour contrary to the intention of the contract when unforeseen contingencies arise. The need for adjustment and amendment of the contract leads to the consideration of short-term contracting. Short-term contracts make the problems of negotiation between bilateral monopolists relevant. Each party has an incentive to realize the gain potential by engaging in exchange, but also to capture the largest possible proportion of this potential.

Even though a small numbers condition does not obtain at the outset, this condition tends to evolve as the contractual partners invest in *transaction-specific capital* and acquire *transaction-specific skills*. This process makes maintenance of the contractual relation all the more important for the parties to the contract, as the consequences of termination become severe. Market contracting becomes risky as the pay-off resulting from hold-up strategies increases.

The relative advantages of relying on internal organization instead of market contracting consist, according to Williamson, of the attenuation of incentives by subgroups in an organization to behave opportunistically, as their behaviour can be monitored more closely and an incentive system designed to further the interests of the organization. In addition, disputes may be more easily settled within an organization than across markets. As to the bounded rationality issue, the advantages include the possibility of a step-by-step approach to the exchange process, and a process of convergent expectations serving to reduce uncertainty.

The theory of the firm inspired the outlining of similar theories concerning legislative bodies (Weingast and Marshall, 1988; North 1990a) and government bureaux (Moe, 1984). The purpose of legislative institutions (political rules) is to facilitate exchanges between the members of the legislature by providing enforcement mechanisms (Weingast and Marshall, 1988). Exchange problems found in legislatures cause transaction costs which are reduced by legislative rules structuring the decision-making process. The organization of, for example, the US Congress has thus evolved to serve the interest of its members. A key point is that non-market forms of exchange may be better suited to this purpose than pure market exchange.

The two key components of this neo-institutional theory are, on the one hand, interests – the goals and preferences of the legislators –

and, on the other, transaction costs. It assumes that legislators represent the interests of their district, especially those of the politically active interest groups. Within Congress, for example, many different interests are represented, but in order to achieve policy decisions by means of majority voting, each legislator must enter into exchange with legislators representing other interests in order to serve the interests he or she represents.

The transaction costs rise in relation to the particular exchange problems faced within such exchange, especially the problem of enforcement. If a legislator agrees to support one bill for which he or she has no particular interest in exchange for support for 'his/her' bill, there may be a temptation to break the agreement in a number of cases. If one bill comes up for a vote before the other, as is usually the case, the last bill may be voted against despite agreements to the contrary. A bill may also be renegotiated if it provides a continuing benefit flow while the other bill provides a one-shot benefit. It may be justified by new public attitudes to the issue, the new nature of the bill if amended, etc. In general, making a contract sufficiently detailed to cover such contingencies and the problem of opportunism are conducive to high transaction costs for the market trading of vote alternatives. It suggests a potential for other institutions to reduce transaction costs and facilitate bargains.

The legislative committee system constitutes such an institution. It has three elements: a decentralization of jurisdiction to committees which have veto rights over changes of the status quo through the control of the agenda, a seniority system to assign legislators to positions in the committees, and a bidding mechanism in the case of vacancy.

Controlling changes regarding the status quo means that the problems of renegotiating a contract are solved. Although there may be a majority for renegotiating, the committee can control the agenda and prevent changes. In effect, a legislator trades influence over a number of policy areas in exchange for disproportionate influence over the policy area of his/her particular concern, thereby also relieving the problem of lack of simultaneity. This is a more efficient way of reducing transaction costs through reducing the possibility of ex post opportunism than the alternative market solution of writing a complex contingent claims contract.

Another body of literature within economic neo-institutionalism is the property rights school originating with Coase. It has been mainly concerned with the effect of property rights on economic outcomes or the emergence of property rights. It involves the study of the effect of common property on the allocation of resources, and uses models where rationality on the societal level is more or less implicitly assumed as well as models focusing on the interests of various actors. Demsetz's (1967) analysis concerns how property rights develop such

that they internalize external effects when the benefits of internalization exceed the costs of internalization, that is, defining and enforcing
rights. A number of factors, among them the value of the resource to
which the rights would be attached, influence the cost-benefit ratio.
This model assumes efficient economic rules (property rights).

On the other hand, North (1981) presents an interest group model
of property rights in which property rights develop in accordance with
the interests and cost-benefit analysis of groups with strong bargaining
power. This type of analysis is also very close to political science as it
requires modelling of the political process and the political rules in
society.

*Institutional teleology*

If the raison d'être for institutions is said to be to economize on transaction costs (Demsetz, 1967), then rationality enters either through a
rational choice of institutions or by means of the invisible hand of
competition. The rational or effective solution may be reached through
one of two paths: (a) design or (b) selection. If institutional change is
rational, then the latter mechanism could provide an optimal result for
the whole of society, even if individual action was motivated by self-
interest.

North describes three main problems with the efficiency interpretation of the origin of institutions. First, no neat supply function of new
institutional arrangements can be taken for granted: how can one identify the menu of organizational forms that a society devises in
response to changing relative prices? Secondly, the bargaining
problem involves high transaction costs which may prevent the parties
from reaching an institutional agreement to the benefit of the affected
parties. Thirdly, the problem of inertia (Matthews, 1986: 913–15)
arises, as complex institutions serving several purposes may prove
difficult to change.

Institutions may be efficient in the sense that they serve well the
interests of those who have created them. But whether these institutions produce policy outcomes that are the most beneficial for society
at large depends on the relationship between the legislature and
society. North (1981) shows that a ruler in an effort to further his/her
interests may devise property right systems that are inefficient for
society as a whole due to survival considerations and agency and
measurement costs constraints. A choice of institution taken without
the participation (or perfect representation by agents) of all affected
parties may result in external effects, making for a difference between
'participant efficiency' and 'global efficiency'.

The natural selection argument when applied to public sector institutions and the fundamental economic rules is hampered by the fact that
there is no autopilot steering the development of such institutions

along the right path. Changes in such rules are made by decisions and not by aggregate changes in a population of institutions. Institutional decisions depend on the perceptions and interests of the affected parties and their relative bargaining strength. The visible hand may be influenced by competitive pressures but it is certainly not as efficient in 'eliminating inefficiency as the invisible hand of competition is claimed to be.

If efficiency will not come about by the rationality of a selection process, then rationality by design remains the only option. The rational choice of institutions is the choice which 'the collectivity believes, on average, will generate the least ex post regret', according to Shepsle (1989: 139n). In this case, the efficient set of institutions would be the intended result of a collective choice process, a so-called 'equilibrium institution'.

One finding in the social choice literature is that outcomes of voting procedures cannot be predicted only on the basis of knowledge of voters' preferences. 'An outcome X was said to be an equilibrium if there existed no Y preferred to it by a decisive coalition of agents (normally a simple majority of the set of agents)' (Shepsle, 1989: 136). In voting processes, such equilibria generally do not exist when a collective choice is to be made between three or more alternatives and there is no core solution. Every alternative X can be beaten by an alternative Y which is preferred to X by a decisive coalition of voters. In fact, not only can every alternative be beaten, but any alternative can also be chosen depending on the point at which the decision process is stopped (Kelly, 1986).

The actual voting process does not reveal the flux predicted by formal theory, which has led to the rediscovery of institutions (Riker, 1980; Shepsle, 1989). Within a given set of institutions, formal or informal rules, equilibria generally do exist. In fact there are often several equilibria (Shepsle, 1986). Rules may restrict the agenda, the issues voted upon, the dimensions of an issue voted upon together or separately, the alternatives allowed to enter the voting process and in which sequence, etc.

However, those who find that the policy outcomes provide constraints unfavourable to them due to a particular configuration of institutions may seek to change these institutions. They have institutional interests which are derived from their policy interests. We enter an infinite regress where no choice of institutions can be unconstrained, leading to a lack of stable outcomes of the collective choice process. Following this line of thought, a rational choice of efficient institutions is impossible. The whole notion of 'equilibrium institution' as the outcome of a rational selection among alternative sets of rules involves pieces of social teleology, or the idea that somehow society arrives at the best solution despite all kinds of opportunistic behaviour.

Vanberg and Buchanan (1989) separate the concept of 'constitutional preferences' or institutional interests into two components: constitutional theories (cognitive) and constitutional interests (evaluative). An individual's constitutional theories are his/her conceptions about what will be the actual outcomes of alternative rules. Constitutional interests on the other hand are the valuations of the various outcomes. Since theories are to some degree uncertain, individuals are placed behind a 'veil of uncertainty' (Vanberg and Buchanan, 1989: 54). The greater the homogeneity of interests, the greater the likelihood of an equilibrium solution.

In general, even if an equilibrium is reached there is no guarantee that it will be efficient or rational or optimal. The inability to reach accurate constitutional theories may in fact be useful in overcoming the bargaining problem by giving priority to efficiency concerns in the formation of institutions. The other side of the coin when efficiency is concerned is, however, that the lack of information makes it more difficult to know what institutions are efficient for society. Institutional efficiency can be guaranteed neither through a rational choice process nor through a process of natural selection.

## THE PRINCIPAL–AGENT MODEL

Whenever human interaction involves considerable transaction costs due to the intertemporal nature of the interaction as well as the complexity of the agreement involved, principal–agent problems arise (Stiglitz, 1987). The principal–agent relationship is constitutive of state institutions, in particular public policy-making in democracy. Public policy or the making and implementation of policies in the public sector involves the problems typical of principal–agent relationships within the private sector. In the policy process and the implementation stages there is the typical attempt of the population as the principal to *monitor* the efforts of politicians and bureaux as the agents to live up to the terms of the contract agreed upon.

The principal–agent problem of designing a *compensation system* or contract that motivates the agent to act in the interests of the principal as well as to monitor the observation of the agreement is not confined to private sector credit and insurance institutions. The principal–agent model, where the outcome of the activities of the agent depends on the effort of the agent and an unobservable random variable, allows us to analyse a number of policy problems within an integrated framework, such as institutional choice, for example.

There are two types of transaction costs involved in social interaction. First, there are the information costs that arise in acquiring knowledge about the prerequisites for collective action. Each participant would want to know not only the preferences of the other participants but also the technology to be used in the collective undertaking.

Secondly, there are the motivation costs that stem from coordinating two or more participants in a collective action. The resort to a principal–agent model in a democratic state is a method for dealing with the transaction costs that arise in collective action.

Public activities by means of the state result in a double principal–agent relationship in a democracy. On the one hand there is the relationship between the population as the principal and its agents in their capacity of rulers of the population. On the other hand the rulers may wish to employ a staff to be active in the implementation of the wishes of the rulers, which entails that the latter become the principal of the former. This double principal–agent relationship between the electorate, government and administration is more relevant than the distinction between politics and administration.

The principal–agent structure of the state is characterized by ambiguity, opportunistic behaviour, moral hazard and adverse selection. The fact that democratic state institutions rest upon a principal–agent structure in no way prohibits the agent from reversing the relationship and regarding itself as the principal. No benevolent assumptions have to be made about the conduct of state activities. The possibility of reversing the principal–agent structure of the state, having the population serve the interests of the state, makes it all the more urgent that institutional mechanisms be found that limit the range of opportunistic behaviour as well as the dangers of moral hazard and adverse selection. However, there are transaction costs involved in restricting the degrees of freedom of the agent.

Strictly speaking, the referendum model involves the smallest possible margin for the agent to act on behalf of the principal. The population would decide each issue by means of a majority vote to be implemented by those occupying state authority positions. This assumes that the activities of the agent are completely observable by the population and that each issue can be decided and implemented on its own terms. The transactions costs involved in monitoring the actions of the agent on such a close basis would be staggering.

If every policy were to be clearly separable to be voted completely on its own merits, then the fiscal illusion expansion of the public sector could be halted. However, this would require a control over the agenda that would prohibit Arrowian cycles and preference manipulation (Moulin, 1983; Nurmi, 1987). As long as the agenda comprises more than two alternatives and as long as majority rule is employed within a group of more than two people, there are bound to arise mismatches between the preferences of the individual in the population and those declared as the winning alternative by the agent on the basis of the referendum. How can the electorate in a liberal democracy constrain its public agents – politicians and civil servants – to act according to the contract agreed upon in various settings: in the constitution, on the election day or in the employment relation?

Making the agent in the political body the automatic implementor of the wishes of the population is not a practical solution to the problem of having the agent serve the principal in the public sector. Typical of the democracies of the world today is the distance between the electing body and the elected. This gives rise to all the kinds of principal-agent problems that are encountered in the analysis of the private sector (Ross, 1973; Mueller, 1986; Williamson, 1986; Ricketts, 1987). How would the population as the principal interact with the set of political parties and politicians as their agents given that there is uncertainty about what action the principal wishes the agent to take as well as the fact that the action of the agent cannot be perfectly or costlessly monitored?

The standard public choice models of the interaction between voters and politicians as well as between politicians and public bureaux deal with the basic principal-agent problem of how one group of people are to monitor the activities of another group in a contractual relationship characterized by fundamental fuzziness arising from limited observability, bounded rationality, asymmetrical information and strategic moves (Mueller, 1989). How is the political contract between the electorate, the politicians and the civil servants to be handled given the transactions costs within the public sector of deciding and implementing public policies?

Within any institutional setting there are bound to be serious problems of ambiguity about the rewards to be given to the agent, about the desired actions to be taken by the agent, about the causal link between actions and outcomes, as well as about the actual state of the environment of public policy. Here we will discuss two models that derive their sense from a principal-agent framework, although other models could be interpreted in the same way, such as for instance, the Hotelling-Downs model (Enelow and Hinich, 1984) or the Breton model of the logic of demand for and supply of government policies (Breton, 1974).

*Asymmetrical information, moral hazard* and *adverse selection* characterize the relationships between the electorate and their agents. Ambiguity will arise as to whether the actions taken by the agent under the circumstances were the correct or desired ones as well as about whether the outcomes are deemed sufficiently acceptable by the principal to call forth the rewards demanded by the agent. The politicians may pledge that the actions desired by the principal were not realistic in the new context or that the outcomes were determined by the situation. The politicians could claim that the differences between the desired outcomes and the actual outcomes is confined within the election contract, due to moral hazard. Opportunism in the interpretation of the ambiguous terms of the political contract may be an attractive strategy. The Brennan and Buchanan (1980) model of the revenue-maximization Leviathan deals with the principal-agent relation between the electorate and the policy-makers.

Policy-making in a democracy not only involves deciding on a programme structure as well as the ends and means of a programme. It also comprises the implementation stage, the activities of public servants as administrators or professionals. The implementation of policies gives rise to the typical double principal–agent problem within the public sector referred to by the troublesome conceptual pair: politics versus administration. In addition to the electoral cycle of picking the politicians and choosing an agenda, civil servants have to be hired by government to execute policy decisions.

The implementation stage requires a set of activities monitored by the state in order to accomplish political objectives. Contracts have to be made between the state and civil servants stipulating what the state expects in return for remuneration. Due to the transactions costs involved in hiring and monitoring public officials, the state typically employs the bureau model for handling various state activities. Basic to the operation of the bureau is a principal–agent relationship between politicians on the one hand and civil servants on the other hand.

The Niskanen theory of the budget-maximizing bureau is one way to model a principal–agent relationship. It emphasizes the asymmetrical information involved in the interaction between politicians and the bureaux. Niskanen's conclusion that the bureau as the agent will always be in a strategically advantageous position in relation to its principal the government has received much attention, but it is far from the only model that approaches bureaucracy as a principal–agent relationship (see Chapter 2).

In a democracy the interests of the citizens have the same status as the principle of consumer sovereignty in a decentralized economy. However, the principle of citizen sovereignty has to be accommodated to the principal–agent problems involved in governing a state. Due to the transaction costs involved in collective action a voluntary exchange approach to the provision of public goods fails. The state offers taxation as the solution to the free-rider problem in collective action. At the same time the necessity of employing an involuntary exchange mechanism for managing human interaction creates the two principal–agent problems in political life. The *first* one refers to the monitoring of the politicians by the citizens whereas the *second* one deals with how the politicians are to monitor the civil servants implementing the public policies.

## CONCLUSION

Institutions may be interpreted as the humanly devised constraints on social interaction. There is a basic choice between pursuing one's interests within an established framework or making an effort to change this framework. When these courses of action may be regarded as alternative means of serving one's interests, egoistic or altruistic, then the determinants of institutions may be analysed in the same analytic framework as rational actions within a given institutional structure. This way of considering the relationship between institutions and interests gives interests precedence over institutions which is exactly opposite to the position maintained in the sociological version of neo-institutionalism.

Common sense takes a casual position in relation to two of the fundamental components of a social system, namely its rules or norms and the interests that motivate the people in that system. It notes that both the science of politics and that of economics analyse how interests of various kinds populate different kinds of institutions, affecting the collective outcomes of the interaction within the system. Public institutions seem to harbour many group interests of various kinds besides self-interests such as personal desires and needs. Private institutions may have their foundation in economic-being motives, but there seems to be scope left for broad group interests.

This starting point appears to be reasonable, but it is rejected by two important methodologies in political science, the public interest dogma on the one hand and the holism of the new institutionalism. This argument amounts to a defence of common sense, because the balance between institutions and interests, rules and preferences, procedures and needs, is constant in political life. If the institutions are absent, then individuals and groups cannot interact, coordinating their effort or fighting out their conflicts. If interests are done away with, then why would persons ever orient peacefully or contentiously towards each other?

It is always possible to raise the question about the public institutions of society: *cui bono*? Institutions may be alternated so that interests are aggregated in a more adequate way which presupposes that institutions do not come before interests. If this rational approach to institutional choice were an illusion, then why are we so anxious about evaluating public and private institutions according to political and economic criteria? Let us look at the logic of public sector evaluation.

Neo-institutionalism in the economic approach implies that institutional choice is very important in public policy-making. What kind of criteria should government employ when reforming or introducing institutions: efficiency norms or ethical principles about social justice? More specifically, what would such criteria imply?

# 9

# EFFICIENCY, EFFECTIVENESS AND EVALUATION

The rapid expansion of the public sector in the 1960s and 1970s implied a basic change in the relationship between the public and the private. The strong process of increasing the tax state – publicization as it were – meant that citizens in the welfare state became more reliant on public policy than ever before. Big government means that a considerable portion of the resources of society is mobilized by the national or local governments and allocated by these bodies to various programmes, thus reducing the scope for markets.

The problem of the ownership of the means of production is no longer salient – 'capitalism' versus 'socialism' – and neither are the pros and cons of a planned economy contra a market economy. However, the overriding problem remains of how to strike a balance between the public sector and the private sector in the sense of public policy-making contra market allocation and voluntary exchange mechanisms (Dooley et al., 1979). Basically, this is a normative problem concerning the scope for the two fundamental modes for arriving at collective choices.

What kinds of criteria are we to employ to decide what types of goods and services are to be allocated by means of the budget and through markets? What is an appropriate size for the government redistribution branch? And are there possibilities for mixing public and private modes of interaction?

Two kinds of deliberations are involved here: standards for evaluating public sector programmes as well as normative criteria that identify good or just public policy. Here we shall discuss evaluation, in particular effectiveness and efficiency, whereas Chapter 10 discusses the explicitly normative approach to policy-making, examining two justice models.

The status of evaluation criteria has never been such an issue of contention as the problem of normative criteria of policy-making, although there is perhaps not such a profound epistemological difference between the two. The policy sciences (Lerner and Lasswell, 1951) have always had a practical orientation, looking for ways to improve public management (Metcalfe and Richards, 1987). Values and policy are inextricably intertwined, be it instrumental values such as effectiveness and efficiency or ultimate values such as justice and equity (Paul and Russo, 1982). Here, we face the fundamental problem of introducing clear concepts about efficiency that may be employed in the study of public policies.

Actually, the conception of policy analysis as a discipline in itself implies not only a theoretical ambition to understand how policies operate in the public sector, but also the practical skills for suggesting intelligent proposals for reform and improvement, as stated in the policy movement (Nagel and Neef, 1979; Meltsner and Bellavita, 1983).

As emphasized by Aaron Wildavsky in *Speaking Truth to Power* (1979), policy analysis is certainly not an applied social science discipline serving the ends of public institutions. The importance of scientific understanding and analysis of the *is* of the public sector cannot be over-emphasized. But there are also questions of the *ought* of public programmes that policy analysis wishes to address, one of which concerns how to evaluate the actual performance of public programmes according to efficiency criteria.

## DEFINITIONS

Whatever model of policy-making and policy implementation one adopts the question of public sector efficiency is bound to come up. In the various models of bureaux and bureaucracy behaviour there is a contention between hypotheses about the performance of bureaux that must be decided by means of empirical research. Some definitions take a prejudged approach to the problem of policy or bureau performance, stating from the outset that policy-making is rationality or that bureaucracy is rigidity.

A public policy programme in one or a couple of bureaux is simply a set of people – a part of government – that may or may not operate efficiently. Whatever approach one adheres to with regard to decision-making, implementation or management, the problem of policy or bureau performance is an open one, meaning that we need empirical performance evidence in relation to policies or bureaux.

Thus, even if we manage to pin-point the various characteristics stated as typical of bureaucracy – impersonality, hierarchy, legitimate authority, size maximization, uncontrol, rigidity – we still must have evidence of inefficiency before we draw the conclusion that bureaux are wasteful. The same applies to the variety of public policy models and implementation models. How do we conceptualize efficiency more precisely in the public sector?

Although there exist several definitions of organizational efficiency in the literature we use the oft-quoted Etzioni concepts of organizational efficiency and organizational effectiveness. In his *Modern Organizations* Amitai Etzioni states: '(1) The actual effectiveness of a specific organization is determined by the degree to which it realizes its goals. (2) The efficiency of an organization is measured by the amount of resources used to produce one unit of output' (1964: 6).

Table 9.1  *Effectiveness and productivity*

**Effectiveness**

|  |  | Goal accomplishment | Goal failure |
|---|---|---|---|
| **Productivity** | Cost minimization | I | II |
|  | Waste | III | IV |

The argument is that there is a basic distinction here: on the one hand, productivity is the 'amount of resources used to produce a unit of output', and on the other, effectiveness is the 'degree to which an organization realizes its goals' (Etzioni, 1964: 8). The distinction between productivity and effectiveness or goal attainment allows for the possibility that bureaux may score well on one dimension but poorly on the other. Often 'efficiency' is employed when evaluating performance, but it is an ambiguous word meaning either productivity or effectiveness. This can be illustrated in a 2×2 table (Table 9.1).

Categories II and III deserve some further comment. Category II may appear to be a contradiction: how could public institutions be efficient and at the same time produce outputs that have no relation to their ends or that may even be counterproductive in terms of their purposes? Category III appears almost as peculiar: how can public institutions be effective and at the same time be wasteful in terms of the employment of their resources?

One may ask whether the Etzioni distinction really helps very much. Would we not regard a bureau that operates meaningless activities in an efficient manner as wasteful? Would we not deny the rationale of a bureau that though achieving its tasks does not allocate its resources in an optimal way? The Etzioni distinction, however, clearly demonstrates that we must not only focus narrowly on cost minimization but also pay attention to the desired output or outcome, the standard as it were.

Overall efficiency in policy-making and bureaux cannot be a function of goal attainment solely, or only be interpreted in terms of cost minimization. Both elements must enter the efficiency equation, as Roland McKean states in his *Efficiency in Government through Systems Analysis*:

> The consequences of an action fall into two types: (1) those positive gains which we like to increase, or the achievement of objectives, and (2) those negative effects which we like to decrease, or the incurrence of costs. Neither type by itself can serve as an adequate criterion: the maximization of gains without regard to cost or resource limitation is hardly a helpful

test, and the minimization of cost regardless of other consequences of the alternative actions is nonsense. (1958: 34)

If we conclude that overall efficiency in the public sector must include both Etzioni aspects, then we may suggest that efficiency is to maximize gains minus costs, or effectiveness considering efficiency. However, the criterion maximize gain/costs requires that gains and costs can be compared in terms of some common standard, which is doubtful in relation to bureau outputs.

Certainly, some goals are more important than others, meaning that costs may be easier to accept in some activities than in others. Efficiency in the public sector is a function of both the provision of goods and services in relation to objectives and the allocation of resources, meaning productivity, as argued in *The Search for Government Efficiency* (Downs and Larkey, 1986).

## MEASUREMENT ASPECTS

Efficiency in the sense of productivity is measured by means of longitudinal data covering output and cost measures for a decade or two. Efficiency is a matter of comparisons over time. Effectiveness, on the other hand, may be approached in a direct way, by asking whether a programme currently reaches its goals. The measurement problems in relation to productivity and effectiveness may be approached by means of a series of performance equations.

First, there are the two equations for estimating productivity: performance output/resource input as well as resource input/input costs, which lead to the basic efficiency measure in the public sector: output of services/input costs. Secondly, we have the basics of the effectiveness measure: outcomes/outputs as well as value of outcomes/outcomes, which we use to find the essential effectiveness equation, namely value of outcomes/outputs of services. Combining the two equations we arrive at the following benefit/cost definition of overall efficiency: value of outcomes/resource costs.

Whereas the problems of measuring productivity development over time slices are well-known by now, the measurement of effectiveness also remains problematic in the public sector. Here, we focus primarily on efficiency measurement. To compare the way resources are allocated in order to reach a level of provision we must hold quality constant in some way. Only if the output has equal quality may we compare efficiency in the employment of resources.

Given a certain level of service quality we can establish inefficiency in two ways: social efficiency versus bureau efficiency. In order to provide its citizens with a certain amount of goods and services at a certain quality level society may use one of its basic allocation mechanisms: market or bureau. Speaking of efficiency, we must separate the question of which of these two forms of allocation

Table 9.2   *X-inefficiency and social efficiency*

|  | Social efficiency | Social inefficiency |
|---|---|---|
| Bureau efficiency | I | II |
| Bureau inefficiency | III | IV |

mechanism is the most efficient – social efficiency – from the question as to how bureaux or policy programmes are most efficiently to organize their activities.

It is clearly conceivable that there may be bureau or programme efficiency in the Leibenstein sense of X-efficiency (no slack or fat) but still social inefficiency, if voluntary exchange mechanisms were more efficient. This can be represented in a 2 × 2 table (Table 9.2).

In order to judge whether or not there is inefficiency with regard to a bureau it is not enough to focus only on the bureau itself. First, we must ask whether the market or some type of quasi-market mechanisms could provide the goods or services more efficiently than the bureau. It may be very difficult to decide whether market or bureaucracy is superior in relation to certain goods and services. This seems to require some theory of the nature of goods and services and their relation to the two basic types of decision mechanisms, market versus bureaucracy or public policy.

To judge whether there is bureau efficiency may also be troublesome. Cost differences between bureaux may be the result of differences in the quality or quantity of goods and services supplied. If we hold bureau output constant we may state how much waste there is. The problem then becomes one of identifying the extent to which the bureau could lower its costs while maintaining the same service level. This is not to deny that the efficiency judgement may focus on the oversupply of bureau output, but it is another problem which is more difficult to solve empirically as the demand for bureau goods and services is not easily measured.

Effectiveness and productivity in public resource allocation do not just present difficult theoretical problems. The measurement aspects are as important as they are problematic to handle. Richard Murray (1987) has shown how the basic problems involved in measuring public sector efficiency or productivity can be tackled both theoretically and empirically.

There have been a number of studies of public sector effectiveness and efficiency (Borcherding et al., 1982; Mueller, 1989). The findings in the efficiency and effectiveness analyses are not always easy to interpret, particularly not the study of goal attainment or effectiveness. One may distinguish between different kinds of analyses: (1) studies of productivity development for different programmes in various parts of the public sector over time; (2) comparisons of productivity in the same services that have both private and public principals; (3) studies of effectiveness in different public programmes; (4) comparisons of effectiveness in similar programmes that have either a private or a public principal. When it is possible to make well-judged productivity comparisons between public and private programmes for 'similar' goods and services, then the overall conclusion from a number of studies in various countries appears to be that private provision is more efficient than public provision, all other things being equal.

However, the general findings to the effect that private provision tends to be more efficient and also more effective do not warrant the conclusion that the privatization option is the single relevant alternative in public sector reform. What gives private provision an advantage over public provision is not the ownership factor, but the existence of competition in allocation. Thus, if more competitive mechanisms could be introduced into the public sector, then productivity and efficiency would be enhanced without abolishing the public principal. Let us illustrate this with, on the one hand, systematic cost comparisons between similar units in the public sector and, on the other hand, the employment of the administrative size principle.

## RELATIVE COST COMPARISONS

The identification of bureau inefficiency is a difficult task as it calls for rather precise empirical measurements. It is necessary to make a number of decisions as to the type of activity behaviour involved as well as to the nature of the bureau output in question. It seems promising to make an initial distinction between administrative bureau behaviour and service bureau behaviour. This is an analytic distinction as we may expect to find both types of behaviour in most large public bureaux, boards or authorities.

A second distinction concerns the separation between a cross-sectional approach and a longitudinal one. Suppose we have a number of public administration units – central agencies, regional or local government entities, local state units; we may inquire into the relative efficiency of these bureaux either by taking a longitudinal approach or by resorting to cross-sectional comparison.

The efficiency judgement along one dimension is not the same as that along the other dimension. A bureau may be more efficient than another; yet, it may not perform as efficiently as it used to do, or vice versa. There may be two different types of inefficiency: administrative inefficiency and service inefficiency.

The public sector is typically divided up into various sectors of activity on the basis of a more or less hierarchical structure. The lower units in the structure are oriented towards the provision of goods and services whereas the higher entities or agencies are more concerned with administrative work, preparing budgetary requests, policy proposals and deciding on matters of principle relating to the implementation of laws. There is also administrative work within the lower entities dealing with personnel administration and overall fiscal management of the unit.

It is possible to isolate these administrative functions and analyse them separately from the service functions in order to study administrative efficiency. The analysis of administrative efficiency may focus on the longitudinal development of the administrative function in relation to the service function in order to find out whether the administrative function at various levels expands more rapidly than the service function – a process that could be called 'bureaucratization' (Meyer, 1985).

Alternatively, the analysis of administrative efficiency may examine cross-sectional variation in the size of the administrative function in order to find out whether, for example, all local governments employ the same amount of administrative resources for the provision of their services; or we may wish to look at differences in the size of the central agencies between various sectors of activity.

The cross-sectional analysis of administrative efficiency is highly suitable for testing the hypothesis about administrative economies of scale. The economies of scale hypothesis means that the administrative component in various local governments – to be separated from the service functions – will vary as a function of overall size, or that the size of the administrative overhead will fall relatively speaking as the size of the organization increases (Blau, 1973).

Service inefficiency is of a different kind. It may also be studied by means of cross-sectional or longitudinal analyses, but it is essential to bear in mind the importance of the concept of service level. The public provision of goods and services in terms of bureau operations may display large variation measured by some cost index – the 'same' programme varying in cost quite substantially between various local state units, regional or local governments; however, we cannot simply attribute the cost variation to service inefficiency as it may be a function of variations in the quality or quantity of the goods or services provided. Only by holding the level of service constant may we explain a cost variation by means of inefficiency.

Thus, the service inefficiency hypothesis requires elaborate analysis of the provision of public goods and services in order to distinguish inefficiency from costs that derive from the choice of higher service levels or costs that are incurred as a function of environmental exigencies. The study of service inefficiency links up with the analysis of public policy variations at central, regional and local levels of government (Sharpe and Newton, 1984). To what extent is there X-inefficiency in bureau operations? The concept of X-efficiency emphasizes that it is important to take a broad overview of the factors that have an impact on bureau outputs, whether in service production or in administrative functions (Leibenstein, 1966).

It is often stated that government activities can only be measured in terms of costs. The value of the goods and services produced does not show up in the national accounts, simply because the demand for these goods and services is not revealed in standard prices. The willingness to pay shows up in the election process, which does not indicate the marginal value of various goods and services very adequately. So-called Lindahl prices are the taxes various groups are willing to pay for bundles of goods and services. Thus, marginal value for each good and service is not adequately revealed in budget-making.

Yet government provision does not only entail costs. Big government is not first and foremost administration of public goods, but the production of a number of divisible goods and services. Public management has to ensure that the production is effective and efficient. How effectiveness and efficiency are to be handled in the public sector is the basic task for public management and is still a matter of dispute. Effectiveness and efficiency apply to both administration and service provision. How is a mechanism to be installed in the public sector that promotes effectiveness and efficiency in administration and service production? Whereas the combination of prices and the profit motive is conducive to effectiveness and efficiency in the private sector, no such mechanism has yet been devised in public management. Therein lies the problem of a large sector for publicly provided goods and services.

Private sector efficiency is accomplished not primarily because organizations are private and not because they function in markets where prices are employed. The advantage of the market over the public sector and budget-making stems from the strong institutionalization of competition. But competition is not necessarily tied to the private sector or market allocation. Competition follows from comparison and organizations may be compared within the public sector as well. Public management should be based on systems of relative cost comparisons.

A system of relative cost comparison may form the basis for systematic and continuous evaluations of the costs and performance records of public organizations. The new idea is that similar organizations should be compared by means of standardized indicators and that the outcome of the evaluation should be tied to the budgetary process, punishing the high spenders and low performers as well as rewarding the high performers and low spenders. Such relative cost comparisons of organizations with a similar output – universities and colleges, county councils, local governments, regional state authorities – may cover efficiency in both the basic functions of public organizations: administration and service production.

Thus, decentralization may be combined with three-year budgetary frames and performance scanning. Yet, as important as these new developments is the stress on outputs and outcomes instead of inputs; as long as this ex post perspective is not tied to systematic cost and performance comparisons something crucial will be missing.

## THE SIZE HYPOTHESIS

The size hypothesis is a seminal idea in organizational analysis. It predicts that the relative size of an organization's administrative component will decline as a function of the overall size of the unit. It has profound implications for the analysis of administrative effectiveness and efficiency in the public sector.

The size hypothesis is an example of a theory that relates the structure of organizations to their context. According to the so-called contingency theory, structural properties describe salient characteristics of institutions, and contextual variables may, to a considerable extent, explain such properties.

The findings of the Aston Programme for Organizational Analysis support such an approach: 'The structure of an organization is closely related to the context within which it functions, and much of the variation in organization structures might be explained by contextual factors' (Pugh et al., 1969: 91).

Relative size of an organization's administration is a structural property of an organization, and overall size is one basic contextual characteristic (Hall, 1974). Size of an organization is related to several structural properties such as functional specialization, role specialization, standardization and formalization (Pugh et al., 1963; Pugh and Hickson, 1976). It should be pointed out that size has many dimensions which may have quite dissimilar relationships with structural properties (Kimberly, 1976; Astley, 1985). Furthermore, size is a conspicuous property in public sector organizations.

From a theoretical point of view, the size hypothesis states that organizations should display administrative economies of scale. The size hypothesis may be derived from general theoretical generalizations about organizational structure and organizational context. According to the theory of organizational differentiation: 'Increasing size generates structural differentiation in organizations, along various dimensions at decelerating rates' (Blau, 1974: 302).

This implies both that the proportionate size of the average structural component decreases with increases in organizational size, and that the larger the organization the wider the supervisory span of control (Blau, 1974: 305–9). Since the administrative component of an organization constitutes a structural component the implication is that 'large-scale operations reduce the proportionate size of the administrative overhead, specifically of the complement of managers and supervisors' (Blau, 1974: 311).

Increasing organization size is conducive to structural differentiation at a decelerating rate because increasing size also creates a need for more coordination and communication among differentiated structures. Thus, there is the opposing force that 'Structural differentiation in organizations enlarges the administrative component' (Blau, 1974: 314).

Size, then, has two effects on the administrative component of an organization, the direct one decreasing the relative size of the administration and the indirect one increasing the administration. In the size hypothesis, it is assumed that the direct effect will at first be larger than the indirect one but that structural complexity increasing the administrative component will outweigh the administrative economy of scale effect later on as organization size gets bigger and bigger. Thus: 'The rate of savings in management overhead with increasing size is higher among comparatively small than among competitively large organizational units, although, or perhaps because, the management overhead is bigger in small than in large organizational units' (Blau, 1974: 319).

Conceptually, the size hypothesis raises some crucial problems in methods of conceptualizing and measuring administrative efficiency by means of distinctions between various kinds of staff in organizations. The distinction between administrative and non-administrative functions or operational functions is well-entrenched in administrative theory (Hood and Dunsire, 1981). Yet, it is not easy to apply to various types of organizations.

Sometimes a distinction between administrators and production- or service-oriented personnel appears straightforward. It may show up in official documents where a budgetary item singles out administration as a specific function. In other cases it might be far more difficult to decide what is to count as administration and what belongs to operational activities. The administrative component may include general management, supervisory staff, personnel administration, planning or supportive staff in general.

In their analysis of employment security agencies, Blau and Schoenherr (1971) employed three measures of administrative ratios. They differentiated between a managerial ratio (percentage of supervisory personnel), a staff ratio (percentage of total personnel time devoted to staff and technical activities) and a clerical ratio (percentage of personnel with low skills). According to Blau and Schoenherr only the first two measures capture the administrative component of an organization. One may also argue in favour of a broader concept of the administrative component as they suggest that all kinds of supportive personnel should be included (Hall, 1974: 124–8).

However, in studies of the size hypothesis a narrower specification of the concept of administration is the usual approach. Looking at hospitals, Anderson and Warkov (1961) identified the administrative component as the personnel employed in general hospital administration. Testing the size hypothesis in the American higher education system Blau (1973) distinguished between the ratio of administrators to faculty and the clerical–faculty ratio.

The higher up in the administrative hierarchy a bureau is, the less illuminating becomes the distinction between administrators and production personnel. Central government bureaux are typically involved in general administrative tasks which implies that it is of little relevance to measure the size of their administrative component. This is not to deny the usefulness of the distinction between the administrative component of an organization and its non-administrative components, but it is a warning against the assumption that the administrative component of an organization can be easily identified and measured. In order to employ the size hypothesis it is necessary to specify what is to count as administration and service production for each kind of organization studied.

Empirically, the status of the size hypothesis is undecided. In his overview of theories of organizational growth and development, William Starbuck (1965) states that the empirical evidence is inconclusive about how increasing organizational size relates to the size of the administrative component of an organization. However, reviewing the literature, Hall argues that the evidence on the whole supports the size hypothesis:

> The extensive studies of the size of the administrative component in organizations relative to their overall size yield the conclusion that there is a tendency toward a curvilinear relationship, in that the administrative component tends to decrease in size as organizational size increases, but in very large organizations, the relative size of the administrative component again increases – although not up to the level that it assumes in small organizations. (1974: 138)

What is important to underline here is the fact that a systematic employment of the size principle could be used to enhance administrative efficiency within both national government entities and local government entities. Organizations that provide similar services could be compared on the basis of the relative size of their administrative component in order to find out whether there are administrative scale economies. If not, then perhaps mechanisms could be devised to ensure that, for example, universities of different sizes or small and large local governments do capture the possible economy of scale in administration. This raises the issue of whether effectiveness- or efficiency-promoting mechanisms can be implemented at all in the public sector due to institutional obstacles. The asymmetry theory claims that these hindrances are powerful resistances to change.

## INSTITUTIONAL OBSTACLES

The asymmetry theory states that the forces that have an interest in and promote public sector expansion are stronger than the forces that have an interest in and wish to strengthen the private sector. The fundamental asymmetry operates at three levels of the public sector: decision-making, production and financing. The decision asymmetry refers to the lack of a balance between collective decisions that are valid for the whole population and the benefits from collective action that are private in the sense that they are better for some special interest groups than for the general interests of citizens (Kristensen, 1987a).

The production asymmetry occurs in public resource allocation proper due to the absence of efficiency criteria guiding the interaction between the interests of various producer groups like bureaucrats or professionals, on the one hand, and consumer groups, on the other, looking in vain for clear measures of effectiveness or productivity.

Finally, the financial asymmetry refers to the gulf between the consumption of goods and services in the public sector and the actual payment for this consumption. Whereas consumption of particular goods and services is mostly free of virtually any charges the overall level of supply of the public sector is paid for by means of general taxes and charges. This fosters the asymmetry between those who benefit from the public sector and those who produce its goods and services. Is there really such a profound asymmetry bias in the institutional web of the public sector?

The public sector is basically a collective household mobilizing resources and transforming these into an output of goods, services and money. The basic mechanism for operating the system is the budget, a national one supplemented by regional or local government budgets. These public budgets are collective for a group of people living within a geographical area. The distinctive properties of the budget mechanism for allocating resources and redistributing money marks the public sector off from market mechanism allocation. Public budgets have a supply side as well as a demand side. According to the argument above the interaction between supply and demand in public budget-making is basically asymmetric in favour of the supply side. The budget is too large in the sense of quality supplied, but it is also too expensive in the sense of efficiency.

When making decisions about budget allocation and budget redistribution narrow interests in the supply of various budgetary programmes that benefit some at the expense of others have an edge over the interests of broad citizens' groups in the supply of goods and services that benefit all. The dividends from several budget items are vital to special interest groups whereas general interests tend to be diffuse and hardly motivate people to presume as they will not benefit differentially.

When producing goods and services in the public sector the budget only recognizes the costs as there exists no procedure by which demand could be effectively identified. Who could tell where the marginal value of a quantity or quality of a budgetary item equals its marginal cost? This means that producers may always claim that enough is not enough and that more resources will have a great impact in terms of effectiveness, with the result that requests will always chase appropriations whatever the level of budgetary expenditures. Since the goods and services produced in the public sector are often imponderables – who would not want better health care when ill, who would deny the cultural value of academic institutions and who would deny that more redistribution towards the poor, the sick or the needy is not of marginal value? – there is no natural way to evaluate costs in the public sector.

Paying for the consumption of budgetary programmes is based on the formula that the total budget must somehow cover its costs whatever financial instrument is used. Since every programme costs very little in terms of its percentage of the total there will be an excess demand for each budgetary item. However, as the overall cost for the total budget is shared by so many, there is little incentive for everyone to combat general increases in overall finances. The incentive to look for the supply of special goods, services and money is stronger than the general interest in holding down the overall budget.

According to the asymmetry theory the modern state rests upon a fundamental confusion of the two basic functions of budgeting: *resource allocation* and *redistribution*. The welfare state and its programmes have no basis whatsoever in the rationales for the use of the budget instrument, that is, provision of public goods proper and the rectification of market failures. The welfare state is big government because it attempts redistribution in goods and services, not in terms of money. Choice is to be government choice so that everyone gets the same service for the same price. The reason for this is the strong position of producer groups.

If the asymmetrical relationships that are contained in the public sector increase the risk of inefficiency in public programmes, then what are the remedies? Some would argue in favour of privatization (Kristensen, 1987b). A number of empirical studies may be quoted in support of the hypothesis that efficiency is often higher in private production than in public provision (Mueller, 1989). However, several public programmes are not easily privatized either because of the risk of market failure or due to the resistance of interest groups or citizen groups.

We end here with the much discussed theme of decentralization as a strategy for enhancing effectiveness and efficiency in the public sector. However, the meaning of 'decentralization' is also subject to debate. It may refer to several processes of change: (1) geographical transfer of bureaux from the urban core to the periphery; (2) privatization; (3) emphasis on implementation instead of planning and policy-making; (4) transfer of functions from the state to local governments; (5) transfer of decision opportunities from the central to the local level in the public sector; (6) participation of the local level; (7) access or influence of the local level on the centre; (8) formalization of implicit institutions; (9) integration of organizations.

To explain the decentralization concept one might choose meanings (4), (5) and (6). Should the centralization or decentralization mechanism be used with regard to the provision of a good service? There is no definitive answer here, as it depends on the calculation of 'pros' and 'cons' in relation to each item of provision. The advantages of centralization are equality and coordination; the disadvantages, hierarchy and excessive standardization. The advantages of decentralization are flexibility and adaptability; the disadvantages, traditionalism and inequalities.

## CONCLUSION

Maybe public management is a nuisance as some critics of the Weberian ideal-type model imply? Or perhaps public management is waste writ large as public choice models imply? In big government public management is bound to attempt to enhance efficiency in both administration and service provision. And efficiency can be promoted by the introduction of systems for relative costs comparisons. This is a missing element in public management, the continuous and systematic competition between similar organizations in terms of how they relate inputs to outputs.

In order to make hypotheses about inefficiencies in public programmes amenable to scientific test in relation to specified sets of data we suggest a number of distinctions. First, we must distinguish between social efficiency and bureau or programme efficiency, as some goods and services are more efficiently provided for by the market whereas others better suit public management. The best way to increase bureau or programme efficiency may be to insert more quasi-market institutions into the public sector.

Secondly, the analysis of bureau efficiency may be conducted in four different modes (Table 9.3). Focusing on different sector-oriented systems within the public sector, the distinction between the administrative function and the service function seems promising. Bureau or policy inefficiency may mean either that the administrative component in the system is too large according to some standard or

Table 9.3   *Modes of bureau efficiency*

|                     | Cross-sectional | Longitudinal |
|---------------------|:---------------:|:------------:|
| Administration      | I               | II           |
| Goods and services  | III             | IV           |

that the provision of goods and services is too costly given some standard. Administrative inefficiency may be interpreted as a process phenomenon – bureaucratization – to be revealed by means of a longitudinal approach. Or administrative efficiency may mean that economies of scale in the administrative function are seized upon – a cross-sectional interpretation.

The study of efficiency in the service function of a public institution or programme is more complicated as there are more explanations of cost variations in the provision of public programmes than simply a lack of efficiency. Service inefficiency may be regarded as a residual when the amount of cost variation that stems from variations in external conditions of the choice of service level (quality or quantity) has been recognized. But there are other equally valid evaluation criteria, for example, social justice, which we shall now consider.

## APPENDIX: SOME MEASURES OF KEY TERMS

1  Productivity = output/input.
2  Effectiveness = effects of output/input.
3  Labour productivity = output/labour input.
4  Cost productivity = output/costs.
5  Value added productivity = output × prices of purchases/labour input = value added/labour input.
6  Efficiency of a private firm = output × prices/prices = productivity × input, or revenues/costs = output/input × prices of output/prices of input = productivity × prices of output/prices of input (Murray, 1987).

The distinction between inner or outer efficiency, or productivity and effectiveness, may be stated in a system of equations.

*Productivity or inner efficiency*: Input/Costs × Output/Input, which gives us Output/Costs.

*Effectiveness or outer efficiency*: Effects/Output × Benefits/Effects, which gives us Benefits/Output.

Combining the two equations we have: Output/Costs × Benefits/Outputs, which gives us Benefits/Costs.

# 10

# ETHICS AND NORMATIVE POLICY MODELS

To speak about ethics in relation to public policy may provoke serious disagreement about the nature of policy analysis and policy studies. Since Weber social scientists have been accustomed to the distinction between *is* and *ought* and the traditional focus of the conduct of scientific inquiry on matters of fact whether in a theoretical or in an empirical mode (Weber, 1949). However, one may agree with Robert Goodin in *Political Theory and Public Policy* that:

> Even if facts and values could be separated – and there is much in policy debates to put paid to the myth that they can – this book strongly argues that they should not be. Empirical and ethical theory ought both to be used, and used in tandem, to guide public policymaking. (1982: 4)

At the same time it seems important to bear in mind the relevance of the Weberian call for ethical neutrality for the analysis of policy (Weber, 1949; Brecht, 1959). Since policy analysis is heavily oriented towards questions of ends and means as well as values, it seems important to stick to the distinction between the scientific study of policies and the moral inquiry into the proper solutions of policy problems without any positivist pretension that one task is more meaningful than the other.

Public policies are justified by the resort to moral concepts such as social justice. And the ethical interpretation of the notion of justice may be employed in the understanding of ongoing policy-making. These norms may be regarded as offering standards against which existing policy programmes may be evaluated. Thus, it is relevant to ask how public policies relate to various theories of justice. Following the public choice models we would predict a vast gulf between ideal conceptions and realities. The basic problem in the normative analysis of public policy is how to derive specific and determinate solutions which may be implemented by government under the label of social justice (Bromley, 1989; Heap, 1989). This is at the heart of the redistribution branch of government.

## NORMATIVE POLICY APPROACHES

This is not the place to introduce a comprehensive and detailed examination of normative policy models. We only wish to display how social justice may be interpreted in a policy context (Walzer, 1983).

Questions about the size of the public sector and the role of public policy in society used to be answered in terms of so-called positive approaches, searching for the determinants of growth and displaying the consequences of big government. The time is ripe for the standard positive models of, for example, incrementalism and the demographic approach to be supplemented by more normative deliberations concerning the public and the private. The problem of identifying decision criteria for the demarcation of the public and the private sectors is indeed formidable, with relevance for questions about the proper role of public policy.

A social choice is a decision as to which social state in a set of alternatives is to be implemented. Formally, the arrival at a collective choice amounts to the specification of a social welfare function in the economists' jargon, where the level of welfare in society is dependent, somehow, upon the utility of its citizens. The pros and cons of public policy and market as mechanisms for collective choice are dependent on how well each mechanism specifies the social welfare function.

A social decision involves two things: a consideration of what is feasible and a deliberation about what is desirable. There are thus two kinds of evaluation criteria that are relevant in deciding between policy and market: the capacity of each choice mechanism to consider technology, or to identify the set of alternatives open to participants in the choice process; and value (a set of ethical properties), or the capacity of the choice mechanism to pick the best alternative. Well-known approaches to normative policy-making or the specification of a social welfare function include the following.

### The utilitarian framework

The policy relevance of the utilitarian definition of social justice seems straightforward. What could be more obvious than that policies should promote the utility of citizens? Many policies are undoubtedly enacted under the explicit claim that they promote the common interest according to some utility interpretation (Sen and Williams, 1982).

Why, then, not declare that the basic objective of public policy is to satisfy the utilitarian criterion on justice? And why not employ some utility yardstick as the technique for evaluating various policies? The utilitarian model thus appears to be highly salient to policy-making, but it suffers from severe theoretical problems due to the difficulties inherent in the concept of utility. There is actually a set of utilitarian models and no agreement has as yet been forthcoming about which one to use in public policy.

First, there is the classical utilitarian model, according to which total utility is to be maximized. Secondly, there is the average utility model, maximizing the average utility of citizens over all conceivable programmes. Thirdly, we have the Harsanyi (1977) impersonality model, which maximizes the utility that a detached person would enjoy were his/her behaviour to become a rule. Fourthly, there is the neo-classical utility model of von Neumann and Morgenstern, which replaces the measurement of utilities with a probability experiment.

The difficulty with the utilitarian approach is that utility is a notoriously difficult concept to handle both operationally (what is actually measured) and theoretically. Are all kinds of utility worthy of justice? Suppose some public policy that scores high on some utility measurement is still considered unjust, then what should be done? And it is not difficult to find examples of policies that may give the majority a higher utility score than other policies while simultaneously doing injustice to the minority. How would policy-making be conducted employing the utilitarian criteria (Sen, 1982)?

## A contractarian framework

The difficulties in the concept of utility and in the notion of utility aggregation prompted Rawls (1971) to suggest a principle of justice that is independent of any measure of utility, well-being or pleasure – justice as fairness. The fairness principle is a Kantian rule which everybody would choose as the guiding principle of public policy were they to pick normative principles under a veil of ignorance. The difference principle states that the advantages of the least favoured are to be maximized given the priority of such liberty as is possible, with the same degree of liberty being accorded to everyone. The difference principle is a combination of an efficiency principle – Pareto optimality – and a strong principle of equality as a redistribution criterion.

Starting from the natural differences in individual capacities the lot of the poor is to be maximized, given free opportunity for everyone. Thus, redistribution schemes are to be introduced up until the point at which the harm they do to the incentive system has the consequence that the position of those worst off deteriorates due to the loss in total output. Thus, there is a real trade-off between total income in a society and equality, given the simple rule that the liberty of all takes precedence over equality. Below we discuss to what extent this is a clear principle for public policy-making.

## The procedural framework

Whereas the utilitarian models, as well as the Rawlsian model, could be employed to justify various policy programmes, the models suggested by Buchanan and Nozick, although very different in basic assumptions, envisage a state with minimal commitment to public policy. Buchanan (1977) would favour policies that are conducive to efficiency as defined by the Pareto principle.

He postulates two different policy programmes: the protective state and the productive state. The first kind of public policy is oriented towards internal and external security, guaranteeing the sanctity of contract. The second kind of policy would be oriented towards the genuinely collective services. This is the only foundation for public policy, with the exception that citizens may decide by majority rule to redesign the property rights according to some principle of legitimacy. How such redistributions are to be justified is not clarified, but the conception of social justice only maintains that it rests uniquely in the policy process in a constitutional setting.

No end state is just in itself as utilitarians or Rawls would argue; if unanimity is accepted as the decision principle we would be guaranteed Pareto-optimality in the public goods provision, but Buchanan is prepared to relax the unanimity rule in favour of majoritarian principles due to the existence of staggering decision costs (Buchanan and Tullock, 1962; Buchanan, 1986). But why would majorities always promote just or efficient policies?

More radical in the rejection of policy-making is the Nozick (1974) entitlement principle stating that social justice follows naturally from the just endowment of entitlement and the proper transfer of rights according to a just process of interaction. No policy is ever needed except those that clarify and ascertain justice in both property rights and in property rights transactions. In the Nozick minimal state the best public policy is no policy, which is not in line with the distributional tasks of the state according to two normative models to be discussed below.

## DISTRIBUTIONAL MODELS AND PUBLIC POLICY

The renewed interest in distributive problems during the 1970s has implied a new perspective on public policy. It asks questions about the basic purpose of public policies, whether and to what extent they promote social justice. Public policy – marginal or comprehensive, rational or symbolic – has distributive implications which need to be evaluated in terms of some theory of justice. If government is looked upon as a tool for social reform, then what is the overall objective behind all public programmes? A number of public policies may be operated for neutral reasons of efficiency, the state substituting for market failure, but the question of who should benefit cannot be avoided.

We focus upon two alternative solutions as to the proper ends of public policy, one of which claims that the state should maximize total welfare or utility and the other that government ought to guarantee individual rights (Frey, 1984; Waldron, 1984; Dworkin, 1987). What does this mean for public policy-making?

The present conflict between utilitarianism and contractarianism refers to the definition of social justice. What is a just act is a broader problem than the question of ends for public policy. Once the general problem of justice in ethics has been framed in terms of what government should do, the question of justice in society has been turned into a problem of redistribution which is highly relevant for public policy. Each existing social state may be looked upon as a possible distribution of welfare between individuals or groups of individuals that may be altered by the choice of public policies.

Each policy promotes certain interests at the expense of others, but the question remains: what is a just public policy? In the face of conflicting interests between major social groups, how is the state to act if it wishes to enhance social justice?

This is a normative question to the same extent as the problem of finding a social welfare function that picks the distributive solution within a space of production possibilities in a welfare economics framework. Allowing for Pareto-optimal moves a final choice has to be made of how the interests of one group are to be related to the interests of another group. Which interests is it just to promote and to what extent? The redistributive problem appears in all public policies, whether in taxation or in allocation. How is it to be solved?

The distribution problem may be avoided by removing it from day to day public policy, but it will crop up elsewhere. Buchanan (1975) argues that the distributive problem is a constitutional one, to be solved in terms of a constitutional contract at the border between anarchy and Leviathan. The constitution will be the redistributive contract, outlining the size of the protective state and the productive state. But which is the correct constitution? Since there can be no independent criteria of social justice in the Buchanan positivist economics, the just constitution is the contract that everybody agrees on – the Wicksell unanimity rule or Pareto-optimality in welfare economics.

However, when people are in disagreement, when the interests are fundamentally opposed, then which is the solution that everybody should be in agreement on? If the redistribution problem is such a contentious one in day-to-day policy-making, why would it become less so when transferred to a constitutional setting? The question of who is to benefit is transformed into who decides if the Buchanan (1977) solution is resorted to, process replacing criteria of justice. Why would unanimity result in a just society?

It has been argued that the distribution problem is a pseudo-problem, demanding the statement of a final end state which society is to be moved towards (Nozick, 1974). And all end states are impossible to implement, because social life is not predictable or controllable.

The Nozick solution to the redistribution problem is to focus on fair procedures. Any social state with its distribution of welfare between various interests is just as long as it has evolved in terms of a set of just procedures. Therefore, what is a just procedure? According to Nozick (1974) a person is entitled to what he/she has inherited or acquired. Why? Because such a society is better than a different society where these principles of entitlement are not upheld – better meaning according to some ideal end state?

It has been claimed that an ethical solution to the distributive problem demands that all real life interests be removed as non-relevant. The choice of a solution is to be an ethical one, meaning that a disinterested attitude is the correct one to adopt. Thus, Rawls (1971: 136–42) states that the redistribution problem should be solved under a veil of ignorance; and Harsanyi (1977) demands that the person who evaluates his/her interests be in an equiprobable predicament in relation to the various social strata.

First, this is not the real life redistribution problem that public policy faces every day. And in whatever manner it is solved, the real life distributive question remains: how do we choose between alternative distributions of welfare? To choose under a veil of ignorance or under the assumption of equiprobability may well mean to choose the maximin rule or to maximize average utility, but what does it mean to choose in real life policy predicaments when interests have to be compared and traded off against each other?

Secondly, the replacement of a set of criteria for choosing between various distributions in so-called ethical positions only means that the problem reappears in a different shape. Thus, we wish to know how the advantages are to be distributed between various groups before one is allowed a choice under a veil of ignorance. And we wonder about the criteria of distribution that guide the welfare of the various groups in which a person has an equiprobable chance of ending up.

In whatever way the redistribution problem is framed, it is a question about criteria of justice. Government may find these criteria in the calculation of overall utility or in the safeguarding of individual rights. How is public policy to implement these two solutions to the distributive problem?

## ENDS IN PUBLIC POLICY-MAKING

It seems difficult to dispense with the notion of ends in relation to public policy. According to the rational interpretation of public policy the concepts of means and ends are highly relevant to the analysis of the making and implementation of policies. The criticism of the means–end paradigm makes two types of claims, one weaker and one stronger. The weak version states that public policies sometimes are characterized by ambiguous goals and unreliable technologies. The means–end model is an ideal-type which is appropriate for the analysis of policy-making and policy implementation where actual cases of policy-making are always more or less approximate to the rational model but never identical (Simon, 1957).

The strong version implies that the means–end model is always inappropriate as public policies cannot have identifiable goals and must lack reliable means (Pressman and Wildavsky, 1984). Public policy-making is an ongoing continuous process where ends cannot be separated from means or outcomes (Ham and Hill, 1984); and the systemic uncertainty makes tactics and strategy the pervasive properties of public policies where solutions look for choice opportunities among participants in a fluid decision-making process (March and Olsen, 1976).

However, if the garbage can model is true of every process of policy-making and implementation, then perhaps there should be as few public policies as possible? Why enhance the spread of policy failure or policy pathologies? What, then, happens to justice in social life? We are reminded of the distinction between a strong and a weak version of the garbage can model (Chapter 3). According to the strong interpretation all public sector programmes tend towards a garbage can process, meaning that it is rather meaningless to ask what policy analysts in the bureaucracy (Meltsner, 1976) should do. The weak version only warns us against the possibility of the occurrence of a garbage can development in various public sector areas.

If, then, there is a proper place for public policy-making and the garbage can model stands for those processes where things have gone wrong for some reason or other, then we are back to the problem of evaluating the goals in the making and implementation of public policies. What ends should be promoted in public policies?

Goals are states considered desirable by some persons or group of individuals. State activities in the form of public policies are oriented towards the accomplishment of ends by the employment of means – although these ends and means may fall far short of the requirement of a rational decision model or an ideal-type of bureaucracy. In the multiplicity of public policy objectives in big government (Rose, 1984), could there be some common denominator among the goals? There exist some basic alternative interpretations of the proper ends of public policies, inter alia utilitarianism and contractarianism according to the basic justice distinctions between utility, desert and needs (see Miller, 1976).

According to the former, public policies should promote the overall well-being – happiness – of the citizens of a country, whereas the latter states that public policies should implement the rights of individuals derived from some agreement between these persons as to the kind of state they would be willing to enter and support could they make a proper choice of institutions. If public policy is the effort to implement programmes that realize goals, then how should the ends be identified? What are the systematic criteria for choosing between ends? To what extent do utilitarian and contractarian theories contribute to the problem of finding criteria for selecting the proper ends in policy-making and policy implementation?

## A SIMPLE MODEL OF UTILITARIANISM

We will outline a basic model of utilitarianism in order to investigate the basic proposition of utilitarianism, that is the Greatest Happiness Principle (Broad, 1930; Sidgwick, 1967). Although the modern debate about the place of utilitarianism in ethics involves a number of complex issues (Harsanyi, 1977; Sen and Williams, 1982; Smart and Williams, 1987), the emphasis here is on the policy implications of the fundamental idea in Benthamite utilitarian approaches: to maximize the greatest happiness of the greatest number (Lyons, 1965; Hodgson, 1967; Regan, 1980; Parfit, 1984). We will not enter the extensive debate about the inherent difficulties in the utilitarian approach related to measuring utility cardinally or making interpersonal utility comparisons (Sen, 1970). If we assume that the utilitarian approach could work, then what are the distributional implications for policy-making?

A society has a certain number of individuals where each individual possesses a certain number of happiness-conducive factors. These happiness-conducive factors may in some way be related to money. Furthermore, each individual experiences these with a specific 'intensity of happiness' which measures the amount of happiness per unit of happiness-conducive factors, meaning that he/she experiences the happiness of having a sum of money to a certain degree.

By means of these two concepts we can define the happiness of an individual as a function of both money and the intensity of feelings. Happiness is dependent on these two concepts and mathematically it is clear that the same amount can be acquired by infinitely many combinations of money possession and intensity of feeling.

A society of a number of individuals has a total amount of happiness which is merely the summation of each individual's happiness. It is evident that in the utilitarian model the crucial concept is the intensity of happiness feelings. In the short-term perspective we can assume that each individual's possession of money is rather fixed; thus the determinant of the individual's happiness and total happiness in society is the various individuals' intensities of feelings.

In utilitarian theory it is assumed that a given amount of happiness could be redistributed among the individuals to achieve a more 'fair' society by following the Greatest Happiness Principle. From the definition of happiness it is clear that a redistribution of happiness follows from a redistribution of the possession of money, which is to be carried out by the state through public policy. Thus the problem is how to redistribute money.

We will assume that when an individual's possession of money changes, then his or her intensity feelings also change. It also seems reasonable to assume that when the possession of money increases, then the intensity feelings increase as well, at least up to a certain

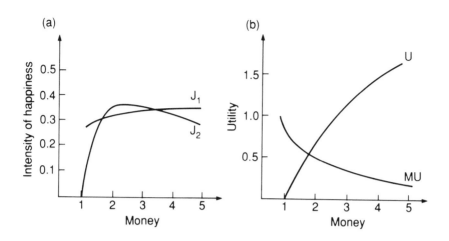

Figure 10.1  *Utilitarian happiness functions*

limit. Mathematically, we may model the relation between intensity and money by means of two equations as outlined in Figure 10.1a.

The relation between intensity and money may be non-linear, as for example $J_1$ in Figure 10.1a, or the intensity function may be modelled as involving a local maximum, curve $J_2$ in the figure. Let us first look at the non-linear relationship defined asymptotically in the figure, that is, when a millionaire earns his tenth million it may not give him as much satisfaction as when he earned his first. Given this non-linear relationship, if it is assumed that every individual has the same upper limit of his/her intensity function, then total happiness (TH) is not affected at all by the distribution of money. Every society has the same level of happiness independent of the distribution of money. If we suppose that the upper limit varies for each individual, then happiness would vary with the distribution of money in such a way that an unequal society comprises the largest total amount of happiness.

Let us now proceed to an intensity function which raises towards a maximum and then decreases towards zero. This means that the more money you get beyond a certain limit the less intensely you feel about it (curve $J_2$ in Figure 10.1a). Thus, individual happiness would be an increasing function of the possession of money, but the rate of increase is marginally decreasing (Figure 10.1b).

Here we have the standard case always referred to when it is argued that utilitarianism implies equality (Musgrave, 1959). However, whether a decreasing marginal utility curve (MU) for money is the true curve depends on matters of fact. Why is it an indisputable truth that the marginal utility curve of money is the one in Figure 10.1b?

Let us assume a society with two individuals 1 and 2 having the money bundles $M_1$ and $M_2$ where the first bundle contains less

Table 10.1  *Total happiness and income redistribution*

| c | TH |
| --- | --- |
| 0 | 1.000 |
| 2 | 1.380 |
| 5 | 1.477 |
| 5.5 | 1.480 |
| 6 | 1.477 |
| 9 | 1.380 |

money than the second bundle; let us examine total happiness in society when a sum of c is transferred from one to the other. Individual 1 has a sum of money equal to 1 (thousand pounds) and individual 2 has money equal to 10 (thousand pounds). Calculating total happiness for some different rates of c, we arrive at the results shown in Table 10.1.

In Table 10.1 maximizing happiness means that income should be shared equally for a universe of two individuals. This is actually the standard distributive solution conceived of in utilitarianism. Let us quote from one of the classic texts, *The Economics of Welfare* by A.C. Pigou:

> it is evident that any transference of income from a relatively rich man to a relatively poor man of similar temperament, since it enables more intense wants to be satisfied at the expense of less intense wants, must increase the aggregate sum of satisfaction. (1962: 89)

However, the Pigou redistributive solution is not self-evident. Distributing happiness to the members of a society is indeterminate as long as we do not know the nature of the intensity function of individuals. This is an empirical problem – maybe it is impossible for government to determine. The standard utilitarian solution assumes the existence of a special intensity function, namely the marginal diminishing utility of money. Is it self-evidently true?

The well-known attack by Robbins on the Pigou welfare propositions in *An Essay on the Nature and Significance of Economic Science* included a sharp rejection of the utility function assumed by Pigou. Let us quote at some length:

> But suppose that we differed about the satisfaction derived by A from an income of £1000, and the satisfaction derived by B from an income of twice that magnitude. Asking them would provide no solution. Supposing they differed. A might urge that he had more satisfaction than B at the margin. While B might argue that, on contrary, he had more satisfaction than A. We do not need to be slavish behaviourists to realize that here there is no scientific evidence. (1932: 139)

Robbins' argument continued by stating that the typical utilitarian utility function employed as a basis for equality in income distribution was a concealed value premise:

since in our hearts we do not regard different men's satisfaction from similar means as equally valuable, it would be rather silly, if we continued to pretend that the justification for our scheme of things was in any sense *scientific*. It can be justified on grounds of general convenience. Or it can be justified by appeal to ultimate standards of obligation. But it cannot be justified by appeal to any kind of positive science. (1932: 141)

This is not the place to discuss whether the second line of Robbins' attack is correct. The problem with the Pigou utilitarian solution is that in the conduct of public policy governments cannot take the Pigovian utility function for granted when redistributing income or wealth. The decreasing marginal utility of money is the same as assuming risk aversion (Varian, 1987), but what is the ground for treating *all* people as risk-averse? If one accepts Robbins' call for explicit value premises as the foundation for redistributive solutions, then entirely different solutions may be advanced. Let us transfer the analysis of such a normative framework for public policy solutions to the redistributive question.

## A SIMPLE MODEL OF RAWLSIANISM

In order to clarify the meaning of the Rawls solution we employ a simple model of an economy consisting of two persons, A and B. And we assume that each on his own may provide himself with a certain amount of income, $M_A$ and $M_B$. However, if they cooperate they may increase their earnings considerably in terms of a joint effort, that is, $M_{A\&B} > M_A + M_B$. How is this additional income to be divided? Let us suppose that the contribution of A, the rich person, is much larger than the contribution of B, the poor person. If income was to be determined by the marginal productivity theory, then the rule of division would be perhaps something like 90 per cent and 10 per cent. However, Rawls states that desert is not a just principle of income distribution:

The marginal product of labor depends upon supply and demand. What an individual contributes by his work varies with the demand of firms for his skills, and this in turn varies with the demand for the products of firms. An individual's contribution is also affected by how many offer similar talents. There is no presumption, then, that following the precept of contribution leads to a just income unless the underlying markets forces, and the availability of opportunities which they reflect, are appropriately regulated. And this implies . . . that the basic structure as a whole is just. (1971: 308)

Justice or fairness demands a different principle of distribution. Suppose that government sets itself the task of accomplishing this redistribution by means of public policy taxing A and transferring the taxation revenues to B. The market outcomes are to be changed by public policy moving the social state towards the criterion of justice – the difference principle.

Evaluating the Rawlsian solution we face three distinct problems:

1  What does the difference principle actually imply in terms of redistribution solutions?
2  Given the specification of the redistributive solutions, could government implement them?
3  If the solutions are known and they are implementable, are they really just?

In order to discuss these problems in more detail we start from a model of an economy where the rate of taxation affects the amount of total production, and thus the amount of income to be divided between A and B. And we will employ the four rules in Rawls' *A Theory of Justice* (1971) to derive determinate solutions to the distribution problem: (a) the liberty principle, (b) the fair opportunity rule, (c) Pareto-optimality and (d) the difference principle.

For the sake of simplicity we assume that the pre-tax production, Q, is unity and that all accrues to A; t denotes the rate of taxation levied on A in order to transfer income to B. And following the efficiency–equality trade-off principle we assume that total production will decrease as a function of the rate of taxation, as displayed in Figure 10.2. The higher the rate of taxation, the lower the total income due to the disincentive effect of taxation on work effort. The more exact shape of the curve will be discussed in terms of three model possibilities. How is the amount of production due to the cooperation between A and B to be divided between A and B, given the three possibilities or cases outlined in Figure 10.2?

Case 1: Let us assume that the relationship between total income and tax rate is a linear one. We see that the maximal possible production occurs where the rate of taxation is zero. Which combination of production and transfer payments are we to choose? There are three possible criteria: (a) to maximize production; (b) to maximize the share of the least advantage, that is, B; (c) to share equally, meaning 50 per cent each, that is, a tax rate of 0.5.

If we choose to maximize production, then B would hardly be interested in this solution and it is also a solution that the Rawlsian framework rejects. The difference principle has precedence over the rule of maximizing production. If we follow the difference principle, then $Q_A = Q_B$. Following the difference principle in this case means that the total production will be half as large as possible. And the total income thus derived will be divided equally between A and B. When the relationship between total production and rate of taxation is linear, then the equality solution is the same as the difference solution.

Case 2: Suppose that the function is concave, meaning that A will not reduce his willingness to cooperate as quickly as in the linear case. The production loss is here much smaller and the equality solution and the difference principle solution are not the same.

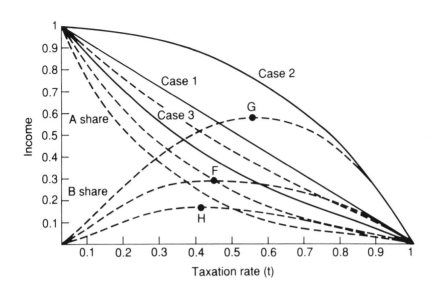

Figure 10.2 *Rawls' justice solutions*

Case 3: Let us finally assume that the function is convex, meaning that the rich person reduces his labour effort at an increasing rate in the beginning. Then, we have a much larger production loss. In this case the equality solution is not the same as the difference principle solution, as maximizing the position of the least advantaged means choosing a tax rate such that he/she would get more than when the rate $t = 0.5$.

We are now in a position to answer the three questions about the Rawlsian solution to the distributive problem raised above. The Rawlsian solutions are depicted in Figure 10.2 as F, G, and H. They all maximize the share of the least advantaged, B, given the restriction on the amount of tax revenues to be raised by levying a tax rate of t on the production or income created by the cooperative efforts of A and B, transferring income from A to B.

At F, the linear case, the difference rule solution is the same as the strict equality principle. By moving towards the left on the linear function only the share of A can be raised. Choosing F means a total loss in income which Rawls is prepared to accept because the difference principle has precedence over the maximum output principle. By choosing a tax rate of 0.5 we maximize the share of B and we are only to accept inequalities if they benefit B.

Thus, we cannot choose a tax rate of, for example, 0.3, because it will only give B a share of the total production of $0.3 \times 0.7 = 0.21$ whereas the difference solution would give 0.25. However, the loss to society is substantial. And to A the difference solution of $0.5 \times 0.5 =$

0.25 is much inferior to any solution to the right, for example, $0.7 \times 0.7$ = 0.49. The difference solution claims that $0.25 + 0.25 = 0.5$ is more just than $0.21 + 0.49 = 0.7$. Why this is so one could wonder. This is the first case.

Let us proceed to the concave curve, that is, case 2. The difference solution is at G where the share of B is maximized by means of a tax rate of 0.7 which benefits B more than A. B would get $0.7 \times 0.71$ = 0.49 leaving A with only $0.71 - 0.49 = 0.22$. Maximizing the share of the least advantaged may thus mean the creation of another inequality which Rawls has not recognized. Again, moving towards the right, decreasing the tax rate levied on total income means that total income becomes larger and the share of A increases. Why is it more just to favour B differently than, for example, to choose the equality solution?

Finally, we discuss the convex function, that is, case 3. Here the difference solution is at H, meaning that we should accept more inequality moving towards the right from the tax rate of 0.5 because such a move to a tax rate of 0.4 would increase the share of B. Since the production loss is heavy B only receives a share of 0.19 and A gets 0.27. If we move further to the right we will increase total production and the share of A: for example, at tax rate 0.3 we will have $0.18 + 0.42 = 0.60$. Why is the first solution more just than the second?

## CONCLUSION

Public policy is a tool of government to enhance justice in society by redistributing income from those who have to the have-nots. Redistribution may also relate to goods and services, meaning that public allocation has redistributive implications. What, then, is justice?

Here we emphasize that the solutions that may be derived from theories of justice tend to be indeterminate and difficult to implement by government action. The state may aim at maximizing total utility or safeguarding individual rights to primary goods. It may seem self-evident that government ought to maximize the greatest happiness of the greatest number. However, such an aggregation rule is not easy to implement, because government needs to know the relationship between the possession of happiness-creating factors like money and the intensity of happiness. Different distributions of happiness-creating factors are possible in relation to the same overall level of total happiness, meaning that government lacks a criterion for which distribution to choose. Only by making a few empirical assumptions open to refutation is it possible to arrive at the equality solution.

The Rawlsian solution – the difference principle – creates a heavy strain on government. When deciding about the amount of transfer payments that will maximize the lot of the least advantaged, government must know the impact on total production from the tax rate. Is the efficiency–equity trade-off a linear, convex or concave function? However, the serious problem with the difference principle solutions is their claim to justice. The three Rawlsian solutions – F, G, H – are by no means self-evident. Society would benefit from moving away from these solutions. Why is Rawls' claim just? Both the utilitarian and the Rawlsian solutions are indeterminate, but the contractual position in the Rawlsian interpretation seems to pick solutions that are hardly self-evidently just whereas the utilitarian solutions are unfeasible by government action.

Distributional theory is a vital concern for public policy and the theory of the state. Distributional theory has to come up with determinate solutions as to what government should do to promote social justice. Two frequently discussed normative models are utilitarianism and contractarianism. However, the utilitarian approach does not arrive at unambiguous solutions and it makes too heavy demands on the cognitive capacities of government; the Greatest Happiness Principle is simply not implementable. The Rawlsian approach allows the derivation of three alternative solutions, but they are not evidently desirable. Normative public policy has to consider both feasibility in terms of government implementation and desirability in terms of social justice.

# CONCLUSION

# WHAT ARE THE POLICY SCIENCES?

The decline of the public administration approach opened up the public sector to a variety of new approaches. One of these new perspectives is what was sometimes called 'policy analysis' or more broadly the 'policy sciences'. Overcoming the petrifaction of public administration it claimed to have a comprehensive new framework with which to approach the public sector. A number of different approaches followed in the wake of the dissolution of the public administration school – organizational theory, decision analysis, evaluation research, steering theory, management sciences – all of which were intended as new partial approaches to the study of the public sector.

But, given that the policy approach was launched as a candidate to replace public administration as a basic framework, is there really a distinct policy approach to the public sector? Could the policy approach really arrive at a general theory of public policies?

When the public policy approach was launched after the Second World War it embodied an entire new approach to the interpretation of the state and local governments. Not only were the traditional principles of the public administration perspective outdated, but the study of public policy required new scientific techniques and approaches. This belief in a special policy perspective or policy methodology was continually reiterated in one form or another as the policy perspective became popular, its application widened and the number of policy studies began to rise sharply in the late 1960s.

## THE POLICY ORIENTATION

Policy analysis would not only be a scientific discipline of its own with its special techniques for the study of the public sector, but would also offer serious guidance to practical men in power as to how to go about handling social problems in society. Already in the first major volume in what was to become the policy tradition – the classical *The Policy Sciences* edited by D. Lerner and H.D. Lasswell (1951) – there was this combination of two basically separate enterprises: a science of policy-making and a science for policy-making.

Lasswell identifies the scope of policies with the set of choices. He states: 'The word "policy" is commonly used to designate the most important choices made either in organized or in private life'

(Lasswell, 1951: 5). Perhaps such a general definition of the concept of a policy was never strictly adhered to, as the connection between policy and the public sector has remained a very close one.

Lasswell states that the policy orientation comprises three elements: (1) the methods by which the policy process is investigated; (2) the results of the study of policy; (3) the findings of the disciplines making the most important contributions to the intelligence needs of the time (Lasswell, 1951: 4). It is not clear what the difference is between the first two elements in the policy orientation. In any case Lasswell hinted at a separation between two kinds of policy studies that has characterized much of the policy movement. Policy analysis could mean either the analysis of the policy process – description and explanation – or the elaboration of the methods to be used in ongoing policy-making – prescription or recommendation.

In Lasswell's perspective policy analysis is not simply the understanding of policies as important public or private choices 'explaining the policy-making and policy-executing process'. The other side of the coin is the activist notion. The policy analyst should also locate data and provide interpretations of the policy problems at a given point – policy problems being 'the fundamental and often neglected problems which arise in the adjustment of man in society', in the 'world revolutionary process of the epoch'.

However, not only in the policy sciences but in all the approaches to the public sector we find this tension between objectivity and subjectivity, between value neutrality and value relevance and between explanation and prescription. Why create a special discipline for the analysis of the public sector if it does not hold the promises of improvement in public policy-making and implementation? Surely the methodology employed in explaining policy outcomes in terms of the policy process could also be used to remodel the tools used in ongoing policy-making? Thus, policy analysis could devise a set of intellectual instruments with which to improve the various steps in the policy circle, from demands over decision to implementation and outcomes, which are fed back into the process.

Almost from the start the ideas of the policy sciences have contained this tension between description and recommendation. We may quote from Lasswell one more time: 'the policy science approach has the further implication that it includes, in addition to knowledge about the policy-making process itself, the assembling and evaluating of knowledge – from whatever source – which appears to have an important bearing upon the major policy problems of the time' (Lasswell, 1951: 14).

Thus, the policy orientation involves some fundamental questions which have been answered differently as the policy movement has developed. Let us quote from Christopher Ham and Michael Hill's *The Policy Process in the Modern Capitalist State*, where they distinguish between 'analysis of policy' and 'analysis for policy': 'The distinction is important in drawing attention to policy analysis as an academic activity concerned primarily with advancing understanding, and policy analysis as an applied activity concerned mainly with contributing to the solution of social problems' (1984: 4).

On the one hand we have the problem of identifying the characteristic properties of the policy process in the public sector. On the other hand there is the question of the proper techniques to be employed in the policy-making process in order to arrive at public programme improvement. In addition, there is the problem of congruence between the theoretical position and the practical recommendations.

The balance between the theoretical and practical tasks of policy analysis could be struck in different ways. Lasswell underlined the practical aspects of the policy orientation, but warned strongly against too close a contact between policy analysts and the political life. Yehezkal Dror advocates the opposite position in *Public Policymaking Reexamined* (1974).

## OPTIMAL POLICY-MAKING

Public programmes are based on greater or lesser knowledge about the causal mechanisms operating in society. They also involve normative considerations about the priority of goals and the appropriateness of means. Is there a social science theory that could improve the cognitive and normative foundations of the making and implementing of public choices? Perhaps all research into the public sector should be directed towards the task of finding means of improving policy-making? Could there be an optimal way of structuring the policy process?

Dror takes a very optimistic view on the practical lessons to be learnt by policy analysis. He states: 'Contemporary literature in the field of systems analysis, economics, decisionmaking theory, management sciences, and political science, as well as in other disciplines, already includes much material relevant to constructing an optimal model of policymaking' (1974: 31). What would optimal policy-making look like and how could it be derived from the study of the public sector?

Dror identifies the following components in optimal policy-making: (1) use of qualitative knowledge; (2) rational as well as extra-rational components; (3) economic rationality; (4) involvement of metapolicy-making; (5) feedback mechanisms. As there is little quantitative information available directly for policy-making purposes, qualitative data have to suffice. By extra-rational mechanisms are meant intuition, non-routine behaviour and guesstimate. There are different needs for resources for both policy and non-policy purposes as well as for various kinds of policy purposes, involving short- and long-term policies and metapolicy-making.

Policy-making may be of three kinds: (1) metapolicy-making on how to conduct policy-making, (2) making policy on substantive issues, and (3) re-policy-making or making policy based on the feedback information about the policies enacted and implemented. Feedback of information is relevant for both metapolicy-making and substantive policies, where in the first case data would have structural implications for improving the process of policy-making, whereas in the second case information could be used to alter already existing programmes in order to increase the probability of positive outcomes.

Thus, a policy science would be a set of principles guiding both the overall process of policy-making and the minute details in every single policy. Such a set of policy rules would ensure optimal policies – it is hoped. However, these principles are not enough, as there also has to be an 'optimal policy-making structure' (Dror, 1974: 198).

Would we really be prepared to call a policy 'optimal' simply because it satisfied the formal conditions that Dror lays down? Perhaps optimal policy-making would require commitment to some substantive values or goals? Perhaps optimality in policy-making also requires some structuring of the policy-making process? Dror lays down a few conditions on an optimal policy-making structure, but they are also only of a formal kind: participation by many and diverse groups; a minimum amount of formalization of the policy process assigning various policy tasks to different groups; redundance between groups and tasks as well as isolation of some groups from others; integration of groups and periodical reexamination and reform of the structure (Dror, 1974: 197–213). Again, we may wish to demand stronger requirements in order for a policy-making structure to be considered optimal.

The idea of optimal policies or optimal policy-making processes is an elusive one. It is far from obvious how prescriptions for the identification of optimality could be derived from the existing knowledge about the public sector, which is heavily heterogeneous and spread across several social science disciplines. Yet would not the idea of creating a new interdisciplinary policy science imply a possibility that we could start gathering systematic knowledge with a policy orientation?

Dror develops another typical idea in the context of developing an independent field of research, in this case the policy sciences, namely the establishment of a set of policy specialists situated not too far from state power. He writes:

> One of the main recommendations that emerges from comparing the optimal model with actual policymaking is to establish and reinforce special organizations for policy analysis. . . . Establishing special organizations that are charged with taking a fresh look at basic policy issues is a necessary (though not sufficient) step toward approximating optimality in public policymaking. (Dror, 1974: 261)

The idea of a set of specialists on public policy and policy implementation located in separate institutes may sound attractive, because it would lend an aura of legitimacy and responsibility to the entire enterprise. But it is highly questionable, because it builds on the weak hypothesis that policy analysis would turn out different results if practised in one institutional setting rather than another. Whatever the organization involved in policy analysis may look like, it is still the case that the quality of the findings and the recommendations depend upon how the inquiry has been conducted, not its formal aspects. Some have argued that policy analysis is distinct as a discipline and not in terms of organizational paraphernalia. What methods would a policy analyst typically use?

## THE TOOLS OF POLICY ANALYSIS

The separation of policy analysis into analysis of policy or analysis for policy may seem abstruse. Why could social science knowledge not perform both functions at the same time? In the work of scholars sometimes associated with the so-called Policy Studies Organization there is a strong underlining of the need for policy analysis to be both theoretical and practical. To Nagel and Neef, for example, any radical distinction between knowledge to be used in policy-making and knowledge that models the policy process would be very difficult to uphold. To quote:

> Policy analysis or policy studies can be broadly defined as the study of the nature, causes, and effects of alternative public policies. Sometimes policy analysis is more specifically defined to refer to the methods used in analyz-ing public policies. The main methods, however, are no different from those associated with social science and the scientific method in general. (Nagel and Neef, 1979: 221)

Yet there is one major development within the policy orientation that maintains that policy analysis is more a craft than a science.

Edward S. Quade states the argument for the interpretation of policy analysis as analysis for policy in *Analysis for Public Decisions* (1976). According to this practical interpretation of the policy orientation, it would be preferable if policy analysis acknowledged from the start that it cannot adhere to the strict requirements of the social sciences. He states:

> science is concerned primarily with the pursuit of truth, and it seeks to understand and predict. Policy analysis seeks to help a decision-maker make a better choice than he would otherwise have made. It is thus concerned with the more effective manipulation of the real world – even if this may have to be accomplished without full understanding of the underlying phenomena. (Quade, 1976: 21)

It sounds somewhat strange that policy analysis cannot be evaluated properly by means of a truth condition. The notion that policy analysis deals with the manipulation of the real world and not the search for truth about phenomena may seem a clear-cut recognition of its limits. However, should one accept such a demarcation of the scope of policy analysis? To many in the policy school Quade's restriction is both too narrow and basically confused about the ends and means of policy analysis. How could a policy hypothesis be used to manipulate real world phenomena if it was not also true of that world?

The identification of policy analysis as analysis for policy is typically based on a number of approaches that are said to constitute a specific policy focus. To this set of policy tools Quade adds the following: operations research, systems analysis, cost-effectiveness analysis, cost-benefit analysis. (For an overview of various administrative doctrines, see Hood and Jackson, 1991). Quade himself outlines a model of policy analysis that involves both intellectual cogitation and social interaction with policy-makers. He states:

> There are thus three stages associated with policy analysis. First, discovery, attempting to find an alternative that is satisfactory and best among those that are feasible; second, acceptance, getting the findings accepted and incorporated into a policy or decision; third, implementation, seeing that the policy or decision is implemented without being changed so much that it is no longer satisfactory. (Quade, 1976: 254)

It is obvious that Quade has some more or less radical model of rational decision-making in mind. What is striking about this iden-tification of policy analysis is that it makes no distinction between 'policy' and 'policy analysis'. I do not understand why a policy analyst would be concerned about the process of policy-making and policy implementation. Perhaps new circumstances developed in the policy process that call for a different policy? Perhaps one discovers at the implementation stage that the drawbacks of a policy had been under-estimated, meaning that a policy change is indeed most welcome? Surely policy analysis could help policy-makers improve both policies and implementation of policies. Any such good advice from policy analysis depends on the truth of their positions, not how eagerly they look for policy success. To quote Nagel and Neef again: 'policy analysis is not something new methodically' (1979: 221–2).

## ART AND CRAFT IN POLICY ANALYSIS

It is questionable whether these strong demands on the originality and scope of policy analysis were characteristic of the policy movement in general. Another major development in the policy orientation was to uphold the view of policy analysis as analysis of policy. In *Speaking Truth to Power* (1979) by Wildavsky the practical ambitions behind the policy school are moderated while its intellectual claims are stated more specifically. Wildavsky narrows down the goals of the entire school as well as identifying more concretely how policy analysis is to go about achieving them.

Yet, even in Wildavsky's cautious interpretation there is this same
idea that policy analysis constitutes a distinct social inquiry to be
pursued by means of its own methodological structure. Policy analysis
is both an art and a craft, Wildavsky claims. What, more specifically,
are the methods and tools used in the conduct of policy analysis?

Perhaps the main argument with Wildavsky is that policy analysis is
not some conventional technique employed in ongoing public
decision-making and implementation. Policy analysis is an art where
the creativity that is necessary for arriving at a deep understanding
cannot be produced by the mechanical application of information
systems like planning, programming, budgeting systems (PPBS), zero-
based budgeting (ZBB) and management by objectives (MBO),
program, evaluation, review technique (PERT) and social indicators.
Wildavsky states: 'Policy analysis is an applied subfield whose content
cannot be determined by disciplinary boundaries but by whatever
appears appropriate to the circumstances of the time and the nature of
the problem' (1979: 15). Here we again confront this idea that there
exists a distinct social science of public policies – applied social
research with an interdisciplinary orientation. Perhaps it is self-
evidently true that policy analysis is what is hoped for in the policy
school. Yet sometimes it may pay to question the most basic assumptions.

Why would policy analysis be more of an applied social science than
pure social research, whatever could be meant by this distinction when
it occurs in the social sciences? Why could social theory not model the
policy process and its various components in a manner that is relevant
for practical politics? Moreover, in the same way, the requirement of
interdisciplinarity does not make sense, because there would certainly
be valid contributions forthcoming from political science, economics,
sociology and psychology separately.

Policy analysis is an art, because it is based on the conduct of social
inquiry employing the standard canons of scientific study. Wildavsky
writes:

> Analysis is imagination. Making believe the future has happened in the
> past, analysts try to examine events as if those actions already had occur-
> red. They are strongly committed to 'thought experiments' in which they
> imagine what might have been in order to improve what may come to pass.
> Theories are discarded instead of people. Naturally, this is risky. (1979: 16)

Creativity in art like originality in social research will not be
forthcoming through the application of some set of tools as in the practice of a craft. What matters more than craftmanship is scientific
fantasy, unrestrained by any constraints that could be involved in an
applied research setting.

Policy analysis is a craft, because it is a problem-solving activity.
Wildavsky writes: 'Policy analysis, to be brief, is an activity creating

problems that can be solved. Every policy is fashioned of tension between resources and objectives, planning and politics, scepticism and dogma. Solving problems involves temporarily resolving these tensions' (1979: 17).

As a policy in real life involves ends and means, so policy analysis must be a set of theories about the relationship between ends and means. Policy analysis implies rationality – means searching for ends – as well as responsibility – proper resources achieving suitable objectives. Since policy analysis deals with contested and value-ingrained materials, it must be practical, evaluative and reconstructive.

Yet even practical recommendations have to be based on solid theoretical foundations. What matters more than the identification of the objectives and the resources in policy-making organizations is the causal hypothesis about how means have an impact on ends. The arrival at relevant guesses about the means–end relationship depends on both dogma and scepticism, but so do all kinds of knowledge about people in general. Wildavsky writes: 'These, then, are the tasks and tensions of policy analysis: relating resources to objectives by balancing social interaction against intellectual cogitation so as to learn to draw the line between scepticism and dogma' (1979: 19).

Few would argue with this sound identification of policy analysis. Actually, there is only one drawback. While it certainly identifies what typically goes on in policy studies, it fails at the same time to distinguish how the policy orientation differs from the ordinary conduct of social inquiry.

## CONCLUSION

'Public policy', like some other words such as 'politics', 'public administration' and 'public management', has a double meaning standing for both the science of something and the object studied. It could either mean the public sector as it appears in various phenomena – public resource allocation, income redistribution and public regulation – or it could stand for some framework for or approach to the interpretation of these appearances. As a matter of fact, public policy as an academic discipline was launched in the form of new courses, departments, institutes or schools where policy analysis would be practised, replacing the outdated public administration framework.

However, two difficult problems arise in relation to the ambition to identify a distinct social science enterprise, the policy analysis orientation:

1 Does such a distinct approach to the understanding of the public sector exist that we may comfortably speak about policy analysis as an art and craft in its own right?

2  Could policy analysis in the future deliver a new general framework
   for the study of the public sector?

I would be inclined to answer 'no' to both these questions. Nor do I
see the advantages of pursuing the policy school's ambitions. Policy
analysis is first and foremost analysis. As such it requires both the
rational and the irrational components in the ordinary conduct of
social inquiry.

Since the public policy vogue faded there has been an intense search
for new ways of modelling the public sector and its organizations.
New concepts, models and approaches that are relevant for the
reorientation of traditional public administration are now forthcoming,
focusing on the place of motivation or *interests* and *institutions* or rules
within the public sector.

The common focus on the public sector, amorphous as it is in the
era of big government, used to be bureaucracy. Since the bureaucracy
concept is elusive, if not essentially contested, there are disadvantages
in the traditional public administration framework. There was no
clarification either of the extent to which public sector problems are
due to the operation of bureaucracies, or the extent to which public
bureaucracies are different from private bureaucracies. It is true that
the concepts of bureaucracy tie in with another crucial notion – the
state, but the emerging public policy approach in the 1960s and 1970s
did not manage to explain fully how bureaux in the public sector
operate.

It was recognized that there were drawbacks in starting from the
bureaucracy perspective. The crux of the matter was that there is no
connection between the meaning and the reference of the term.
Bureaux exist all over the public sector at various levels of government
– that is the denotation of the concept. However, what is the connotation of the concept? Here, we find fundamental dissensus and contrary
proposals as to what are the distinctive properties of bureaux: efficiency, impersonality, social rationality or waste, partiality and
rigidity.

However, it is doubtful whether the launch of the policy approach
solved all the problems inherent in the public administration
approach. Just like the public administration approach, public policy
models failed to clarify how interests and institutions interact within
the public sector. If the classical public administration framework, the
top-down policy-making model or the so-called Napoleonic state
concept are not enough for understanding the public sector in its
various manifestations – allocation, redistribution and regulation –
then we must move towards some new approach which recognizes the
role of private incentives and public institutions. Clearly, there is a set
of proper functions for government, but how are we to go about inter-
preting its rules and the motivation of its personnel?

# BIBLIOGRAPHY

Aberbach, J.D., Putnam, R.D. and Rockman, B.A. (1981) *Bureaucrats and Politicians in Western Democracies*. Cambridge, MA: Harvard University Press.

Albrow, M. (1970) *Bureaucracy*. London: Macmillan.

Alchian, Armen A. (1950) 'Uncertainty, Evolution and Economic Theory', *Journal of Political Economy*, 48: 211–21.

Alchian, Armen A. and Demsetz, Harold (1972) 'Production, Information Costs and Economic Organization', *American Economic Review*, 62: 777–95.

Alt, J.E. and Chrystal, A.K. (1983) *Political Economics*. Berkeley: University of California Press.

Amacher, R.C., Tollison, R.D. and Willett, T.D. (1976) *The Economic Approach to Public Policy*. Ithaca, NY: Cornell University Press.

Anderson, J.-E. (1975) *Public Policy-Making*. London: Nelson.

Anderson, T.R. and Warkov, S. (1961) 'Organizational Size and Functional Complexity', *American Sociological Review*, 26: 23–8.

Ankar, D. and Ståhlberg, K. (1980) 'Assessing the Impact of Politics: A Typology and Beyond', *Scandinavian Political Studies*, 3: 1191–208.

Appleby, P.H. (1949) *Policy and Administration*. Alabama: University of Alabama Press.

Argyris, C. (1960) *Understanding Organizational Behavior*. Homewood, IL: Dorsey Press.

Argyris, C. (1964) *Integrating the Individual and the Organization*. New York: Wiley.

Arrow, K.J. (1963) *Social Choice and Individual Values*. New Haven, CT: Yale University Press.

Arrow, K.J. and Scitovsky, T. (eds) (1969) *Readings in Welfare Economics*. London: Allen & Unwin.

Ashford, D.E. (ed.) (1978) *Comparing Public Policies*. Beverly Hills, CA: Sage.

Astley, W.G. (1985) 'Organizational Size and Bureaucratic Structure', *Organizational Studies*, 6: 201–28.

Atkinson, A.B. and Stiglitz, J.E. (1980) *Lectures on Public Economics*. London: McGraw-Hill.

Baier, V.E., March, J.G. and Saetren, H. (1986) 'Implementation and Ambiguity', *Scandinavian Journal of Management Studies*, 2: 197–212.

Bardach, E. (1977) *The Implementation Game*. Cambridge, MA: MIT Press.

Barone, E. (1935) 'The Ministry of Production in the Collectivist State', in Hayek (1935).

Barrett, S. and Fudge, C. (eds) (1981) *Policy and Action*. London: Methuen.

Barry, B. (1971) *Sociologists, Economists and Democracy*. London: Collier-Macmillan.

Barry, B. (1973) *The Liberal Theory of Justice: A Critical Examination of the Principal Doctrines in 'A Theory of Justice' by John Rawls*. Oxford: Clarendon Press.

Barzel, Yoram (1982) 'Measurement Cost and the Organization of Markets', *Journal of Law and Economics*, 25: 27–48.

Bator, F.M. (1957a) 'The Anatomy of Market Failures', *Quarterly Journal of Economics*, 72: 351–79.

Bator, F.M. (1957b) 'Simple Analytics of Welfare Maximization', *American Economic Review*, 47: 22–59.

Baumol, W.J. (1965) *Welfare Economics and the Theory of the State*. London: Bell & Sons.

Baumol, W.J., Bailey, E.E. and Willig, R.D. (1977) 'Weak Invisible Hand Theorems on the Sustainability of Multiproduct Natural Monopoly', *American Economic Review*, 67: 355.

Bender, J. and Moe, T.M. (1985) 'An Adaptive Model of Bureaucratic Politics', *American Political Science Review*, 79: 755–74.

Bendix, R. (1956) *Work and Authority in Industry*. New York: Wiley.

Benson, J.K. (1982) 'A Framework for Policy Analysis', in Roger, D.L. and Whetten, D.A. (eds), *Interorganizational Theory, Research and Implementation*. Ames: Iowa State University Press.

Benveniste, G. (1972) *The Politics of Expertise*. Berkeley, CA: Glendessary Press.

Berg, S.V. and Tschirhart, J. (1988) *Natural Monopoly Regulation*. Cambridge: Cambridge University Press.

Bergson, A. (1954) 'On the Concept of Social Welfare', *Quarterly Journal of Economics*, 68: 233–52.

Bergson, A. (1969) 'A Reformulation of Certain Aspects of Welfare Economics', in Arrow and Scitovsky (1969).

Bergson, A. (1982) *Selected Essays in Economic Theory*. Cambridge, MA: MIT Press.

Bernard, C. (1938) *The Functions of the Executive*. Cambridge, MA: Harvard University Press.

Bilas, R.A. (1971) *Microeconomic Theory*. New York: McGraw-Hill.

Blau, P.M. (1955) *The Dynamics of Bureaucracy*. Chicago, IL: University of Chicago Press.

Blau, P.M. (1973) *The Organization of Academic Work*. New York: Wiley.

Blau, P.M. (1974) *On the Nature of Organizations*. New York: Wiley.

Blau, P.M. and Schoenherr, R. (1971) *The Structure of Organizations*. New York: Basic Books.

Blau, P.M. and Scott, W.R. (1963) *Formal Organizations: A Comparative Approach*. London: Routledge & Kegan Paul.

Blaug, M. (1980) *The Methodology of Economics*. Cambridge: Cambridge University Press.

Bodenheimer, E. (1962) 'Prolegomena to a Theory of the Public Interest', *Nomos*, 1: 205–17.

Bohm, P. (1976) *Social Efficiency: A Concise Introduction to Welfare Economics*. London: Macmillan.

Borcherding, T.E. (1977) *Budgets and Bureaucrats: The Sources of Governmental Growth*. Durham, NC: Duke University Press.

Borcherding, T.E. (1984) 'A Survey of Empirical Studies about Causes of the Growth of Government' (mimeo). Paper presented at the Nobel Symposium on the Growth of Government, Stockholm.

Borcherding, T.E., Pommerehene, W.W. and Schneider, F. (1982) 'Comparing the Efficiency of Private and Public Production: The Evidence from Five Countries', in Bös, D., Musgrave, R.A. and Wiseman, J. (eds), *Public Production*. New York: Springer-Verlag.

Braybrooke, D. and Lindblom, C. (1963) *A Strategy of Decision*. New York: Free Press.

Brecht, A. (1959) *Political Theory*. Princeton, NJ: Princeton University Press.

Breit, W. and Hochman, H.M. (eds) (1969) *Readings in Macroeconomics*. New York: Holt, Rinehart & Winston.

Brennan, G. and Buchanan, J.M. (1980) *The Power to Tax*. Cambridge: Cambridge University Press.

Brennan, G. and Buchanan, J.M. (1985) *The Reason of Rules*. Cambridge: Cambridge University Press.

Breton, A. (1974) *The Economic Theory of Representative Government*. London: Macmillan.

Bridge, G. (1977) 'Citizen Choice in Public Services: Voucher System', in Savas (1977).

Broad, C.D. (1930) *Five Types of Ethical Theory*. London: Routledge & Kegan Paul.

Bromley, D.W. (1989) *Economic Interests and Institutions*. Oxford: Blackwell.

Brown, C.V. and Jackson, P.M. (1978) *Public Sector Economics*. Oxford: Martin Robertson.

Browne, A. and Wildavsky, A. (1984) 'Should Evaluation become Implementation?', in Pressman and Wildavsky (1984).

Bruin, G. (1991) *Decision-Making on Public Goods*. Amsterdam: Het Spinhuis.

Buchanan, J.M. (1960) *Fiscal Theory and Political Economy*. Chapel Hill: University of North Carolina Press.

Buchanan, J.M. (1965) 'A Theory of Economic Clubs', *Economica*, 32: 1–14.

Buchanan, J.M. (1967) *Public Finance in Democratic Process*. Chapel Hill: University of North Carolina Press.

Buchanan, J.M. (1968) *Demand and Supply of Public Goods*. Chicago, IL: Rand McNally.

Buchanan, J.M. (1975) *The Limits of Liberty: Between Anarchy and Leviathan*. Chicago, IL: Chicago University Press.

Buchanan, J.M. (1977) *Freedom in Constitutional Contract*. College Station: Texas A&M University Press.

Buchanan, J.M. (1978) 'Markets, States and the Extent of Morals', *American Economic Review*, 68 (2): 364–8.

Buchanan, J.M. (1984) 'Politics without Romance: A Sketch of Positive Public Choice Theory and its Normative Implications', in Buchanan, J.M. and Tollison, R.D. (eds), *Theory of Public Choice*. Vol. II. Ann Arbor, MI: University of Michigan Press.

Buchanan, J.M. (1986) *Liberty, Market and State*. Brighton: Wheatsheaf.

Buchanan, J.M. (1987) *The Constitution of Economic Policy*. Stockholm: Nobel Foundation.

Buchanan, J.M. (1988) 'Market Failure and Political Failure', *Cato Journal*, 8 (1): 1–13.

Buchanan, J.M. and Stubblebine, W.C. (1969) 'Externality', in Arrow and Scitovsky (1969).

Buchanan, J.M. and Tollison, R.D. (eds) (1972) *Theory of Public Choice*. Vol. I. Ann Arbor, MI: University of Michigan Press.

Buchanan, J.M. and Tollison, R.D. (eds) (1984) *The Theory of Public Choice*. Vol. II. Ann Arbor, MI: University of Michigan Press.

Buchanan, J.M. and Tullock, G. (1962) *The Calculus of Consent*. Ann Arbor, MI: University of Michigan Press.

Buchanan, J.M. and Wagner, R.E. (1977) *Democracy in Deficit*. New York: Academic Press.

Buchanan, J.M., Tollison, R.D. and Tullock, G. (eds) (1980) *Toward a Theory of the Rent-Seeking Society*. College Station, TX: Texas A&M University Press.

Caiden, N. and Wildavsky, A. (1974) *Planning and Budgeting in Poor Countries*. New York: Wiley.

Caldwell, B.J. (1984): *Appraisal and Criticism in Economics*. Boston, MA: Allen & Unwin.

Cassinelli, C.W. (1962) 'The Public Interest in Political Ethics', *Nomos*, 1: 44–53.

Castles, F.G. (ed.) (1982) *The Impact of Political Parties*. Beverly Hills, CA: Sage.

Cawson, A. (ed.) (1985) *Organized Interests and the State*. London: Sage.

Cerych, L. and Sabatier, P. (1985) *Implementation of Higher Education Reform in Europe*. Hanley, Staffs: Trentham Books.

Charlesworth, J.C. (ed.) (1968) *Theory and Practice of Public Administration: Scope, Objectives and Methods*. Philadelphia, PA: American Academy of Political and Social Science.

Chisholm, D. (1987) 'Ill-structured Problems: Informal Mechanisms and the Design of Public Organization', in Lane (1987).

Clark, B. (1983) *The Higher Education System: Academic Organization in Cross-national Perspective*. Berkeley: University of California Press.

Clarke, R. and McGuiness, T. (eds) (1987) *The Economics of the Firm*. Oxford: Blackwell.

Coase, R.H. (1937) 'The Nature of the Firm', *Economica*, 4: 386–405.

Coase, R.H. (1960) 'The Problem of Social Cost', *Journal of Law and Economics*, 3: 1–44.

Coase, R.H. (1988) *The Firm, the Market and the Law*. Chicago, IL: University of Chicago Press.

Cohen, M. and March, J.G. (1974) *Leadership and Ambiguity: The American College President*. New York: McGraw-Hill.

Cohen, M., March, J.G. and Olsen, J.P. (1972) 'A Garbage Can Model of Organizational Choice', *Administrative Science Quarterly*, 17: 1–25.

Cohen, M., March, J.G. and Olsen, J.P. (1976) 'People, Problems and the Ambiguity of Relevance', in March and Olsen (1976).

Colm, G. (1962) 'The Public Interest: Essential Key to Public Policy', Nomos, 1: 115–28.

Cornes, R. and Sandler, T. (1986) The Theory of Externalities: Public Goods and Club Goods. Cambridge: Cambridge University Press.

Crozier, M. (1964) The Bureaucratic Phenomenon. Chicago, IL: University of Chicago Press.

Cyert, R.M. and March, J.G. (1963) A Behavioral Theory of the Firm. Englewood Cliffs, NJ: Prentice-Hall.

Dahl, R.R. (1947) 'The Science of Public Administration: Three Problems', Public Administration Review, 7: 1–11.

Daniels, N. (ed.) (1985) Reading Rawls. Oxford: Blackwell.

Danziger, J.N. (1978) Making Budgets: Public Resource Allocation. London: Sage.

Davis, S.M. and Lawrence, P.R. (1977) Matrix. Reading, MA: Addison-Wesley.

Dempster, M.A.H. and Wildavsky, A. (1979) 'On Change: Or, There is No Magic Size for an Increment', Political Studies, 27: 371–89.

Demsetz, H. (1967) 'Toward a Theory of Property Rights', American Economic Review, 57: 347–59.

Demsetz, H. (1970) 'The Private Production of Public Goods', Journal of Law and Economics, 13: 293–306.

Demsetz, H. (1982) Economic, Legal, and Political Dimensions of Competition. Amsterdam: North-Holland.

Demsetz, H. (1988) 'Why Regulate Utilities?', in Stigler (1988)

Derthick, M. (1972) New Towns In-Town. Washington, DC: Urban Institute.

Derthick, M. and Quirk, P. (1985) The Politics of Regulation. Washington, DC: Brookings.

Doel, H. van den (1979) Democracy and Welfare Economics. Cambridge: Cambridge University Press.

Dolbeare, K.M. (ed.) (1974) Public Policy Evaluation. Beverly Hills, CA: Sage.

Donaldson, L. (1982) 'Divisionalization and Size', Organizational Studies, 3: 321–37.

Dooley, M.P., Kaufman, H.M. and Lombra, R.E. (1979) The Political Economy of Policy-Making. Beverly Hills, CA: Sage.

Downs, A. (1957) An Economic Theory of Democracy. New York: Harper & Row.

Downs, A. (1960) 'Why the Government is Too Small in a Democracy', World Politics, 12: 541–63.

Downs, A. (1961) 'The Public Interest: Its Meaning in a Democracy', Social Research, 29: 1–36.

Downs, A. (1967) Inside Bureaucracy. Boston, MA: Little, Brown & Co.

Downs, G. and Larkey, P. (1986) The Search for Government Efficiency. Philadelphia, PA: Temple.

Dror, Y. (1974) Public Policymaking Reexamined. New York: Leonard Hill Books.

Dunleavy, P. (1985) 'Bureaucrats, Budgets and the Growth of the State: Reconstructing an Instrumental Model', British Journal of Political Science, 15: 293–328.

Dunleavy, P. (1991) Politicians, Bureaucrats and Democracy. London: Harvester Wheatsheaf.

Dunleavy, P. and O'Leary, B. (1987) Theories of the State. London: Macmillan.

Dunsire, A. (1973) Administration: The Word and the Science. Oxford: Martin Robertson.

Dunsire, A. (1978) Implementation in a Bureaucracy. Oxford: Martin Robertson.

Dunsire, A. (1987) 'Testing Theories: The Contribution of Bureaumetrics', in Lane (1987).

Dunsire, A. and Hood, C. (1989) Cutback Management in Public Bureaucracies. Cambridge: Cambridge University Press.

Dworkin, R. (1987) Taking Rights Seriously. London: Duckworth.

Dye, T. (1966) Politics, Economics and the Public. Chicago, IL: Rand McNally.

Dye, T. (1976) Policy Analysis. Alabama: University of Alabama Press.

Easton, D. (1965) A Framework for Political Analysis. Englewood Cliffs, NJ: Prentice-Hall.

Eatwell, J., Milgate, M. and Nennan, P. (eds) (1987) *The New Palgrave Dictionary of Economics*. London: Macmillan.

Eavery, C.L. (1984) 'Bureaucratic Agenda Control: Imposition or Bargaining', *American Political Science Review*, 78: 719–33.

Eckstein, H. and Gurr, T.R. (1975) *Patterns of Authority: A Structural Basis for Political Inquiry*. New York: Wiley.

Edelman, M. (1971) *Politics as Symbolic Action*. Chicago: Markham.

Eggertson, T. (1990) *Economic Behaviour and Institutions*. Cambridge: Cambridge University Press.

Eisenstadt, S.N. (1959) 'Bureaucracy, Bureaucratization and Debureaucratization', *Administrative Science Quarterly*, 4: 302–20.

Elmore, R.F. (1978) 'Organizational Models of Social Program Implementation', *Public Policy*, 26: 185–228.

Elmore, R.F. (1982) 'Backward Mapping: Implementation Research and Policy Decision', in Williams (1982).

Enderud, H. (1977) *Four Faces of Leadership in an Academic Organization*. Copenhagen: Nyt Nordisk Forlag.

Enelow, J.M. and Hinich, M.J. (1984) *The Spatial Theory of Voting*. Cambridge: Cambridge University Press.

Etzioni, A. (1964) *Modern Organizations*. Englewood Cliffs, NJ: Prentice-Hall.

Etzioni, A. (1967) 'Mixed-Scanning: A "Third" Approach to Decision-Making', *Public Administration Review*, 27: 385–92.

Etzioni, A. (1975) *A Comparative Analysis of Complex Organizations*. New York: Free Press.

Etzioni-Halevy, E. (1983) *Bureaucracy and Democracy: A Political Dilemma*. London: Routledge & Kegan Paul.

Eulau, H. (1963) *The Behavioral Persuasion in Politics*. New York: Random House.

Evans, P.B., Rueschemeyer, D. and Skocpol, T. (eds) (1985) *Bringing the State Back In*. Cambridge: Cambridge University Press.

Fairchild, H.P. (1955) *Dictionary of Sociology*. Totowa, NJ: Littlefield, Adams.

Fenno, R.F. (1966) *The Power of the Purse*. Boston, MA: Little, Brown & Co.

Ferejohn, J.A., McKelvey, R.D. and Packel, E.W. (1984) 'Limiting Distributions for Continuous State Markov Voting Models', *Social Choice and Welfare*, 1: 45–67.

Feyerabend, P. (1975) *Against Method*. London: Verso.

Fishburn, P.C. (1973) *The Theory of Social Choice*. Princeton, NJ: Princeton University Press.

Frey, B.S. (1978) *Modern Political Economy*. London: Martin Robertson.

Frey, B.S. (1988) 'Explaining the Growth of Government: International Perspectives', in Lybeck and Henrekson (1988).

Frey, R.G. (ed.) (1984) *Utility and Rights*. Oxford: Blackwell.

Friedman, M. (1953) *Essays in Positive Economics*. Chicago, IL: University of Chicago Press.

Frohlich, N., Oppenheimer, J.A. and Young, O.R. (1971) *Political Leadership and Collective Goods*. Princeton, NJ: Princeton University Press.

Frohlich, N., Oppenheimer, J.A. and Young, O.R. (1978) *Modern Political Economy*. Englewood Cliffs, NJ: Prentice-Hall.

Fudge, C. and Barrett, S. (1981) 'Reconstructing the Field of Analysis', in Barrett and Fudge (1981).

Furubotn, E.G. and Pejovich, S. (1972) 'Property Rights and Economic Theory: A Survey of Recent Literature', *Journal of Economic Literature*, 10: 1137–62.

Galbraith, J.K. (1967) *The New Industrial State*. London: Hamilton.

George, V. and Wilding, P. (1984) *The Impact of Social Policy*. London: Routledge & Kegan Paul.

Glymour, C. (1980) *Theory and Evidence*. Princeton, NJ: Princeton University Press.

Goodin, R.E. (1982) *Political Theory and Public Policy*. Chicago, IL: Chicago University Press.

Goodman, N. (1965) *Fact, Fiction and Forecast*. Indianapolis, IN: Bobbs-Merrill.

Goodman, N. (1972) *Problems and Projects*. Indianapolis, IN: Bobbs-Merrill.
Goodsell, C.T. (1983) *The Case for Bureaucracy*. Chatham, NJ: Chatham House.
Gordon, I., Lewis, J. and Young, K. (1977) 'Perspectives on Policy Analysis', *Public Administration Bulletin*, 25.
Gouldner, A.W. (1954) *Patterns of Industrial Bureaucracy*. Glencoe, IL: Free Press.
Graaff, J. de van (1957) *Theoretical Welfare Economics*. Cambridge: Cambridge University Press.
Grant, W. (1985) 'Corporatism and the Public–Private Distinction', in Lane (1985).
Grant, W. and Nath, S. (1984) *The Politics of Economic Policymaking*. Oxford: Blackwell.
Grinyer, P.H. (1982) 'Discussion Note: Divisionalization and Size', *Organizational Studies*, 3: 339–50.
Gulick, L. and Urwick, L. (eds) (1937) *Papers on the Science of Administration*. New York: Institute of Public Administration.
Gunsteren, H. van (1976) *The Quest for Control*. New York: Wiley.
Gwartney, J.D. and Wagner, R.E. (eds) (1988) *Public Choice and Constitutional Economics*. Greenwich, CT: Jai Press.
Hall, R.H. (1974) *Organizations: Structure and Process*. Englewood Cliffs, NJ: Prentice-Hall.
Ham, C. and Hill, M. (1984) *The Policy Process in the Modern Capitalist State*. Brighton: Wheatsheaf.
Hanf, K. and Scharpf, F.W. (eds) (1978) *Interorganizational Policy Making: Limits to Coordination and Central Control*. London: Sage.
Hanke, S.H. (1987) 'Privatization', in Eatwell et al. (1987).
Hansen, T. (1981) 'Transforming Needs into Expenditure Decisions', in Newton (1981).
Hanson, J.L. (1974) *A Dictionary of Economics and Commerce*. London: Macdonald & Evans.
Hardin, G. and Baden, J. (1977) *Managing the Commons*. San Francisco: Freeman.
Hardin, R. (1982) *Collective Action*. Baltimore, MD: Johns Hopkins University Press.
Hargrove, E. (1975) *The Missing Link: The Study of the Implementation of Social Policy*. Washington, DC: Urban Institute.
Harsanyi, J.C. (1977) *Rational Behavior and Bargaining Equilibrium in Games and Social Situations*. Cambridge: Cambridge University Press.
Harsanyi, J.C. (1986) 'Advances in Understanding Rational Behavior', in Elster, J. (ed.), *Rational Choice*. Oxford: Blackwell.
Hayek, F.A. von (ed.) (1935) *Collectivist Economic Planning*. London: Routledge & Kegan Paul.
Hayek, F.A. von (1944) *The Road to Serfdom*. London: Routledge & Kegan Paul.
Hayek, F.A. von (1955) *The Counter-Revolution of Science*. New York: Free Press.
Hayek, F.A. von (1973) *Law, Legislation and Liberty*. Vol. 1. Chicago, IL: Chicago University Press.
Head, J.G. (1974) *Public Goods and Public Welfare*. Durham, NC: Duke University Press.
Heap, S. Hargreaves (1989) *Rationality in Economics*. Oxford: Blackwell.
Heclo, H. and Wildavsky, A. (1974) *The Private Government of Public Money*. London: Macmillan.
Hedberg, B., Nystrom, P.C. and Starbuck, W.H. (1976) '"Camping on Seesaws": Prescriptions for a Self-Designing Organization', *Administrative Science Quarterly*, 21: 41–65.
Hempel, C.G. (1965) *Aspects of Scientific Explanation*. New York: Free Press.
Hernes, G. (ed.) (1978) *Forhandlingsökonomi og blandingsadministratasjon*. Oslo: Universitetsforlaget.
Herring, E.P. (1936) *Public Administration and the Public Interest*. New York: McGraw-Hill.
Hesse, M. (1974) *The Structure of Scientific Inference*. New York: Free Press.
Hibbs, D.A. (1987) *The American Political Economy: Macroeconomics and Electoral Politics*. Cambridge, MA: Harvard University Press.
Hibbs, D.A. and Fassbender, H. (eds) (1981) *Contemporary Political Economy*. Amsterdam: North-Holland.

Hill, L.B. (ed.) (1992) *The State of Public Bureaucracy*. New York: Armonk.

Hirschman, A.O. (1970) *Exit, Voice and Loyalty*. Cambridge, MA: Harvard University Press.

Hjern, B. and Hull, C. (1982) 'Implementation Research as Empirical Constitutionalism', *European Journal for Political Research*, 10: 105–15.

Hjern, B. and Hull, C. (1984) 'Going Interorganizational: Weber meets Durkheim', *Scandinavian Political Studies*, 7: 197–212.

Hjern, B. and Porter, D.O. (1981) 'Implementation Structures: A New Unit for Administrative Analysis', *Organizational Studies*, 2: 211–27.

Hodgson, D.H. (1967) *Consequences of Utilitarianism*. London: Oxford University Press.

Hodgson, G. (1988) *Economics and Institutions*. Cambridge: Polity Press.

Hofferbert, R. (1974) *The Study of Public Policy*. Indianapolis, IN: Bobbs-Merrill.

Hogwood, B.W. and Gunn, L.A. (1984) *Policy Analysis for the Real World*. Oxford: Oxford University Press.

Hogwood, B.W. and Peters, G.B. (1983) *Policy Dynamics*. Brighton: Wheatsheaf.

Hogwood, B.W. and Peters, G.B. (1985) *The Pathology of Public Policy*. Oxford: Clarendon Press.

Holler, M. (ed.) (1984) *Coalitions and Collective Action*. Wurzburg: Physica Verlag.

Hood, C. (1976) *The Limits of Administration*. London: Wiley.

Hood, C. (1987) 'British Administrative Trends and the Public Choice Revolution', in Lane (1987).

Hood, C. (1990) 'Public Administration: Lost an Empire, Not Yet Found a Role?', in Leftwich, A. (ed.), *New Developments in Political Science*. Aldershot: Gower.

Hood, C. and Dunsire, A. (1981) *Bureaumetrics: The Quantitative Comparison of British Central Government Agencies*. Farnborough: Gower.

Hood, C. and Jackson, M. (1991) *Administrative Argument*. Aldershot: Dartmouth.

Hood, C. and Schuppert, G.F. (eds) (1987) *Delivering Public Services in Western Europe*. London: Sage.

Hotelling, H. (1931) 'Stability in Competition', *Economic Journal*, 39: 41–57.

Hyneman, C.S. (1950) *Bureaucracy in a Democracy*. New York: Harper.

Indik, B.P. (1964) 'The Relationship between Organizational Size and Supervisory Ratio', *Administrative Science Quarterly*, 9: 301–12.

Ingram, H.M. and Mann, E.E. (eds) (1980) *Why Policies Succeed or Fail*. Beverly Hills, CA: Sage.

Jenkins, B. and Gray, A. (1983) 'Bureaucratic Politics and Power', *Political Studies*, 31: 177–93.

Johansen, L. (1978a) *Public Economics*. Amsterdam: North-Holland.

Johansen, L. (1978b) *Lectures on Macroeconomic Planning*. Vols 1–2. Amsterdam: North-Holland.

Johansen, L. (1979) 'The Bargaining Society and the Inefficiency of Bargaining', *Kyklos*, 32: 497–522.

Johnsen, E. (1968) *Studies in Multiobjective Decision Models*. Lund: Studentlitteratur.

Jones, G.W. (ed.) (1980) *New Approaches to the Study of Central–Local Relationships*. Farnborough: Gower.

Jonsson, E. (1985) 'A Model of a Non-Budget-Maximizing Bureau', in Lane (1985).

Jordan, G. (1981) 'Iron Triangles, Wholly Corporatism and Elastic Nets: Images of the Policy Process', *Journal of Public Policy*, 1: 95–123.

Jordan, G. (1990) 'Sub-governments, Policy Communities and Networks: Refilling Old Bottles', *Journal of Theoretical Politics*, 2: 319–38.

Kahn, A. (1988) *The Economics of Regulation: Principles and Institutions*. Cambridge, MA: MIT Press. (Original edition 1971.)

Kaplan, A. (1964) *The Conduct of Inquiry*. San Francisco: Chandler.

Kaufman, H. (1976) *Are Government Organizations Immortal?* Washington, DC: Brookings.

Kaufman, H. (1981) *The Administrative Behavior of Federal Bureau Chiefs*. Washington, DC: Brookings.

Kaufman, H. (1985) *Time, Change and Organization*. Chatham, NJ: Chatham House.

Kelly, J.S. (1986) *Social Choice Theory*. Berlin: Springer-Verlag.

Kimberly, J.R. (1976) 'Organizational Size and the Structuralist Perspective', *Administrative Science Quarterly*, 21: 571–97.

Knight, K. (1976) 'Matrix Organization: A Review', *Journal of Management Studies*, 13: 111–30.

Konukiewitz, M. (1985) 'Taming the Housing Market', in Lane (1985).

Kooiman, J. and Eliassen, K.A. (eds) (1987) *Managing Public Organizations*. London: Sage.

Kristensen, O.P. (1987a) *Vaeksten i den offentlige sektor*. Copenhagen: Jurist- og Ökonomforbundets Forlag.

Kristensen, O.P. (1987b) 'Privatization', in Kooiman and Eliassen (1987).

Krupp, S. (ed.) (1966) *The Structure of Economic Science*. Englewood Cliffs, NJ: Prentice-Hall.

Kuhn, T.S. (1962) *The Structure of Scientific Revolutions*. Chicago, IL: Chicago University Press.

Laffer, A.B. (1978) 'Taxation, GNP, and Potential GNP', *Proceedings of the Business and Economics Statistics Section*. Washington, DC: American Statistical Association.

Laffer, A.B. (1981) 'Government Extractions and Revenue Deficiencies', *Cato Journal*, 1: 1–21.

Lane, J.-E. (ed.) (1985) *State and Market: The Politics of the Public and the Private*. London: Sage.

Lane, J.-E. (ed.) (1987) *Bureaucracy and Public Choice*. London: Sage.

Lange, O. (1969) 'The Foundations of Welfare Economics', in Arrow and Scitovsky (1969).

Lange, O. and Taylor, F.M. (1964) *On the Economic Theory of Socialism*. New York: McGraw-Hill.

Larkey, P., Stolp, C. and Winer, M. (1981) 'Theorizing about the Growth of Government: A Research Assessment', *Journal of Public Policy*, 2: 157–220.

Lasswell, H. (1951) 'The Policy Orientation', in Lerner and Lasswell (1951).

Lasswell, H. (1962) 'The Public Interest: Proposing Principles of Content and Procedure', *Nomos*, 1: 54–79.

Laver, M. (1986) *Social Choice and Public Policy*. Oxford: Blackwell.

Layard, P.R.G. and Walters, A.A. (1978) *Microeconomic Theory*. New York: McGraw-Hill.

Le Grand, J. and Estrin, S. (eds) (1989) *Market Socialism*. Oxford: Clarendon.

Lehmbruch, G. and Schmitter, P.C. (eds) (1982) *Patterns of Corporatist Policy-Making*. London: Sage.

Leibenstein, H. (1966) 'Allocative Efficiency versus "X- Efficiency"', *American Economic Review*, 56: 392–415.

Lerner, A.P. (1944) *The Economics of Control: Principles of Welfare Economics*. New York: Macmillan.

Lerner, D. and Lasswell, H.D. (eds) (1951) *The Policy Sciences*. Stanford, CA: Stanford University Press.

Levy, F., Meltsner, A.J. and Wildavsky, A. (1974) *Urban Outcomes*. Berkeley: University of California Press.

Leys, W.A.R. (1962) 'The Relevance and Generality of "The Public Interest"', *Nomos*, 1: 237–50.

Leys, W.A.R. and Perry, C.M. (1959) *Philosophy and the Public Interest*. Chicago, IL: Committee to Advance Original Work in Philosophy.

Likert, R. (1961) *New Patterns of Management*. New York: McGraw-Hill.

Lindahl, E. (1967) 'Just Taxation – A Positive Solution', in Musgrave and Peacock (1967). (Original edition 1919.)

Lindbeck, A. (1984) 'Redistribution Policy and the Expansion of the Public Sector' (mimeo). Paper presented at the Nobel Symposium on the Growth of Government, Stockholm.

Lindblom, C.E. (1959) 'The Science of "Muddling-Through"', *Public Administration Review*, 19: 79–88.

Lindblom, C.E. (1965) *The Intelligence of Democracy*. New York: Free Press.

Lindblom, C.E. (1977) *Politics and Markets*. New York: Basic Books.

Lindblom, C.E. (1988) *Democracy and Market System*. Oslo: Norwegian University Press.

Lindblom, C.E. (1990) *Inquiry and Change*. New Haven, CT: Yale University Press.

Lindgren, B.W. (1971) *Elements of Decision Theory*. New York: Macmillan.

Lippman, W. (1955) *Essays in the Public Interest Philosophy*. Boston, MA: Little, Brown & Co.

Lipsey, R.C. and Lancaster, K. (1956) 'The General Theory of Second Best', *Review of Economic Studies*, 24: 11–32.

Lipsky, M. (1980) *Street-Level Bureaucracy*. New York: Russell Sage.

Little, I.M.D. (1973) *A Critique of Welfare Economics*. Oxford: Oxford University Press.

Loerhr, W. and Sandler, T. (eds) (1978) *Public Goods and Public Policy*. Beverly Hills, CA: Sage.

Lybeck, J.A. (1986) *The Growth of Government in Developed Economies*. Aldershot: Gower.

Lybeck, J.A. and Henrekson, M. (eds) (1988) *Explaining the Growth of Government*. Amsterdam: North-Holland.

Lynn, N. and Wildavsky, A. (eds) (1990) *Public Administration: The State of the Discipline*. Chatham, NJ: Chatham House.

Lyons, D. (1965) *The Forms and Limits of Utilitarianism*. London: Oxford University Press.

McCubbins, M.D. and Sullivan, T. (eds) (1987) *Congress: Structure and Policy*. Cambridge: Cambridge University Press.

McKean, R.N. (1958) *Efficiency in Government through Systems Analysis*. New York: Wiley.

McLean, I. (1987) *Public Choice*. Oxford: Blackwell.

Majone, G. and Wildavsky, A. (1984) 'Implementation as Evolution', in Pressman and Wildavsky (1984).

Manley, J.F. (1975) *The Politics of Finance*. Boston, MA: Little, Brown & Co.

March, J.G. (1981) 'Decisions in Organizations and Theories of Choice', in Ven, J. Van de and Joyce, W. (eds), *Perspectives on Organizational Design and Behavior*. New York: Wiley.

March, J.G. (1988) *Decisions and Organizations*. Oxford: Blackwell.

March, J.G. and Olsen, J.P. (eds) (1976) *Ambiguity and Choice in Organizations*. Oslo: Universitetsforlaget.

March, J.G. and Olsen, J.P. (1984) 'The New Institutionalism: Organizational Factors in Political Life', *American Political Science Review*, 78: 734–49.

March, J.G. and Olsen, J.P. (1989) *Rediscovering Institutions: The Organizational Basis of Politics*. New York: Free Press.

March, J.G. and Simon, H. (1958) *Organizations*. New York: Wiley.

Marglin, S.A. (1963) 'The Social Rate of Discount and the Optimal Rate of Investment', *Quarterly Journal of Economics*, 77: 95–111.

Margolis, H. (1982) *Selfishness, Altruism and Rationality*. Cambridge: Cambridge University Press.

Margolis, J. and Guitton, H. (eds) (1969) *Public Economics*. New York: St Martin's Press.

Marini, F. (ed.) (1971) *Toward a New Public Administration: The Minnowbrook Perspective*. Scrawton, PA: Chandler.

Matthews, R.C.O. (1986) 'The Economics of Institutions and the Sources of Growth', *Economic Journal*, 96: 903–18.

May, J.V. and Wildavsky, A. (eds) (1978) *The Policy Cycle*. Beverly Hills, CA: Sage.

Mazmanian, D.A. and Sabatier, P.A. (1983) *Implementation and Public Policy*. Palo Alto: Scott, Foresman.

Melman, S. (1951) 'The Rise of Administrative Overhead in the Manufacturing Industries of the United States: 1899–1947', *Oxford Economic Papers*, 3: 62–112.

Meltsner, A.J. (1976) *Policy Analysts in the Bureaucracy*. Berkeley: University of California Press.

Meltsner, A.J. and Bellavita, C. (1983) *The Policy Organization*. Beverly Hills, CA: Sage.

Merritt, R.L. and Merritt, A.J. (eds) (1985) *Innovation in the Public Sector*. Beverly Hills, CA: Sage.

Merton, R.K. (1957) *Social Theory and Social Structure*. Glencoe, IL: Free Press.

Metcalfe, L. and Richards, S. (1987) *Improving Public Management*. London: Sage.

Meter, D.S. van and Horn, C.E. van (1975) 'The Policy Implementation Process: A Conceptual Framework', *Administration and Society*, 6: 445–88.

Meyer, M.W. (1985) *Limits to Bureaucratic Growth*. Berlin: de Gruyter.

Meyer, M.W. and Brown, M.C. (1977) 'The Process of Bureaucratization', *American Journal of Sociology*, 77: 297–322.

Mierlo, H.J.G.A. van (1985) 'Improvement of Public Provision of Goods and Services' in Lane (1985).

Mill, J.S. (1964) *Utilitarianism, Liberty and Representative Government*. London: Everyman's Library.

Miller, D. (1976) *Social Justice*. Oxford: Clarendon Press.

Miller, G.J. and Moe, T.M. (1983) 'Bureaucrats, Legislators and the Size of Government', *American Political Review*, 77: 297–322.

Milward, H.B. Brinton (1982) 'Interorganizational Policy Systems and Research on Public Organizations', *Administration and Society*, 13: 457–78.

Mintzberg, H. (1973) *The Nature of Managerial Work*. New York: Harper & Row.

Mintzberg, H. (1979) *The Structuring of Organizations*. Englewood Cliffs, NJ: Prentice-Hall.

Mintzberg, H. (1983) *Structures in Fives*. Englewood Cliffs, NJ: Prentice-Hall.

Mises, L. von (1935) 'Economic Calculation in the Socialist Commonwealth', in Hayek (1935).

Mises, L. von (1962) *Bureaucracy*. Westport, CT: Arlington House.

Mises, L. von (1963) *Human Action: A Treatise on Economics*. New Haven, CT: Yale University Press.

Mishan, E.J. (1981) *Introduction to Normative Economics*. Oxford: Oxford University Press.

Mitnick, B. (1980) *The Political Economy of Regulation*. New York: Columbia University Press.

Moe, T.M. (1984) 'The New Economics of Organization', *American Journal of Political Science*, 28: 739–77.

Moe, T.M. (1990) 'Political Institutions: The Neglected Side of the Story', *Journal of Law, Economics and Organization*, 6: 213–53.

Moene, K.O. (1986) 'Types of Bureaucratic Interaction', *Journal of Public Economics*, 29: 333–45.

Morgan, Gareth (1986) *Images of Organization*. Beverly Hills, CA: Sage.

Morgan, Glenn (1990) *Organizations in Society*. London: Macmillan.

Moulin, H. (1983) *The Strategy of Social Choice*. Amsterdam: Elsevier.

Mueller, D. (1979) *Public Choice*. Cambridge: Cambridge University Press.

Mueller, D. (1986) *The Modern Corporation*. London: Harvester.

Mueller, D. (1989) *Public Choice II*. Cambridge: Cambridge University Press.

Murray, R. (1987) 'Productivity Measurement in Bureaucratic Organizations', in Lane (1987).

Musgrave, R.A. (1959) *The Theory of Public Finance*. New York: McGraw-Hill.

Musgrave, R.A. (1962) 'The Public Interest: Efficiency in the Creation and Maintenance of Material Welfare', *Nomos*, 1: 107–14.

Musgrave, R.A. and Musgrave, P. (1980) *Public Finance in Theory and Practice*. New York: McGraw-Hill.

Musgrave, R.A. and Peacock, A.T. (eds) (1967) *Classics in the Theory of Public Finance*. New York: St Martin's Press. (Original edition 1958.)

Myrdal, G. (1961) ' "Value-loaded" Concepts', in Hegeland, H. (ed.), *Money, Growth, and Methodology and Other Essays in Honor of J. Åkermann*. Lund: Gleerup.

Myrdal, G. (1970) *Objectivity in Social Research*. London: Duckworth.

Nagel, E. (1961) *The Structure of Science*. London: Routledge & Kegan Paul.

Nagel, S.S. and Neef, M. (1979) *Policy Analysis in Social Science Research*. Beverly Hills, CA: Sage.

Nath, S.K. (1969) *A Reappraisal of Welfare Economics*. London: Routledge & Kegan Paul.

Newton, K. (ed.) (1981) *Urban Political Economy*. London: Frances Pinter.

Niskanen, W.A. (1971) *Bureaucracy and Representative Government*. Chicago, IL: Aldine-Atherton.

Noll, R. and Owen, B. (1983) *The Political Economy of Deregulation*. Washington, DC: American Enterprise Institute.

North, D.C. (1981) *Structure and Change in Economic History*. New York: Norton.

North, D.C. (1989) 'A Transaction Cost Approach to the Historical Development of Polities and Economies', *Journal of Institutional and Theoretical Economics*, 145: 661–8.

North, D.C. (1990a) 'A Transaction Cost Theory of Politics', *Journal of Theoretical Politics*, 2: 355–67.

North, D.C. (1990b) *Institutions, Institutional Change and Economic Performance*. Cambridge: Cambridge University Press.

Novick, D. (ed.) (1965) *Program Budgeting*. Cambridge, MA: Harvard University Press.

Novick, D. (1973) *Current Practice in Program Budgeting (PPBS)*. London: Heinemann.

Nozick, R. (1974) *Anarchy, State and Utopia*. New York: Basic Books.

Nurmi, H. (1987) *Comparing Voting Systems*. Doidrecht: D. Reidel.

Oates, W. (1972) *Fiscal Federalism*. New York: Harcourt Brace Jovanovich.

Okun, A.M. (1975) *Equality and Efficiency*. Washington, DC: Brookings.

Olsen, J.P. (1983) *Organized Democracy*. Oslo: Universitetsforlaget.

Olsen, J.P. (1988) *Statsstyre og institusjonsutforming*. Oslo: Universitetsforlaget.

Olson, M. (1965) *The Logic of Collective Action*. Cambridge, MA: Harvard University Press.

Olson, M. (1982) *The Rise and Decline of Nations*. New Haven, CT: Yale University Press.

Ostrom, V. and Ostrom, E. (1971) 'Public Choice: A Different Approach to the Study of Public Administration', *Public Administration Review*, 31: 302–16.

Ostrom, V. and Ostrom, E. (1977) 'Public Goods and Public Choices', in Savas (1977).

Page, E. (1985) *Political Authority and Bureaucratic Power: A Comparative Analysis*. Brighton: Harvester.

Page, E. (1987) 'Comparing Bureaucracies', in Lane (1987).

Palgrave, R.H.I. (ed.) (1894) *Dictionary of Political Economy*. Vols I–III. London: Macmillan.

Parfit, D. (1984) *Reasons and Persons*. Oxford: Clarendon Press.

Parkinson, N.C. (1957) *Parkinson's Law or the Pursuit of Progress*. London: John Murray.

Parsons, T. (ed.) (1947) *The Theory of Social and Economic Organization*. New York: Free Press.

Parsons, T. (1968) *The Structure of Social Action*. Vols I–II. New York: Free Press. (Original edition 1937.)

Paul, E.F. and Russo, P.A. (eds) (1982) *Public Policy*. Chatham, NJ: Chatham House.

Peabody, R.L. and Rourke, F.E. (1965) 'Public Bureaucracies', in March, J.G. (ed.), *Handbook of Organizations*. Chicago, IL: Rand McNally.

Peltzman, S. (1988) 'Toward a More General Theory of Regulation', in Stigler (1988).

Pennock, J.R. (1962) 'The One and the Many: A Note on the Concept', *Nomos*, 1: 177–82.

Peters, B.G. (1987) 'Politicians and Bureaucrats in the Politics of Policy-Making', in Lane (1987).

Peters, B.G. (1991) *The Politics of Taxation*. Oxford: Blackwell.

Pfeffer, J. (1982) *Organizations and Organization Theory*. Boston, MA: Pitman.

Pfiffner, J.M. and Sherwood, F.P. (1960) *Administrative Organization*. Englewood Cliffs, NJ: Prentice-Hall.

Phelps, E.S. (ed.) (1962) *Private Wants and Public Needs*. New York: Norton.

Pigou, A.C. (1962) *The Economics of Welfare*. London: Macmillan. (Original edition 1924.)

Pirie, M. (1988) *Privatization: Theory, Practice and Choice*. Aldershot: Wildwood House.
Pondy, L.R. (1969) 'Effects of Size, Complexity and Ownership on Administrative Intensity', *Administrative Science Quarterly*, 14: 47–60.
Popper, K. (1959) *The Logic of Scientific Discovery*. New York: Harper & Row.
Popper, K. (1963) *Conjectures and Refutations*. New York: Harper & Row.
Popper, K. (1972) *Objective Knowledge*. Oxford: Clarendon Press.
Posner, R. (1974) 'Theories of Economic Regulation', *Bell Journal of Economics*, 5: 335–58.
Posner, R.A. (1988) 'The Social Costs of Monopoly and Regulation', in Stigler (1988).
Powell, W.W. and DiMaggio, P.J. (1991) *The New Institutionalism in Organizational Analysis*. Chicago: University of Chicago Press.
Pressman, J. and Wildavsky, A. (1984) *Implementation*. Berkeley: University of California Press. (Original edition 1973.)
Prest, A.R. and Barr, N.A. (1979) *Public Finance in Theory and Practice*. London: Weidenfeld & Nicolson.
Pugh, D.S. and Hickson, D.J. (1976) *Organization Structure in its Context: The Aston Programme I*. Farnborough: Saxon House.
Pugh, D.S., Hickson, D.J., Hinings, C.R., MacDonald, K.M., Turner, C. and Lupton, T. (1963) 'A Conceptual Scheme for Organizational Analysis', *Administrative Science Quarterly*, 10: 301–7.
Pugh, D.S., Hickson, D.J., Hinings, C.R. and Turner, C. (1969) 'The Context of Organizational Structures', *Administrative Science Quarterly*, 14: 91–114.
Putnam, H. (1975) *Mind, Language and Reality*. Cambridge: Cambridge University Press.
Quade, E.S. (1976) *Analysis for Public Decisions*. Amsterdam: Elsevier.
Quine, W.V. (1960) *Word and Object*. Cambridge: MIT Press.
Quine, W.V. and Ullian, J.S. (1970) *The Web of Belief*. New York: Random House.
Quirk, J. and Saposnik, R. (1968) *Introduction to General Equilibrium Theory and Welfare Economics*. New York: McGraw-Hill.
Radomysler, J. (1969) 'Welfare Economics and Economic Policy', in Arrow and Scitovsky (1969).
Ranney, A. (1968) *Political Science and Public Policy*. 19th edn. Chicago, IL: Markham.
Rawls, J. (1971) *A Theory of Justice*. Cambridge, MA: Harvard University Press.
Regan, D. (1980) *Utilitarianism and Co-operation*. Oxford: Clarendon Press.
Rescher, N. (1970) *Scientific Explanation*. New York: Free Press.
Rhodes, R.A.W. (1981) *Control and Power in Central–Local Relations*. Farnborough: Gower.
Rhodes, R.A.W. (1990) 'Policy Networks: A British Perspective', *Journal of Theoretical Politics*, 2: 293–317.
Richardson, J.J. (ed.) (1982) *Policy Styles in Western Europe*. London: Allen & Unwin.
Richardson, J.J. and Jordan, A.G. (1979) *Governing under Pressure*. London: Martin Robertson.
Ricketts, M. (1987) *The Economics of Business Enterprise*. London: Harvester Wheatsheaf.
Riggs, F.W. (1979) 'Introduction: Shifting Meanings of the Term "Bureaucracy"', *International Social Science Journal*, 31: 563–84.
Riker, W.H. (1980) 'Implications from the Disequilibrium of Majority Rule for the Study of Institutions', *American Political Science Review*, 74: 432–47.
Riker, W.H. (1982) *Liberalism against Populism*. San Francisco: Freeman.
Riker, W.H. and Ordeshook, P.C. (1973) *An Introduction to Positive Political Theory*. Englewood Cliffs, NJ: Prentice-Hall.
Robbins, L.C. (1932) *An Essay on the Nature and Significance of Economic Science*. London: Macmillan.
Roethlisberger, F.J. and Dickson, W.J. (1939) *Management and the Worker*. Cambridge, MA: Harvard University Press.
Rose, R. (ed.) (1980) *The Challenge to Governance: Studies in Overloaded Polities*. London: Sage.
Rose, R. (1981) 'What If Anything is Wrong with Big Government?', *Journal of Public Policy*, 1: 5–36.

Rose, R. (1984) *Understanding Big Government: The Programme Approach*. London: Sage.

Rose, R. (1985) *Public Employment in Western Nations*. Cambridge: Cambridge University Press.

Rose, R. (1987) 'Giving Direction to Permanent Officials: Signals from the Electorates, the Market, and from Self-expertise', in Lane (1987).

Rose, R. (1989) *Ordinary People in Public Policy*. London: Sage.

Ross, S.A. (1973) 'The Economic Theory of Agency: The Principal's Problem', *American Economic Review*, 63: 134–9.

Rourke, F.E. (1969) *Bureaucracy, Politics and Public Policy*. Boston, MA: Little, Brown & Co.

Rowley, C.K. and Peacock, A.T. (1975) *Welfare Economics*. London: Martin Robertson.

Rowley, C.K., Tollison, R.D. and Tullock, G. (1988) *The Political Economy of Rent-Seeking*. Dordrecht: Kluwer.

Rudolph, L.J. and Rudolph, S.H. (1979) 'Authority and Power in Bureaucratic and Patrimonial Administration', *World Politics*, 31: 195–227.

Sabatier, P. (1986) 'Top-Down and Bottom-Up Approaches to Implementation Research', *Journal of Public Policy*, 6: 21–48.

Sabatier, P. and Mazmanian, D. (1979) 'The Conditions of Effective Implementation: A Guide to Accomplishing Policy Objectives', *Policy Analysis*, 5: 481–504.

Saltzstein, G.H. (1985) 'Conceptualizing Bureaucratic Responsiveness', *Administration and Society*, 17: 283–306.

Samuelson, P.A. (1954) 'The Pure Theory of Public Expenditure', *Review of Economics and Statistics*, 36: 387–9.

Samuelson, P.A. (1955) 'Diagrammatic Exposition of a Theory of Public Expenditure', *Review of Economics and Statistics*, 37: 35–46.

Samuelson, P.A. (1965) *Foundations of Economic Analysis*. New York: Atheneum.

Savas, E.S. (ed.) (1977) *Alternatives for Delivering Public Services*. Boulder, CO: Westview Press.

Savas, E.S. (1982) *Privatizing the Public Sector*. Chatham, NJ: Chatham House.

Savas, E.S. (1987) *The Key to Better Government*. Chatham, NJ: Chatham House.

Scharpf, F.W., Reissert, B. and Schnabel, F. (1975) *Control Deficits in Multi-Level Problem Solving*. Berlin: International Institute of Management.

Scheffler, I. (1967a) *The Anatomy of Inquiry*. New York: Knopf.

Scheffler, I. (1967b) *Science and Subjectivity*. Indianapolis, IN: Bobbs-Merrill.

Schmidt, M.G. (ed.) (1982) *Wohlfartsstaatliche Politik und bürgerlichen und sozialdemokratichen Regierungen*. Frankfurt am Main: Campus.

Schmitter, P.C. (1983) 'Democratic Theory and Neo-Corporatist Practice', *Social Research*, 50: 885–928.

Schmitter, P.C. and Lehmbruch, G. (eds) (1978) *Trends Toward Corporatist Intermidiation*. London: Sage.

Schotter, A. (1985) *Free Market Economics*. New York: St Martin's Press.

Schubert, G. (1960) *The Public Interest*. Glencoe, IL: Free Press.

Schumpeter, J.A. (1965) *Capitalism, Socialism and Democracy*. London: Allen & Unwin. (Original edition 1942.)

Schumpeter, J.A. (1989) *Essays on Entrepreneurs, Innovations, Business Cycles and the Evolution of Capitalism*. New Brunswick: Transaction.

Self, P. (1972) *Administrative Theories and Politics*. London: Allen & Unwin.

Self, P. (1985) *Political Theories of Modern Government, its Role and Reform*. London: Allen & Unwin.

Selznick, P. (1949) *TVA and the Grass Roots*. Berkeley: University of California Press.

Selznick, P. (1957) *Leadership in Administration*. Evanston, IL: Row & Peters.

Sen, A. (1970) *Collective Choice and Social Welfare*. San Francisco: Holden-Day, Inc.

Sen, A. (1982) *Choice, Welfare and Measurement*. Oxford: Blackwell.

Sen, A. and Williams, B. (eds) (1982) *Utilitarianism and Beyond*. Cambridge: Cambridge University Press.

Shafritz, J.M. and Hyde, A.C. (eds) (1978) *Classics of Public Administration*. Oak Park, IL: Moore Publishing.

Sharkansky, I. (1969) *The Politics of Taxation and Spending*. Indianapolis, IN: Bobbs-Merrill.

Sharkansky, I. (1978) *Public Administration*. Chicago, IL: Rand McNally.

Sharkansky, I. (1979) *Wither the State?* Chatham, NJ: Chatham House.

Sharpe, L.J. (1985) 'Central Coordination and the Policy Network', *Political Studies*, 33: 361–81.

Sharpe, L.J. and Newton, K. (1984) *Does Politics Matter? The Determinants of Public Policy*. Oxford: Clarendon Press.

Shepsle, K.A. (1986) 'Institutional Equilibrium and Equilibrium Institutions', in Weisburg, H. (ed.), *Political Science: The Science of Politics*. New York: Agathon Press.

Shepsle, K.A. (1989) 'Studying Institutions: Some Lessons from the Rational Choice Approach', *Journal of Theoretical Politics*, 1: 131–47.

Shepsle, K.A. and Weingast, B.R. (1981) 'Institutional Equilibrium and Equilibrium Institutions', *Public Choice*, 37: 503–19.

Sherman, R. (1989) *The Regulation of Monopoly*. Cambridge: Cambridge University Press.

Sidgwick, H. (1967) *The Methods of Ethics*, 7th edn. London: Macmillan.

Simmons, R.H. and Dvorin, E.P. (1977) *Public Administration*. Port Washington: Alfred Publishing.

Simon, H.A. (1947) *Administrative Behavior*. New York: Macmillan.

Simon, H.A. (1957) *Models of Man*. New York: Wiley.

Simon, H.A. (1964) 'On the Concept of Organizational Goal', *Administrative Science Quarterly*, 9: 1–22.

Simon, H.A. Smithburg, D.W. and Thompson, V.A. (1950) *Public Administration*. New York: Alfred A. Knopf.

Skocpol, T. (1979) *States and Social Revolutions*. Cambridge: Cambridge University Press.

Skocpol, T. (1985) 'Bringing the State Back In: Strategies of Analysis in Current Research', in Evans et al. (1985).

Smart, J.C. and Williams, B. (1987) *Utilitarianism: For and Against*. Cambridge: Cambridge University Press.

Smith, A. (1962) *The Wealth of Nations*. Vols. I–II. London: Everyman Library. (Original edition 1776.)

Smith, D. and Zurcher, O. (eds) (1944) *A Dictionary of American Politics*. New York: Barnes & Noble.

Sorauf, F.J. (1962) 'The Conceptual Muddle', *Nomos*, 1: 183–190.

Sörensen, R. (1985) 'Economic Relations between City and Suburban Governments', in Lane (1985).

Sörensen, R. (1987) 'Bureaucratic Decision-making and the Growth of Public Expenditure', in Lane (1987).

Spulber, D.F. (1989) *Regulation and Markets*. Cambridge, MA: MIT Press.

Ståhlberg, K. (1987) 'Functional and Dysfunctional Bureaucracies', in Lane (1987).

Starbuck, W.H. (1965) 'Organizational Growth and Development', in March, J.G. (ed.), *Handbook of Organizations*. Chicago, IL: Rand McNally.

Starbuck, W.H. (1976) 'Organizations and their Environments', in Dunnette, M.D. (ed.), *Handbook of Industrial and Organizational Psychology*. Chicago: Rand McNally.

Stigler, G.J. (1975) *The Citizen and the State: Essays on Regulation*. Chicago, IL: University of Chicago Press.

Stigler, G.J. (ed.) (1988) *Chicago Studies in Political Economy*. Chicago, IL: University of Chicago Press.

Stiglitz, J.E. (1987) 'Principal and Agent' in Eatwell et al. (1987).

Stone, R.C. (1969) 'Bureaucracy', in Gould, J. and Kolb, W.L. (eds), *A Dictionary of the Social Sciences*. New York: Free Press.

Streeck, W. and Schmitter, P.C. (eds) (1985) *Private Interest Government*. London: Sage.

Sugden, R. (1981) *The Political Economy of Public Choice*. Oxford: Martin Robertson.

Tarschys, D. (1975) 'The Growth of Public Expenditure: Nine Modes of Explanation', *Scandinavian Political Studies*, 10: 9–31.

Thompson, E.A. and Faith, R.L. (1981) 'A Pure Theory of Strategic Behavior and Social Institutions', *American Economic Review*, 71: 366–80.

Thompson, J.D. (1967) *Organizations in Action*. New York: McGraw-Hill.

Thompson, M., Ellis, R. and Wildavsky, A. (1990) *Cultural Theory*. Boulder, CO: Westview Press.

Thompson, V.A. (1964) *Modern Organization*. New York: Alfred A. Knopf.

Thurow, L.C. (1980) *The Zero-Sum Society: Distribution and the Possibilities for Economic Change*. New York: Basic Books.

Tiebout, C. (1956) 'A Pure Theory of Local Expenditure', *Journal of Political Economy*, 64: 416–24.

Tinbergen, J. (1967) *Economic Policy: Principles and Design*. Amsterdam: North-Holland.

Tollison, R.D. (1982) 'Rent-Seeking: A Survey', *Kyklos*, 35: 575–92.

Trow, M. (1984) 'Leadership and Organization: The Case of Biology at Berkeley', in Premfors, R. (ed.), *Higher Education Organization*. Stockholm: Almqvist & Wiksell.

Trow, M. (1985) 'Comparative Reflexions on Leadership in Higher Education', *European Journal of Education*, 20: 14–49.

Truman, D.B. (1951) *The Governmental Process*. New York: Alfred A. Knopf.

Tufte, E. (1978) *Political Control of the Economy*. Princeton, NJ: Princeton University Press.

Tullock, G. (1959) 'Some Problems of Majority Voting', *Journal of Political Economy*, 67: 571–9.

Tullock, G. (1965) *The Politics of Bureaucracy*. Washington, DC: Public Affairs Press.

Tullock, G. (1970) *Private Wants, Public Means*. New York: Basic Books.

Tullock, G. (1988) *Wealth, Poverty and Politics*. Oxford: Blackwell.

Vanberg, Viktor and Buchanan, James M. (1989) 'Interests and Theories in Constitutional Choice', *Journal of Theoretical Politics*, 1: 49–62.

Varian, H.R. (1987) *Microeconomic Analysis*. New York: Norton.

Veljanovski, Cento G. (1982) 'The Coase Theorems and the Economic Theory of Markets and Law', *Kyklos*, 35: 66–81.

Vickers, J. and Wright, V. (eds) (1988) 'The Politics of Privatization in Western Europe', *West European Politics*, 11 (4).

Vickers, J. and Yarrow, G. (1989) *Privatization: An Economic Analysis*. Cambridge, MA: MIT Press.

Waldo, D. (1948) *The Administrative State*. New York: Ronald Press.

Waldo, D. (ed.) (1971) *Public Administration in a Time of Turbulence*. Scrawton, PA: Chandler.

Waldron, J. (1984) *Theories of Rights*. Oxford: Oxford University Press.

Walzer, M. (1983) *Spheres of Justice*. New York: Basic Books.

Wanat, J. (1974) 'Bases of Budgetary Incrementalism', *American Political Science Review*, 68: 1221–9.

Warwick, D.P. (1975) *A Theory of Public Bureaucracy*. Cambridge, MA: Harvard University Press.

Weber, M. (1923) *Gesammelte Aufsätze zur Wissenschaftslehre*. Tübingen: Mohr.

Weber, M. (1949) *The Methodology of the Social Sciences*. New York: Free Press.

Weber, M. (1978) *Economy and Society*. Vols I–II. Berkeley: University of California Press. (Original German edition 1922.)

Weingast, Barry R. (1989) 'The Political Institutions of Representative Government', *Journal of Institutional and Theoretical Economics*, 145: 693–703.

Weingast, Barry R. and Marshall, William J. (1988) 'The Industrial Organization of Congress; or Why Legislatures, Like Firms, are Not Organized as Markets', *Journal of Political Economy*, 96: 132–63.

Weiss, L. and Klass, M. (eds) (1986) *Regulatory Reform: What Actually Happened*. Boston: Little, Brown & Co.

Westlund, A. and Lane, J.-E. (1983) 'The Relevance of the Concept of Structural

Variability to the Social Sciences', *Quality and Quantity*, 17: 189–201.

White, J. and Wildavsky, A. (1989) *The Deficit and the Public Interest*. Berkeley: University of California Press.

Whiteley, P. (1980) *Models of Political Economy*. London: Sage.

Whiteley, P. (1986) *The Political Economy of Policy-Making*. London: Sage.

Whyte, W.H. (1956) *The Organization of Man*. New York: Simon & Schuster.

Wicksell, K. (1967) 'A New Principle of Just Taxation', in Musgrave and Peacock (1967). (Original edition 1896.)

Wildavsky, A. (1972) *The Revolt against the Masses and Other Essays on Politics and Public Policy*. New York: Basic Books.

Wildavsky, A. (1973) 'If Planning is Everything, Then Maybe it is Nothing', *Policy Sciences*, 4: 127–53.

Wildavsky, A. (1977) 'Changing Forward versus Changing Back. Lindblom: *Politics and Markets: The World's Political-Economic Systems*', *Yale Law Journal*, 217: 34.

Wildavsky, A. (1979) *Speaking Truth to Power: The Art and Craft of Policy Analysis*. Boston, MA: Little, Brown & Co.

Wildavsky, A. (1980) *How to Limit Government Spending*. Berkeley: University of California Press.

Wildavsky, A. (1984) *The Politics of the Budgetary Process*. Boston, MA: Little, Brown & Co. (Original edition 1964.)

Wildavsky, A. (1985) 'The Logic of Public Sector Growth', in Lane (1985).

Wildavsky, A. (1986) *Budgeting: A Comparative Theory of the Budgetary Process*. Boston, MA: Little, Brown & Co. (Original edition 1975.)

Wildavsky, A. (1987) 'Choosing Preferences by Constructing Institutions: A Cultural Theory of Preference Formation', *American Political Science Review*, 81: 3–21.

Wildavsky, A. (1988) *The New Politics of the Budgetary Process*. Boston, MA: Little, Brown & Co.

Wilensky, H. (1967) *Organizational Intelligence*. New York: Basic Books.

Wilensky, H. (1975) *The Welfare State and Equality*. Berkeley: University of California Press.

Williams, W. (1971) *Social Policy Research and Analysis*. New York: Elsevier.

Williams, W. (1980) *The Implementation Perspective*. Berkeley: University of California Press.

Williams, W. (ed.) (1982) *Studying Implementation: Methodological and Administrative Issues*. Chatham, NJ: Chatham House.

Williams, W. and Elmore, R.F. (eds) (1976) *Social Programme Implementation*. New York: Academic Press.

Williamson, O. (1975) *Markets and Hierarchies*. New York: Free Press.

Williamson, O. (1985) *The Economic Institutions of Capitalism*. New York: Free Press.

Williamson, O. (1986) *Economic Organization*. London: Harvester Wheatsheaf.

Willoughby, W.F. (1927) *Principles of Public Administration*. Washington, DC: Brookings.

Wilson, J.Q. (1980) *The Politics of Regulation*. New York: Basic Books.

Wilson, J.Q. (1987) *Bureaucracy: What Government Agencies Do and Why They Do It*. New York: Basic Books.

Wilson, W. (1887) 'The Study of Administration', *Political Science Quarterly*, 2: 197–222.

Wolf, C. (1988) *Markets or Governments*. Cambridge, MA: MIT Press.

Wolff, R.P. (1977) *Understanding Rawls: A Reconstruction and Critique of 'A Theory of Justice'*. Princeton, NJ: Princeton University Press.

Yuhl, G.A. (1989) *Leadership in Organizations*. Englewood Cliffs, NJ: Prentice-Hall.

# Index